THE FULL ROUND

The several lives and theatrical legacy of

STEPHEN JOSEPH

Terry Lane

Duca della Corgna

First published in Italy 2006 by
Duca della Corgna
Castiglione del Lago (PG) Italy
Via Roma 12/14
ediduca@virgilio.it

Copyright © 2006 Terry Lane

The moral right of the author has been asserted

British Library Cataloguing in Publication Data

ISBN 88 – 901721 – 8 – 5

Designed by Terry Lane

Printed and bound in Italy by Stampa & Stampa - Formia (LT) Italy

This book is sold subject to the condition that it shall not, by way of trade or otherwise, be lent, resold, hired out, or otherwise circulated in any form of binding or cover other than that in which it is published and without a similar condition, including this condition, being imposed on the subsequent purchaser

Contents

	Introduction	7
1	Stephen's Father	11
2	Stephen's Mother	15
3	Bringing Up Baby	21
4	The Co-Respondent	23
5	The Wicked Stepmother	27
6	Clayesmore	31
7	The Hall	35
8	Playwright as Biographer	43
9	The House of David	49
10	The Cruel Sea	53
11	Salad Days	61
12	Hard Times	71
13	The New World	83
14	One Great Vision	89
15	Worlds End	101
16	To The Barricades	105

17	Thrift	111
18	P.B.	115
19	Beside the Seaside	121
20	Mahatma Gandhi	131
21	Scarborough	143
22	Makeshift	155
23	A Long Long Trail	161
24	The Potteries	169
25	Catching On	173
26	The Fellow	179
27	Trouble Brewing	191
28	The Last War	199
29	Happily Ever After	213
30	The Full Round	219
	Obituaries	241
	Acknowledgements	247
	Bibliography	248
	References	251
	Index	265

THE FULL ROUND

for Ros

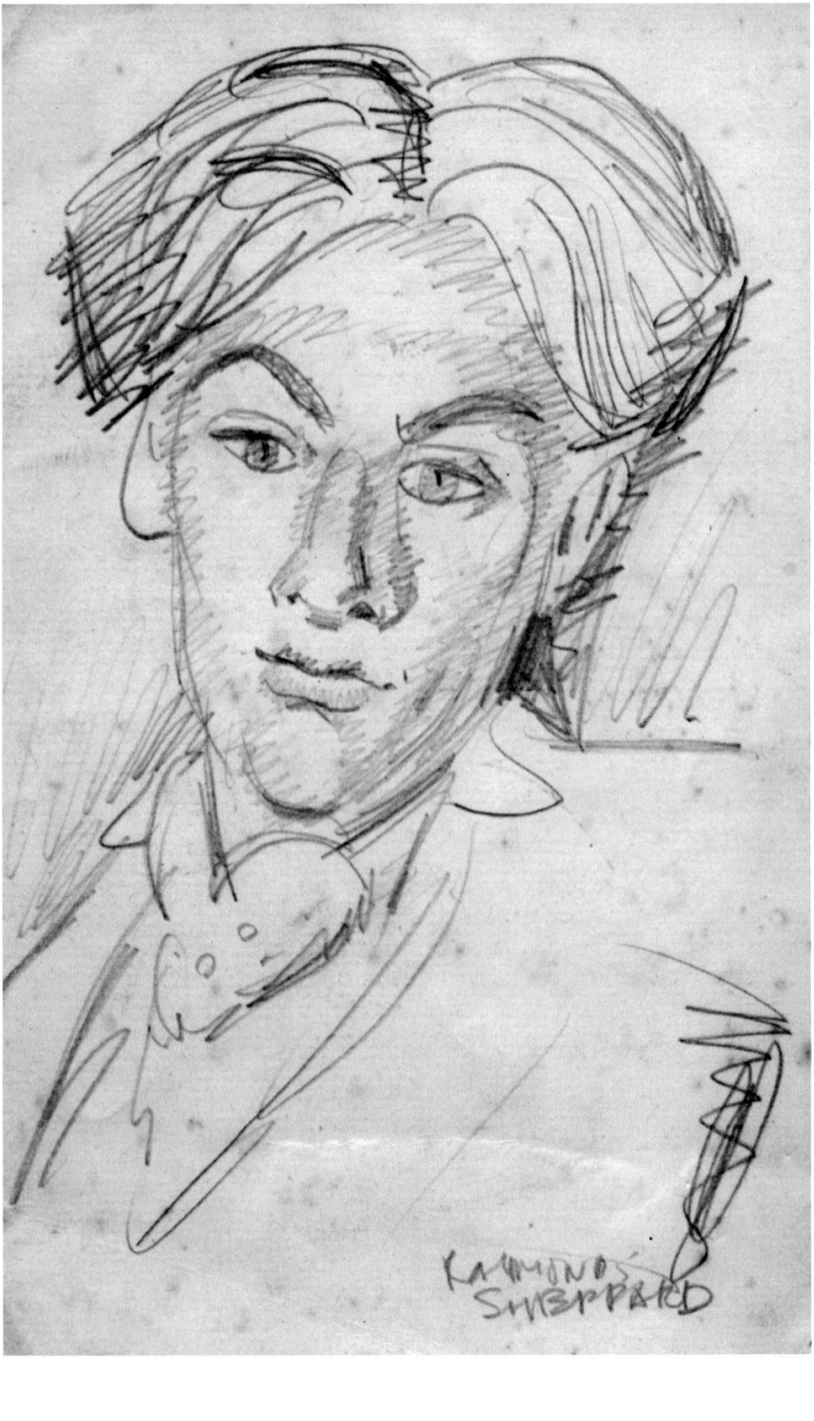
RAYMOND
SHEPPARD

Introduction

Stephen Joseph was the father and the mother of the small theatre movement which swept Britain in the last half century. More than any other individual he is responsible for breaking the conventional mould, and for tearing down the proscenium arch. He was the first person to conceive a Drama school course for Stage Management. He recommended Speech Therapy as a University subject.

He was a man of vision, a gentle giant who established an alternative to orthodox theatre. He had little time for the bourgeois 'west-end' play but sought rather to define the role of theatre in society by tracing it back to its roots. Its essence he easily defined - actors and an audience.

He never identified himself with ideologies Stanislavskian or Brechtian because he knew that to adopt an ideology was to become its slave. Stephen was opposed to tyranny of any sort - he was a convinced and avowed anarchist, both of actions and ideas.

Always ahead of his time, he advocated local radio whilst at university in 1946, and improvisation at drama school shortly after. He was before his time with his concept of fish and chip theatre in which an audience could observe as much or as little as it cared to, and later with Promenade theatre at which a standing audience follows the action around an auditorium, or is surrounded by it.

A decade earlier he had been before his time with Theatre in the Round which became his obsession.

Professor Richard Rothrock of Humboldt State University, shortly before his death, recalled that:

> In a generation illuminated and graced by remarkable people, (Stephen) was probably the most remarkable and the most memorable! Stephen was rich with intellect, knowledge and personality. He seemed to thrive on contradiction. (He was) an intellectual giant.

In the view of Alan, now Sir Alan, Ayckbourn he wasn't a great director,

> He was a great leader, a great theorist . . . he was wonderful on the theory of direction, he taught me so much. He was a rotten writer, but he knew so much about playwriting . . . He was a monumentally bad actor, but he could teach marvellously about acting.

Writer and actor Ian Curteis considered "there is no doubt in my mind that he was a flawed genius," an opinion echoed by Alan Ayckbourn who thought him half madman, half genius. Writer Mike Stott reflects "You always knew he'd never be dull, even if you often felt that you'd been dull by comparison." "There was something in him that was afraid of success, and a melancholy deep enough to prevent his recognising it when it was there," Professor Peter Thomson reflected.

He was always a rather separate, a private man, whom Michael Westmore thought austere. Ever paradoxical, he was foremost an anarchist, and yet a traditionalist amongst whose abiding favourites were Jane Austen, Laurence Houseman and Henry Purcell.

The paradox in part stemmed from being the son of Jewish parents, brought up by a stepmother to be a Christian in the Church of England. The Spartan upbringing imposed by her he carried over into adult life. There was always a utilitarianism about his home and surroundings. His lifestyle was a contrast between driving energy and moody contemplation. His housekeeper would often remark that he should have been a monk, living in an empty cell with only a blanket for luxury.

His unorthodoxy extended to his clothing. He taught in jeans and cowboy boots years before they were ubiquitous. At the theatre he would greet patrons in evening dress with bare feet. In Scarborough Ayckbourn remembers him in leather trousers and shirt open to the navel, cheerfully welcoming the Mayor.

In his introduction to *Actor and Architect* Stephen wrote, "Man cannot... live by washing-machines alone... the theatre must speak, to all people; we have only to take it out of its fetters. We must let the theatre expand, we must explore it, we must allow it to grow..." Elsewhere he wrote "Theatre should be a temple of life. Here is where the great mysteries should be explored."

The outrageous appealed to him. He believed absolutely in the actor as the fundamental, driving source of ideas and energy for the performance. To his students his credo was, "You must think, think, think. I want to stimulate you all to think . . .Make it your own!"

In his Manchester years Richard Rothrock remembers:

> He was a comfortable rebel, a great storyteller, and a marvellous eccentric who cared deeply about the theatre and about people, an extraordinarily articulate man who was impatient for change.
>
> He was an iconoclast, theatrically and socially. Mike Stott observes "barely a day goes by when I don't think 'What would Stephen have said about that?'" Peter Thomson echoes Ayckbourn when he observes "He taught us all so much." He was a charismatic missionary and so filled his actors and students with a sense of purpose and idealism. He was a follower of Krishnamurti, was often inspiring, and could be considerate and patient.

In a letter to the *Scarborough Evening News* Les Freeman wrote of him:

> While scores of other people sat back and shook their heads about the state of the theatre, Stephen Joseph explored the possibilities of changing the existing set up, and his own enthusiasm overflowed, and affected anyone with whom he came into contact.

The Times obituary called him "Perhaps the most successful missionary to have worked in the English Theatre since the Second World War."

The actor Keith Baxter commented:

> He was fiercely and rightly proud of his little space in the Library in Scarborough. He was giving playgoers the sort of nourishment that was on offer hardly anywhere else. But he was no cultural snob either. He was first last and always a man who believed passionately that the theatre was 'important' not in some patronisingly academic fashion, not in some left-wing realpolitik fantasy either. He wanted to speak to ordinary people... beguile their minds and captivate their interest.

He himself wrote that theatre should be an affair, a passionate affair between actors and their audience. . . and Ayckbourn commented that he loved to start things, he hated to finish them. . . "He was a three-day man and then he would go and build something."

Although he wrote articles and books, his best philosophical comments are, like a comedian's best jokes, more or less one-liners.

The art of the theatre depends on the wetness of the British summer.

> Our audiences are middle-aged, middle-class, middlebrow and 90% women.

> All theatres should self-destruct every seven years.

He could be wickedly critical also. Commenting on a *Report on the Provincial Audience* by E.L. Sweeting in 1965 he wrote:

> In the report under discussion (Caryl Jenner's) company is much mentioned. In my opinion its greatest value is that it introduces young people to the sort of second rate acting that they are going to have to put up with if they grow up into theatregoers. Is that good enough?

In his funeral address Hugh Hunt observed that,

> Life was for Stephen an adventure, a challenge, a question and an endless wonder. He met it with the eyes of a child and the mind of a man. Eyes that saw everything as if for the first time, unblurred by the preconceptions of tradition and a mind that he had trained to distinguish between truth and falsehood, emotion and sentiment and, above all, between beauty and its many imitations.

Keith Baxter wrote to the author,

> The last time I remember being with him was on a long walk along the cliffs of Scarborough. He was in fine spirits, bubbling over, and that was pleasing because there were times when the constant battle to keep his theatre alive wore him out. How proud he must be, somewhere, of Alan Ayckbourn's loyalty to his memory and how fine it is that (he) has built on and developed Stephen Joseph's original dream.

There is a studio theatre named after him in the Manchester University Drama Department. Without him the Victoria Theatre Stoke on Trent, the Traverse Theatre in Edinburgh, and the Stephen Joseph Theatre in Scarborough would not exist.

So who was this man, and what were his achievements?

Chapter One

Stephen's Father

Michael Joseph was an accomplished writer, a brilliant editor and a man who judged everything and everyone by his own high opinion of himself.

In 1935 he created his own publishing house. Its imprint was financed by Victor Gollancz under a punitive contractual agreement, from which situation he extricated himself with the assistance of his editorial and production manager Robert Lusty after only six months. His judgement of Lusty was as fine as his judgement of manuscripts, and together they built a reputation for excellence. Office colleague Charles Pick wondered:

> . . I have never fully understood the motives which persuaded Victor Gollancz to finance and to house the new imprint. At no time did there appear to be any particular friendship between him and Joseph. [1]

To Robert Lusty, ten years Joseph's junior, a more contrasting pair could hardly be imagined:

> Victor was fiery, impetuous, dogmatic, arrogant and excitable; Michael was cool, persuasive, charming and cautious. They shared only, a considerable vanity. [2]

Michael Joseph's success came partly as a result of his capacity for hard work, in part from his choice of working colleagues, and from his stable of authors, most of whom he launched: H.E. Bates, John Masters, Richard Llewelyn, Monica Dickens, Vita Sackville West, Richard Gordon. Other writers, Daphne du Maurier and Noel Coward became permanent friends. His *Times* obituary describes him, as one of the most enterprising publishers of his day.

And yet behind all this was a deep seam of insecurity. Early in their relationship he said to Robert Lusty that he envied him his background. [3] Lusty, whose grandfather had sold Kelmscott Manor to William Morris, and whose family was of the quiet yeoman stock of old England, sincerely could not understand why he should pass the remark:

He was a brilliant and accomplished man, but never an easy one to know. Paranoiacally sensitive to his own hurts, he was curiously unthinking towards others. He quite seriously maintained that he had a more sensitive skin than the general run of mankind. A lonely man, (he) would brood for days on end, hardly speaking at all. [4]

No wonder he had few friends and preferred the company of pretty women.

Michael Joseph was born on the 26th September 1897. His mother, Rebecca, was a teacher. His father, Moss, earned a living in several ways, usually in partnership with his brother. They ran a cinema near Marble Arch. Then won the cloakroom concession at Wembley Stadium, which was a very lucrative operation, and after a visit to South Africa to study the diamond market they set up as jewellers near Hatton Garden.

Michael and his brother Lionel were brought up in a house in Osbaldstone Road at Stamford Hill. It was a strictly Victorian home and a strictly Victorian atmosphere. There was no conversation at the dining table, schoolwork was taken seriously, and misdemeanours were punished! There were often rows, which bred a prickly home atmosphere. It was a climate Michael was determined to break out of, but which he nonetheless carried with him into parenthood.

He won a classics scholarship of half-fees to the City of London School when he was eleven. A determined winner, he threw himself into whatever sport presented itself and used all sorts of ruses to win prizes.

Part of the tradition of public schools is the Officer Training Corps. Michael joined the OTC in his last year at school, and enjoyed the technicalities of weapons, the drill and the discipline. He was awarded a place at London University, but the First War was imminent, so he changed his mind and joined the queue of volunteers for the army. When turned down because of his youth he quickly rejoined the queue and insisted he had foolishly given his age as 16, when he was in fact, 26, thus anticipating Hitler's theory that a big whopper is more likely to succeed that a little one. [5]

He was commissioned into the Wiltshire regiment, and war service took him to the major French battlefields. Following action during the first Battle of the Somme he was one of only two officers to survive. During lulls in fighting he wrote, and some of his articles were published in the *Daily Express*.

At the age of eighteen, he had been promoted Lieutenant. His cool-headed bravery in the trenches contributed to his accelerated promotion. The following year he was made Captain. His army career ended abruptly in 1917 due to typhoid.

Whilst he was convalescing in Bournemouth he visited the skating rink for a little exercise and diversion. There he literally bumped into a young lady nervously trying out the ice. She was visiting the town where her mother was convalescent. She was Hermione Ferdinanda Gingold, and they were married in August 1918.

Michael Joseph

Chapter Two

Stephen's Mother

She was a product of her age. She shook off the gloom of the Second World War. She also shook off the sobriety and conservatism of society, just as the voters did the Conservative government after the war. Once she got to America she became something of a gargoyle. To some, her appearances in films like *Gigi* were lacklustre. After watching her onstage in *A Little Night Music*, Ingmar Bergman remarked afterwards, "that Hermione Gingold. . . she does tend to fuck the audience." [1]

If that was true of the 1960s America, her British '40s audience loved her for it. She was heavily roguish, and they loved her for that also. Kenneth Tynan notes:

> Her attitude towards her audiences has always reminded me of the villainous doctor in James Thurber's drawings, who looms unpromisingly over his terrified client and growls: „You're not my patient, you're my meat, Mrs Quist." [2]

Her appearances, spanning the war years made Hermione Gingold one of the best known entertainers of her generation. The fabled *Sweet and Low* revues made her admired and adored by playgoers. It produced the kind of popular reaction these days reserved for pop stars. Feted by her peers and critics, she is included in Tynan's book on heroic acting. The first of five great eccentrics, he describes her as the exemplar of aristocratic waspishness:

> Her every appearance in revue is an adventure - an enquiry into the number of unladylike things a woman can do and say without losing her poise. She gets her laughs by this method, of suddenly and fleetingly letting us glimpse the caged wolf pacing up and down behind the façade of the 'grande dame'.
>
> . . . her voice is a delectable plummy rasp, emerging from her as from a cement mixer... occasionally lunging into them with the masculine

strength and purpose of a growling trombone. . . .[3]

According to her co-star Henry Kendall, many Americans in wartime London believed her to be a female impersonator, "Who is this guy, Hormone Gingold, dressed as a woman." [4]

Witty and idiosyncratic, she was capable of great generosity. She adored the company of men. Those who observed her, remark upon her always having a group of young, attractive, and often androgynous men around her. She was a queen bee surrounded by drones. She needed their support and encouragement to fuel her ego.

Having been married twice, she must have come to perceive men either as brutal bullies or fickle romantics. She describes herself as sexually precocious. Small wonder that after two marriages she should turn to uncomplicated young men. She was unlikely to find a long-term partner who satisfied her intellectual, social and practical needs.

For a while she formed a deep attachment to Tony Ewstrell, a minor leading man of his day, who slept in green silk sheets. He was reputedly homosexual, but whatever their relationship, to her friends she was known as Toni, and signed herself as such thirty years on. [5]

She confided in a friend that she was a dreadful mother [6] and admitted that she had no time for her children,[7] yet the evidence suggests otherwise. She saved her first son Leslie's life, and followed Stephen's progress through his schooling. She, like most people, was capable of reinventing her past. In her book *How to Grow Old Disgracefully,* she describes taking a bath in 1939:

> . . . while I was soaking, my maid poked her head round the door and said, "There's a very tall, good-looking young man at the door who says he's your son..." "He probably is," I said, "Put him in the sitting room and tell him I'll be out in a minute." I jumped out of the bath, put on a bathrobe, combed my hair, and went out to meet my son, Stephen, whom I hadn't seen since he was a baby. [8]

She writes amusingly but her account is not borne out by history. In 1939 Stephen was 18 years old, and although she left the family when he was only three or four, she used to go to see him at public school, where he was between 1935-6. His teacher remembers meeting her on several occasions, notwithstanding their stepmother's stern decree that there should be no communication with their mother. She almost certainly pulled strings to get him into drama school.

Piecing together the early life of 'La' Gingold is complicated by the fact that she is almost our only source, and converts everything into a good joke, as when she sailed to South Africa and the sea was so rough she had to be tied to the mast! She hated aeroplanes, and on one flight from the States to London she left the plane on impulse at a stopover. When the plane arrived at Heathrow, there was her fur coat, but no Hermione! The spectre crossed by sea.

She is equally capable of expropriating good stories from other sources. On the last night of *Sweetest and Lowest*, there were huge crowds outside the theatre trying to get tickets for the performance. Hermione describes sending for sandwiches and drinks to be served to fans who had been queuing all night for seats. [9] Unfortunately, 29 years earlier, the story had been chronicled by her co-star in *Sweetest and Lowest*, Henry Kendall:

> ... the house had been sold out for weeks and the Bow Street Police had to be called in to control the crowds as evening approached. The narrow street outside the theatre was completely blocked with the crowd clamouring for admission. About fifty people had been queuing outside the pit door since seven o'clock the previous evening, and I had coffee and sandwiches sent over from the Ivy... [10]

She leads us to believe her father adored her, but her sister Margaret, was adamant. "Hermione was wrong in her book... Father liked me best." [11] One feels instinctively that Margaret is right. Their father's coolness towards his eldest daughter would also make sense of her performer's desire to be 'loved' by her audience. Some thought her manner rather sour [12] but to most she was kind and generous. She was a perfectionist in her work.

She was born on the 9th of December 1897, the same year as Michael Joseph, of an exotic and well off European family. Her paternal grandfather was Viennese and his wife Turkish. Hermione's father was one of six children. The only daughter of the family married a European Baron and was rumoured to share the favours of the then King of Greece.

James, Hermione's father, became a British citizen. He was a stockbroker and gambled not just his own, but others' fortunes. We must hope that he had more success with his clients' portfolios than he did with his own. He not only exhausted his own capital, he also spent their grandmother's legacy to his two daughters, Margaret and Hermione.

Their mother, Kate Walter, was one of a family of eleven, ten sisters and one brother, who had been brought up in the certain knowledge that luxury and privilege were their due. She complained bitterly and constantly about her health when the reality of her husband's affairs impinged upon her. Kate's family was also Jewish. She appears to have been the only one to make a poor match. She had a husband who womanised, who spent money imprudently, and who beggared them.

Hermione's was a classic riches to rags story. She and her sister were brought up in the top floor of a huge house by a nurse and an under nurse, theirs being a typically Edwardian middle class upbringing. They might see their mother at teatime, their father rarely. She and her sister would occasionally be taken to tea at the Savoy by their father, who often had a lady friend with him.

The family moved from house to garret with some frequency. Her father even disappeared altogether for quite a long spell with her sister Margaret. [13] Hermione claims to have had no great affection for anyone but her father. Her affection appears to have been one-sided. He chose to go off with petite and pretty Margaret, not ugly duckling Hermione. In revenge she tore out the eyes of her sister's dolls and teased her mercilessly. [14]

Rich or poor, Hermione was sent to the Southend Girls' School whose records of her time there were lost in the war, and the family always seemed to be able to go to the seaside for holidays, taking a maid with them. Talent competitions, singing, piano, fencing and acting lessons, led to her being chosen for their companies, first by Sir Herbert Beerbohm Tree and later by William Poel at Stratford and Lilian Bayliss at the Old Vic, all suggesting that her precocity was well recognised.

It was in Bournemouth during one of her mother's fits of hypochondria that she was skating at the ice rink. There, unsteady as only a novice skater can be, she was bumped into by our young officer, convalescing from active service at the front. He pursued her by repeatedly bumping into her. These days a girl might claim sexual harassment, but in 1918 Hermione was swept along by Michael Joseph's persistence and charm.

He spent the last months of his war service as a Machine Gun Corps tutor in Grantham. With one of her mother's sisters, Aunt Dorothy as witness they were married in Grantham Registry Office on the 19th of August 1918, before either was 21 years old. The wedding ring was rolled gold!

There was a mistaken Joseph family belief that it must have been a shotgun marriage. Leslie's widow expressed his firm conviction that since no one in the family knew when the wedding took place, it was because of necessity! That might also have explained the Joseph family's opposition to the union. Moss and Rebecca considered Michael had married beneath him.

Why they should hold that opinion is hard to say. One would expect a stockbroker to be rather more highly regarded socially than a jeweller. We must assume it stemmed from the fact that Hermione was determined to continue her theatrical career and made Michael promise that she could do so. [15]

The acting profession to this day is regarded as distinctly raffish. In 1918, to be an actress was to be a loose woman, and not one to marry into a respectable family!

Stephen

Chapter Three

Bringing up Baby

Michael was demobilised on the 11th of January, 1919; his first son was born on the 12th of August that year. Although delivered in what Hermione describes as the luxury of her parents' house, by a kind doctor, a caring nurse and with the aid of chloroform, her first reaction on being presented with the child was, "Take it away." She named the baby Leslie in memory of her first love, Leslie Hudson who had been killed only weeks after joining the war from which Michael emerged unscathed.

On the strength of his patriotic articles from the front Michael got a job as a junior sub-editor on one of the many weekly magazines then coming out of Fleet Street. He also wrote articles and arts reviews, for other magazines. These were five or six years of struggle during which Hermione found them a just acceptable flat in Lisson Grove, home of that latter-day Galatea created by Bernard Shaw, Eliza Doolittle, the seller of violets. Michael and Hermione's life was no bed of those.

Her agents found Hermione work touring on engagements in the provinces. Between pregnancies she did as much professional work as she could although much was of dubious quality after Stratford and the Old Vic, but it was experience. In between engagements Hermione joined Michael in ploughing through manuscripts which they read and reported on. Two readers earned more than one, and they were both sharpening their critical faculties.

In May 1920 Michael joined the publishing house of the eccentric and legendary Walter Hutchinson, initially as advertising manager. It was not long before he was in the editorial department. Their second son was born on the 13th of June, 1921. The child was named after his father and his uncle. It is likely that Stephen was Hermione's contribution to his name. He was christened Michael Stephen Lionel.

Hermione had adopted a cat after the birth of Leslie. She confesses she loved it more than the baby, and it was to be a constant source of irritation and argument. Michael resented her neglect of the children and the affection she lavished on the cats. She resented with disgust and horror the realities of childbirth. Although the year of Stephen's birth was the year Marie Stopes opened her first birth control clinic in Britain, Hermione had none but the vaguest idea of birth control. 'Sex and contraception just weren't talked about by respectable married couples.'

She struggled to cope on their joint incomes. She preferred domestic work to childcare, shopping, cooking, carrying coal up five flights of stairs. Lighting fires and cleaning were no substitute for work in the theatre. With his salary at Hutchinson's, Michael could afford to offer Hermione either a nurse or a servant. She chose the former.

Out of his experience as editor his first book was published on the 5th of October, 1923. *Short Story Writing for Profit* did so well that it went through four editions in seven months. A year later, almost to the day, he published his second book *Journalism for Profit*.

If Michael's career appeared to be set on an even keel, the same could not be said of his marriage. Hermione was as determined to have a successful career as Michael was. Unfortunately he wanted a wife who would provide him with a stable home life and total commitment to his ambitions to allow him to pursue his own career despite her honesty before marriage and his promise about her work.

Hermione's parents had fallen on hard times. With nowhere to live, Hermione took them into their home, even though she did not get on with her mother. Shortly after Stephen was born Hermione became pregnant for a third time. Their child, a daughter, was stillborn and for a while Hermione's condition was critical.

By this stage there can be little doubt the marriage was collapsing. After three pregnancies in four years and any number of rows, Michael rented a cottage on the Isle of Wight and took his family there for the summer.

On the island he intercepted a letter to the maid. He recognised the writing of his young assistant from Hutchinson's! Although addressed to the maid, it was destined for Hermione.

It led to their last furious argument. Michael locked Hermione in the bedroom, and as she was convinced he had gone for something with which to beat her, she climbed out of the window and left with only her handbag, to catch the ferry and then the train to London.

Once there, she went directly to the home of the man she claimed was her lover, and who was to become her second husband.

Chapter Four

The Co-Respondent

Eric Maschwitz was Head of Light Entertainment on BBC TV from 1958 to 1961. He had joined the corporation in 1926, became editor of Radio Times the following year, and between 1933 and 1937 was Director of Variety. During the war he served as a Lieutenant Colonel in the Intelligence Corps.

Stephen later claimed that his only feelings of filial affection were towards Eric Maschwitz. He told many friends that Maschwitz was the first adult he was able to hold any sort of conversation with, and at least one wartime colleague was convinced that Maschwitz was Stephen's father.[1] Perhaps Stephen was re-inventing his past.

A kindly, generous man, Maschwitz continued his involvement with Stephen and Leslie long after he and Hermione separated. Stephen's *Footlights* productions were transferred to London from Cambridge with the help of his stepfather.

Although a large part of his professional career was salaried in broadcasting, he made a considerable income from writing. His first novel, *A Taste of Honey*, written while he was waiting for Hermione's divorce to go through, can best be described as a Mills and Boon of its day.

One can almost hear Noel Coward telling the story of one Tommy Maskelyn, dark eyes smouldering in charred sockets, ... and writer/diplomat Jerrold Freyne, tallish, slight in build, face colourless (he could be describing himself), who ... had a queer liking for Tommy Maskelyn...[2]

He adapted several popular novels for the stage and co-authored three shows with Val Gielgud. Between 1949 and 1956 he wrote a succession of popular musical comedies creating the contemporary fashion for Zigeuner music. *Balalaika* ran for almost two years. Of his lyrics, Jack Buchanan popularised *Goodnight Vienna* and the entertainer, Hutch, secured the success of *A Nightingale Sang in Berkeley Square*. In 1957 alone *These Foolish*

Things was still earning him royalties of £1000 a year.[3]

In his autobiography he wrote a florid account of his birth:

> Aunts crowded around my little cradle while beyond the windows, in the garden of my fathers' house . . . that highly respectable suburb of Birmingham, Red Admirals and Tortoiseshell, Peacocks and Cabbage Whites performed a series of 'divertissements' among the calceolarias in honour of my birth. [4]

He was born in 1901 in Edgbaston. Eric was descended from Field Marshal von Maschwitz, who was ennobled on the field of battle in the war of the Lithuanians against the Muscovites and Tartars. He took the right to use the appellation 'von' in front of his name.

His great great grandfather had been Director of Salt Mines in Warsaw. His grandfather was a general merchant with a love of music.

His father, gourmet, traveller, prolific reader, tennis player, golfer, stamp collector, and chatterer in seven languages had a splendid cellar! The family business was sanitary pottery which his father exported, embarrassed on one occasion going to the Kremlin with two urinals strapped to the outside of his 'droshky' and passing the Czar coming out as he was going in. He was bankrupted due to losses sustained during the Russian Revolution.

A family given to grand gestures, his father would turn up on birthdays with strawberries and cream for the entire school. Maschwitz won a classical scholarship which took him to Repton, where Victor Gollancz was a master at the time. Gollancz disappeared after encouraging a literary and political review entitled *A Public School Looks at the World*. Parents concerned that Repton was going Red, caused shockwaves to reach MI5 who sent a Major General to investigate. Among Maschwitz's contemporaries were Christopher Isherwood, the performer Douglas Byng and Ben Levy, who as a playwright was to become uncle by marriage to Stephen.

A further scholarship took Maschwitz to Gonville and Caius College in 1919 after which his first job was as an assistant stage manager on *East of Suez* at His Majesty's Theatre. After four unsuccessful days as an A.S.M. the American uncle who had got him the job carted him off to meet Walter Hutchinson in Paternoster Row. There he began his short-lived publishing career as Michael Joseph's assistant editor.

Over tea and cakes and ices he met and became enamoured of Hermione. He says it was at a staff party in a tea-shop basement under the Strand: [5] she, that it was while they were organising charitable teas.[6]

Howsoever, the flamboyantly romantic extrovert Eric was so different from the self-absorbed Michael that it was not long before the moment had been forced to its crisis.

Upon the refugee presenting herself on his doorstep, Eric did the decent thing and left the lady the run of the flat. In later life there were those who said he loved fast cars and fast women, but their contemporaries considered it a marriage of convenience.

For the time being he escaped London and the not inconsiderable social wrath of the day of being a co-respondent, to write *A Taste of Honey* and live for a year on a romantic Mediterranean Island.

Reproduced by kind permission of
Eric Maschwitz Musicals Ltd

Edna Frost

Courtesy, Ashford Press

Chapter Five

The Wicked Stepmother

For there to be a wicked stepmother, there has to be a compliant father. Either that or he must be weak and henpecked. Michael Joseph was no weak man, so we have to accept that he was party to the attitude and behaviour of his wife.

He met Edna Frost at a Chelsea Arts Ball. She was a strikingly beautiful young woman, but it was that bloom which fades with the passing of youth, and in marriage, as her good looks waned, so did her tolerance.

In later life Stephen used to refer to her gleefully as his *wicked* stepmother and would embroider stories about her, of how she had taken to drinking in middle age, as did her sister who was an alcoholic, and that his father had wooed the younger sister. Then when the family realised that they would be left with an elder daughter (and fearing to lose him), they announced his engagement to Edna in *The Times,* thus realising a fait accompli since Michael could not afford a breach of engagement suit.

In this Stephen was like his mother. There were occasions when he was given to changing details and embellishing a good story, and this one is likely to be a somewhat *wicked* romance.[1]

Edna had been a debutante, and at one party David, Prince of Wales, danced with her four times.[2] The fact that the season had not secured her a safe matrimonial partner and that she was 24 when she married Michael suggests a headstrong young lady who had frightened off earlier suitors.

If she was beautiful she was also emptyheaded[3] but having been a debutante she was not only socially desirable, she also brought that breeding which sometimes attends upon wealth.

Her home was in Chester and her parents are most likely to have been from the family-milling firm of Frost and Sons. Father and Grandfather were both Lord Mayor of the city, each being knighted in office.

Father was the longest serving mayor in the city's history and a much-loved man; his wife was a lively independent extrovert. Liberally inclined though they were, in the first instance they did not take kindly to the idea of a divorcee with two children as being a suitable match for their daughter, especially as he was Jewish. Michael never saw his parents again.[4]

When the divorce judge asked Hermione why she wanted a divorce, she is reported to have said, "Because he is so ugly, my Lord."

It says much for Michael's charm and Edna's persistence that they married a month after the decree absolute. Michael was by then an editor with the prestigious literary agents, Curtis Browne.

The Gingold boys were packed off to prep school; both went to Burstow, then to Bradfield College (which has a beautiful copy of a Greek amphitheatre attached to it). Leslie took after his father, was a regular athletic type and was very keen on games and sports of all kinds. He often picked on his younger brother, either to tease or bully. Far from discouraging him, Michael was furious with Stephen for not defending himself from Leslie's belligerence. At home, their stepmother insisted on the boys attending church, and the sight of two obviously Jewish boys in the Anglican pews must have raised the odd eye-brow.[5]

The birth of Michael and Edna's own child, Diana Shirley, did much to emphasize the boys' position in the house. Instead of being members of the family they were interlopers. Whilst Shirley had a magnificent bedroom on the second floor the boys were brought up in the attic with linoleum flooring. Aware of the disparity of attention, Granny Frost was given to calling on the boys at school with presents of sweets and the strictest injunction that they were not to let their stepmother know she had been.[6]

Stephen's marked resemblance to Hermione can have done nothing but increase Michael's dislike of him. Michael considered him unmanly and effete.[7] The boys were nevertheless closely monitored by Edna and a good behaviour slate was kept. Any misdemeanour was listed and when Michael came home out came the swagger stick and the boys were beaten - regularly.

Leslie must have taken a rebellious attitude but Stephen was more servile and these punishments formed his views on injustice and the misuse of power. These he expressed most forcibly in his early plays, and were the first steps to his anarchic philosophy.

The anarchist rejects all forms of external government, and the state. He realises that self-management mirrors the self-regulation and self-organisation of nature. Anarchy holds the ideal of personal and social freedom.

Stephen at school

P.A. Buchanan & Co. Ltd - 1934

Chapter Six

Clayesmore

1935 was a significant year in the Joseph household. Michael left the security of Curtis Browne and established his own publishing house - Michael Joseph Limited. It was the year he moved from Camden Town to a larger detached town house in St. John's Wood. In December Edna's father died, closing an expansive year in a domestically sombre way. For the two young Josephs the year was equally significant. At the age of 14 and having been previously schooled with his brother, Stephen was sent to Clayesmore in Dorset.

It reflects well on Michael that he should have recognised the different temperaments and inclinations of the two boys and have sent his younger son to a very liberally orientated establishment, and one which would develop his interests. As to who lit upon the school, it is most probable that Hermione heard about its theatrical bias, and in some way influenced the choice. She certainly visited the school, took an interest in Stephen's development there and attended speech day in 1936.

Clayesmore was a very unusual school for its time. Founded in Enfield 40 years earlier in 1896 by one of the most original and engaging educationalists of modern times, Alexander Devine, it moved to Pangbourne in 1902, and then to Winchester in 1914 before settling on its present site in 1933. It is situated in the heart of rural Dorset at Iwerne Minster, in a house which was the former home and estate of the second Lord Wolverton. It had been designed by the Victorian architect Alfred Waterhouse, celebrated for his natural history museum in Kensington.

Clayesmore's aim was to treat pupils as individuals and to develop their talents to the fullest extent. Alexander Devine believed that study should awaken interests as well as impart knowledge. He abhorred the narrow curriculum and early specialisation, and above all wanted pupils to think for themselves. He gave an honoured place to music and the arts.[1] The school roll was around 150 boys when Stephen arrived for the autumn term in 1935 at this very free and easy establishment. By great good fortune one of the most influential men in Stephen's life was, at that time, science teacher in the school.

Carl Verrinder had been an Olympic Gold medallist and seemed to the boys in his charge like a Greek god.[2] At weekends he would take groups of boys walking across Dorset, stop over at a Youth Hostel at four shillings a night for supper bed and board before returning the following day. He was a member of the Arts Theatre Club to which he regularly took pupils. One of the productions Stephen saw with him was Shaw's *Back to Methuselah*.

He also produced a succession of shows in the school, plays as well as variety performances with monologues and home based sketches. In these Stephen was often partnered by a boy two years his senior who became a notable character actor and screen gangster, Michael Balfour. These two were good friends and their enthusiasm was shared by a third, Kenneth MacIntosh whose last appointment was as house director at the National Theatre. In 1936 these three performed in Verrinder's production of *Bird in Hand* staged at the Shaftsbury Guild Hall, in a performance seen by Christopher Fry. The school's historian cites these three boys as actors with star quality.

During his time at Clayesmore Verrinder considered he and Stephen to have become 'good buddies', a friendship which was to endure. Stephen was something of an extrovert with decidedly strong opinions. Verrinder would have liked him to stay on at school and do something more ambitious than work in his father's office. He considered the 15 year-old to be highly intelligent and one who didn't need any encouragement: it was always "What are we going to do this term, Sir?"[3]

In 1937 Stephen played *Androcles* for Verrinder in the Bernard Shaw play, despite the school records showing him as having left the previous year. Verrinder's memory is precise, because his wife gave birth to a daughter early in 1937, and Stephen presented them with a large lion nicknamed Andy.

However we interpret the disparity of dates, Verrinder was aware of external reasons for the boy leaving at the age of 16, which is what he would have been in 1936. Certainly records emphasize the bleak nature of this teenager leaving in 1936, having gained his School Certificate with an:

> otherwise undistinguished career - now interested in literature and politics. Wants to go on the stage: Father wants him in his office. Might go to Oxford or Cambridge - left tending pessimistic support.[4]

Verrinder continued to be a good friend. The school's tradition of performing one night a year in London at the Duffy or Toynbee Halls altered whilst Stephen was teaching at Central School. He organised for the cast to perform in the Royal Albert Hall - at that time also home to the Central School of Speech and Drama.

At some point during Stephen's last year or two at school his brother was involved in a sporting accident. Always the outdoor type, Leslie was playing in a cricket match on Kew Green when he was struck on the head by an errant ball.

The incident was of deep embarrassment to Michael who, as a spectator, had to watch his son escorted from the field screaming. The fact that he was in excruciating pain was of no concern to the father whose only thoughts were for his own public humiliation. The boy appeared to recover, but recurring problems occasioned concern and he was sent for specialist diagnosis. The examination was conclusive. He had a tumour on the brain!

Edna's reaction was cold. The boy had cancer - a terminal disease. She had done what she could for her stepchild and was not going to spend money on surgery - the efficacy of which was uncertain. It was sad. As a matter of courtesy Hermione was told.

Michael's reasons for contacting her must be conjectured. There was no National Health Service at the time. He knew that surgery held a possible cure, but that surgery would be expensive. He had been through the war, had seen death, had stared it in the face. He may have been being vindictive in passing the buck to Hermione. He and his wife had brought up her children, now one of them was a goner unless she could do something about it. Edna refused to foot the bill.

Hermione was horrified. Her child was critically ill and required an operation. She discovered the most famous cancer surgeon in London. She could not afford his fee either, but she was married, and although it was largely a marriage of convenience[5] she and Eric were great friends.

Eric had no hesitation in agreeing that the operation should go ahead, and Hermione went to visit Michael in his office, to inform him that Eric Maschwitz would pay for the surgery.[6] It was a tense meeting, and once Hermione had gone, Michael raged through the suite of rooms and flung open every window to rid the office of her scent.[7] His disgust was no doubt due in part to the embarrassment of having a third party do what he should have done himself.

The operation was apparently a success but although he recovered, Leslie's character had altered. His stepsister recalls him changing from a bully into a snivelling wimp.[8] However worse was to follow.

Leslie was apprehended for petty larceny.[9] Michael was stunned and Edna mortified. "How could he do this," she said repeatedly, "after all I've done for him . . .?" People who lived in St. John's Wood didn't do such things. His behaviour was insupportable. The seventeen-year-old was told to leave the house immediately and never to darken its doors again. He left with what possessions he could carry. The rest was burnt.

The precise course of events and dates is now lost, but there can be no doubts that the trauma of Leslie's petty larceny caused a vortex of hysteria, recrimination and retribution. He went to live with the paternal grand parents he barely knew, and Maschwitz found him his first job as an assistant stage manager in the West End. It was a job he did not hold down for long.

It is possible that it was at this time that Michael insisted on Stephen joining him in his office. It may be that Stephen acquiesced for a time, since one of his early plays shows a familiarity with office politics. But in the end one of the Josephian family strengths lay in their determination.

Stephen Joseph was determined on a theatrical career and was not to be deflected.

(Years later, when he was in an army hospital successfully recovering from his second brain tumour, Leslie was much affected by his nurse, a girl from Scotland, bright, attractive, disciplined and determined. She already had a daughter by a previous marriage, and idle conversation led him to ask her where she was from. Margaret was a young lady who had been born in a small town close to Glasgow - Motherwell.

He was so taken by the name and by his cheerful and efficient nurse, that he proposed to her. She provided him with a home and two sons of his own and they settled down in Motherwell.)[10]

Chapter Seven

The Hall

The principles upon which Elsie Fogerty established the Central School of Speech Training and Dramatic Art still obtained thirty years on when Stephen entered as a student. Her desire to act had been frustrated by her father so she turned to teaching. She was the only child of an eminent architect who invested and lost all his working capital in an aborted project for the Austrian government. In his near bankruptcy and decline she supported her parents by her earnings as a speech teacher, which she became par excellence, and without their knowing it the students who paid supported the others for whom she worked free of charge.

She began teaching in rooms in the Royal Albert Hall in 1903, and by 1907 had arranged to take under her tutelage the junior actors of Sir Frank Benson's company from Stratford-upon-Avon. In this way the school at 'The Hall' was born. Her later involvement was critical to the success of the first performance of T.S. Eliot's *Murder in the Cathedral* at Canterbury in 1935. She was a specialist in Greek drama, and orchestrated the chorus for that production. She is described as inspiring her students with the desire for knowledge;[1] she set out to uncover the Dionysian spirit in drama, and to make explicable to a contemporary audience all the excitement of the great classical tragedies.

There can have been few important actors she did not advise privately. She coached Edith Evans and John Gielgud complained that she never sent him a bill.[2] Her most renowned students at The Hall were Olivier and Ashcroft.

She was noted for the simplicity of her productions and revelled in a lack of scenery. She was keen on the individual rather than the masses and was a convinced follower of Adler.[3] For years she took no salary for running the school.

Here was another liberally enlightened atmosphere into which Stephen enrolled in 1937. He almost certainly went in on a scholarship, the school being always short of men.[4] It seems likely that Hermione rescued him from the family firm by using her influence to secure his admission. She had just had a great success in the *Gate Review* and was at the school theatre one day, heavily made-up and with too much lipstick under a large brimmed black straw hat, very actressy. Stephen was embarrassed by her presence and as she left he remarked to a fellow student, Victor Lucas, "That's my mother, she can't stand the sight of me."[5]

Whilst it sounds like a self-pitying indulgence, the truth is probably quite simple. These were the days when children should be seen and not heard. Hermione had attended functions at Clayesmore, and effected Stephen's entrance to the Hall, but she barely spoke to him on any occasion. If it is true that her divorce decree ruled against it, so did her desire as a rising star, not to acknowledge a mature son. She had glowed like a meteor on each occasion, and then been gone without a word. It was after seeing a performance or her revue with fellow pupil Ruth Bernstein that Ruth took Stephen to the Stage Door of the theatre and requested an interview with Hermione. Once in her dressing room Ruth Bernstein introduced Stephen to his mother! (Reuth, as she later styled herself, insists on this point just as she said she became Hermione's understudy and then denied having said it).

The front doors of the Albert Hall were also the entrance to the school premises on the first floor. It was an exhilarating atmosphere, with the sound of orchestral rehearsals filtering into the school. Students would sneak into the upper circle to watch celebrated conductors like Malcolm Sargent and soloists such as Pablo Casals preparing for the evening concerts.

The school's examination room was immediately behind the Great Organ, which frequently burst forth at full blast during inappropriate moments in exams. Elsie Fogerty used to take groups of her pupils to the British Museum to study the attitudes of the Elgin Marbles. She had a way of being very direct with her students. To Mary David she remarked, "You must have been among people who don't think charm important; you don't even make the most of your very pretty hair."[6]

Contemporaries at The Hall remember Stephen as a tall, thin, gangling youth, untidy and very much a loner. He came to the school in a grubby threadbare jacket, baggy grey trousers, scuffed and unpolished shoes, with his chapped wrists sticking out from his too short sleeves:

> He had a wryly humorous self-mockery, which was generally understood by us all to stem from his perception of his mother's dislike and neglect of him, and a way of making rather aggressive and only half humorous remarks which sometimes rubbed people up the wrong way. . . a

defensive mockery of himself and others, accompanied usually by a half smile.[7]

The first year was taken up with technical aspects of the actor's craft. Mime with Irene Mawer, diction classes with the renowned Clifford Turner, phonetics under Walter Ripman, but Ruby Ginner was perhaps by now a little too old to satisfactorily demonstrate the abandon of the Greek Bacchanalia. The schools' Director of Drama was E. Martin Browne who experimented with the students to assist his productions of T.S. Eliot's verse dramas. In 1938 he directed the first performance of Eliot's *The Family Reunion* at the school with a student cast.

Miss Elsie Fogerty, then in her seventies, and a CBE, lectured on the Greek Drama and taught speech therapy. She had the durability of one half her age. When she slipped on the stone steps of the Albert Hall alarmed students rushed to her aid. With perfect composure she sat up and told them, "It's all right my dears, as soon as I felt myself going I simply RELAXED." She always insisted that you could achieve nothing on the stage without the ability to relax. . . the body, the muscles, the nerves, the wrists.[8]

The Hall's canteen was the hub of the students' universe, the same group of friends meeting around the table. Victor Lucas, Luke, still enjoys a successful career as an actor and writer. Arthur Wilkinson, Wilky, gave up the theatre soon after the war and established his own electronics business. Alan Broadhurst, Brocky, became an actor manager in repertory, and gave Stephen his first 'job' after the war. Beryl Dunn was one of the friends who admired him more deeply than he realised, as was Mary David, who provided the author with letters, photographs, manuscripts and many recollections of their times together.

Stephen had spent much of his teenage years writing juvenile playlets. Rejected by his mother as a baby, mocked by his father as a child, made scapegoat by his stepmother. Jewishness was never discussed in the Joseph household. Michael had rejected his own Jewish parents. His children, in their pews, were aware of how different they were from the Christian congregation. So his need to trace the roots of persecution led to his first play being inspired by the Book of Esther.

Haman was written at a time when anti-Semitism was being fanned by Hitler in Europe and Mosley in Britain.[9] The rejection of the Jewish race and its parallel to the holocaust is obvious, though Stephen stops his play short, and does not face the moral dilemma the Book of Esther poses.

Haman proclaims the Persians to be a great race, which miscegenation has polluted. He claims that Persian customs are being fouled by lust for profits and that the Jew must be unmasked for the poison that he is. Commenting on decadence in Persia, Haman sees the fault not within the person. As is the case with malcontents, he seeks outside himself for blame and chances upon it "shuffling along the street," "whispering in the market place," "smiling in another's house." It is "The grim rottenness of the stealthy Jew."

If the writing is somewhat simplistic, it is nonetheless chilling in its penetration of the ego of the anti-Semite, and we are shocked at its bigotry laid bare. Haman's logic is foolish and yet plausible.

The script was typed by fellow student Ruth Bernstein[10] whose floor he sometimes slept on, and was written under a pseudonym to make promotion easier. He adopted the name Lane, acknowledging the inspiration of the independent and adventurous Mrs Lane of the Brittannia Theatre, Hoxton. The play was directed in a 'Greek Frieze' style. Helping with the stage-management of the production Victor Lucas remembers Stephen standing disconsolate alone in the wings during the performance:

> He held his head in his hands in anguish as one of the actors got into a terrible muddle with the lines and made a hash of one of the key scenes. When he saw me he gave one of his customary grins and made some disparaging remark about the whole thing being a disaster.[11]

It was not only Stephen who considered the play a disaster, the production was crushingly dismissed by the adjudicators.

By contrast a highlight of 1938 was to be in the British Premier of Eugene O'Neill's play *Marco's Millions* at the Westminster Theatre, presented under a production company headed by J B Priestley and directed by Michael McCowan who took 25 students from the Webber Douglas and Central Schools to be extras. O'Neill's play is a satire on Occidental materialism in contrast with the contemplative philosophy of the East. The Marco Polo of the title is spiritually blind, and the East exists for him that it may be exploited.[12]

The production had a cast of notable actors - Griffith Jones was Marco, Stephen Murray and Max Adrian his father and uncle respectively but the critical accolade went to two outstanding performances of Robert Harris and Catherine Lacy. For most of the extras it was their first engagement in the professional theatre and they enjoyed the rigours of doubling, trebling and quadrupling a variety of non-speaking roles. It also earned them a welcome addition to their finances during the Christmas/New Year - between terms - period.

In the spring of 1939 a group of students became indignant that not a single Shakespeare play was being staged as part of their curriculum. The protest was instigated by Arthur Wilkinson who wanted a chance to play *Hamlet*. The project was frowned upon by the Vice-Principal of the school as a distraction to studies and so rehearsals took place on the roof of Mary David's flat in Chelsea Old Church Street.

It was Stephen's second production, during which he concentrated more on the lighting and technical aspects than on the actors: an early manifestation of his production technique. The more confident players were left to get on with it, with the occasional tentative suggestions. Alan Broadhurst was Polonius and the Gravedigger, and Victor Lucas, Claudius and the Ghost. The production, remembered with affection by those in it, only just went on in June 1939, as the Hall's authorities were less than happy that the use of the school's stage should have been taken for granted when permission for the production had not been given

> If this is bitter to me, what will it be
> To you, wracked, sensitive, uncherished child They have dashed
> Your half-winged creation to unhappy atoms Tomorrow they will take a brush
> Sweep up the pieces with apologies,
> And mend it all quite neatly;
> And it can never become the creation we have seen,
> Those fretted weeks of effort.
> I wish you less than I believe you,
> That this needless ache may not be so deep.
> I wish you nearer than I know you.
> That I might bear it with you.
> But first, I wish you strong enough to use it, An ugly step, to climb your pedestal
> Of destined greatness.
>
> Stephen's *Hamlet*, 3. vii, 39

The poem was written by Mary David, who was Stephen's stage-manager for the production. *Viva Voce*, the 'organ' of the Pivot Club reviewed three productions in 1939.

> The second . . was *Hamlet* in modern dress. Certainly this was ambitious, but that it was successful and most interesting there can be no doubt. Its most striking feature, which gave great atmosphere

to the production was, perhaps, the beautiful lighting.[13]

It was the first acknowledgement of his stage lighting skill, and the production swelled the funds of the Pivot Scholarship, as did the production that year of Stephen's second play.

> *Wild Sonata*, written and produced by Stephen Joseph, was received with great interest and brought good applause as is natural in the work of a present student. The music was specially composed by Miss Viola Tunnard. . . As a first play it was promising, some of the dialogue and theme being both interesting and unusual. The rather excessive dialogue and deviations from the central idea tended to make it lack unity and to slow down the action. One felt that the cast was not altogether in perfect sympathy with the author.[14]

The end-of-course public production at the Arts Theatre was on the 13th of June, Stephen's birthday. All drama schools hold these shop windows at which directors and agents can assess the ability of the young actors. Stephen not only stage-managed Act III of *She Stoops to Conquer*, he played Gaev in Act IV of *The Cherry Orchard* in which Victor Lucas remembers him as being very good, utilising his own self-denigrating wry humour. . . and getting several laughs, which pleased him very much.[15] He also appeared in Yeats' poetical drama *Dierdre* as Conchubar and was impressive in a long white beard, the play being rehearsed by Miss Fogerty herself.

At some time during the year Robert Atkins directed a play in three acts at the Phoenix Theatre for a Sunday night try-out. The play, translated from the Czech, was *To Be or Not To Be* by Eleanor Kalkowska. Several actors from the Hall were in the cast. Alan Broadhurst and Arthur Wilkinson had speaking parts as did Stephen as the Waiter, who had the unenviable task of opening the play with a few lines of dialogue. Victor Lucas wrote:

> I recall him dashing about the stage very briskly. . . I also recall thinking that Atkins, addressing sarcastic remarks to Stephen at one rehearsal, was treating him as a whipping boy. . . (Atkins) was given to making snide remarks in public at the expense of the more vulnerable members of the cast. In this instance there may have been an element of the unthinking anti-Semitism of the times.

The other piece Stephen wrote between 1938-39 was a pantomime *Beauty and the Beast*. *Viva Voce* describes the 1939 performance as a repeat, so we must assume it was put on in 1938 originally. The reviewer, MJE, describes the achievement as a pantomime of no mean value. All the adjectives are employed - touching, graceful, substantial, debonair. The ugly sisters were described as the cause of ceaseless merriment. "Beauty and the Beast was a great success, and the double performance an innovation well worth repeating." [16]

As a script *Beauty and the Beast* is not strong, but storyline in Panto never needs to be so, the whole never much more than a coat-hanger on which to place the most gaudy characterisations. Performed only at Christmas time, it is a hangover from the pagan ritual of Saturnalia, when the rich exchange places with the poor for a day, the master becoming the servant. In pagan days, it allowed what is now commonplace: an excuse for public cross dressing.

Rehearsal for *Hamlet* (1939)
Jessie Spencer, Alan Broadhurst, Arthur Wilkinson

Central School of Speech Training and Dramatic Art
(Incorporated)

Royal Albert Hall

Patronesses : H.R.H. Princess Louise (Duchess of Argyll)
H.R.H. The Duchess of Kent
President Right Hon. The Earl of Lytton, K.G., G.C.S.I., G.C.I.E.
Vice-President : John Gielgud
Principal : Elsie Fogerty, C.B.E., L.R.A.M.

Programme of a Matinee

given by the Students at the Arts Theatre, W.C.2

on Tuesday, 13th June, 1939, at 2 p.m.

Chapter Eight

Playwright as Biographer

Stephen began writing plays in his attic bedroom to perform with puppets. He used to make the puppets on the family sewing machine until his father discovered him sewing. Then all hell broke loose. Following these lost juvenile playlets is a group of plays which he wrote during the time he was at Central School. Their chief interest is in the way he draws upon family experience and displays the conflict between parents and the developing child.

The Time Has Come, - written on the eve of hostilities - is his most awkward play. It presents a young man's preoccupations, with class struggle, communism and the impending war. His only polemical play, it deals with mans' responsibilities: pacifism, socialism and humanism. It anticipates Priestley's *An Inspector Calls* in which an outside event calls onstage characters who examine their respective responsibilities towards their fellows.

In it he wonders if men will invent and invent until they are killed off by their scientific inventions. It was written almost a decade before the explosion of the first atomic bomb.

He believes in socialism, but not the rulers who shout the loudest making enemies for socialism. Communists hate intelligence, and politics can't be divorced from life. Everything one does and believes is a reflection of politics:

It matters less which nation is victorious than which class is. War and class war. There's no sense - being a pacifist when war's here: that action is too late: The whole world's going to this war.

Where *The Time Has Come* is a play about the issues of the day, *Wild Sonata* examines personal conduct, theft and whether it can be justified; whether what inspires great art can influence our actions.

As a means of communicating with others, the concept of psychokinesis and parapsychology is contained in any number of theosophic observers. In modern parlance it is no more than to observe that violence displayed in one medium will communicate into another; violence on TV breeds violence in society. The artist has a responsibility towards the society in which he functions.

The heroine Diana is a sisterly figure, always selfless. Stephen's step-sister was christened Diana, and a platonic sister figure features in all of these early plays. It is tempting to suppose that he looked for her in Mary David and Heather Black - the lady with whom he later lived, briefly. Neither his mother nor his stepmother could ever be the prototype for a partner in life. Edna's obsession with money is reflected in the character of the shrill landlady who nearly drives the hero to violence:

> To hell with money. . . He would not mind poverty. . . starvation. . . the compulsion. . . to steal it. . . eats into his brain. . . like an insane fast movement of some wild sonata. . . If he is lucky the artist will be recognised during his lifetime, or might never be discovered. That is what makes life exciting. . . If perfection were easily obtained, no one would wish to be perfect.

The play was performed for the Pivot Club at Central School on the 28th of January, 1939. The music was composed by Viola Tunnard, who later wrote the music for many of Joyce Grenfell's songs.

It was dashed off at the time he was working on *Haman* which he considered to be his first serious work.[1]

Showing greater maturity than his earlier works, *Gold and Scarlet* is dated 1941. The David sisters recognise the setting as their home in Llandaff, and the names used - Lisbeth, Ann and Finnimore - as well as the general atmosphere of comings and goings is as it was in that first year of war. *Gold and Scarlet* draws upon the other family crisis Stephen lived through - the potentially fatal brain tumour which Leslie suffered.

The stage direction begs that the play be set without scenery, a style favoured by Elsie Fogerty. His preoccupation with the uninterrupted free flow of drama from scene to scene and the simplicity of the setting indicate a trend he was to develop with his own Studio Theatre Company.

Interestingly, he also explores a device later hallmarked by Brecht of having characters address the audience. No mere Restoration asides, these comments reflect upon the action. They analyse their character's relationships, attitudes to events, and the effects upon the individual of parental authority and of war, both on the warrior and the civilian. The most dramatic of his plays, it is the one in which his feelings towards his father rise most dramatically to the surface: 'I'm too frightened to show him anything but respect.'

The young man in the play has hated his father ever since he can remember. When he was young, his father was strict and without smiles. He comments:

> I was afraid of him as most boys are afraid of their headmaster at school. . .
>
> To me he always seemed so inhuman. The cane; being stingy. . . his always being right. . . I was alone too with my ghosts, my mother wasn't with us.
>
> I wasn't aware of being naughty. . . even when I was punished. I tried to get on well with my father . . . but still he was an enemy.

He doesn't hate his guardian in the way he hates his father, "strangely enough I liked her: she didn't appear to be part of the terror."

In Stephen's home it was his stepmother who chalked up the misdemeanours and the father who carried out the punishment. So of course the child came to look with loathing, not upon the instigator but the perpetrator foolishly carrying out orders: he who does is responsible for his actions, I was only carrying out orders, being the excuse of a sadist.

> My father's under the impression that my mother is the model of sin. They were divorced soon after I was born. She ran away. . . when I hear her on the wireless or at a concert, I feel drawn to her . . . I can quite see why my father did not like her; they're too much alike in one respect. They both revel in flattery from the opposite sex. My failures and weaknesses are always blamed on her.

He realises that one must either do away with, or endure that which one hates. Not that he should murder his father, but admit it is not his father who is evil, but the relationship between them.

Michael Joseph was straight jacketed by the standards of his parents and those around him. His son, determined to break the mould of domestic violence, embraced anarchy. Stephen's hero says "a virtuous search for virtue, is death in life. . . none of us knows how to live. Man has yet to learn the art of living."

Stephen encapsulates his feelings towards his parents with remarkable power and emotion and lays bare the bones of the relationship between them: the vacuity of the step-mother, the vindictiveness of the father punishing the two boys for being their mother's children, in effect punishing his own error of judgement.

In her study *For Your Own Good* Dr Alice Miller observes: "People whose integrity has not been damaged in childhood. . . will feel no need to harm another person or themselves." It seems likely that Edna too was compensating for some unperceived lack in her childhood, perhaps an over strict or distant father.

Having dealt with his own subjective experience, Stephen stands aside and shows us he can be objective, through mockery, about this foolish old lecher. The Father spends much of the play underlining his son's assertion that he is in love with every woman he sees. He brings insensitivity to everything, especially when his son is mentioned:

> He's too much like his mother; he has all her faults

> Of course I have the decency to hide my contempt of him. . .

> I'm sure he respects me and is grateful for what I've done for him. I've been all that a good parent should be. If he doesn't like me, the fault lies with him.

> What a family I've had. A wife who let me down; her son who is a useless weakling.

Having worked out the enmity within his family, Stephen shows us the dignity of man in undertaking that which is necessary for society. It repeats his sense of duty and rejection of pacifism from his earlier play. The writing is powerful and poetic and the structure sound. If the ending is melodramatic, that was no more than the fashion of the day.

It should be remembered that this was an era of 'children should be seen but not heard'. We will notice a very similar attitude towards children when we meet Noel Pemberton-Billing later in the narrative. In another example from slightly earlier, the only son of Kenneth Grahame committed suicide while his parents were enjoying themselves socially and ignoring his desperate pleas to be removed from his miserable school. It is a more tragic irony that the author of one of the best read and best loved children's stories should have been too insensitive to care about the despair of his own child.

On a closer examination of these texts it might be observed that there are strong elements of juvenile self pity. But is it adolescent to remember the slate, the swagger stick, the immature bullying punishment of his father repeating his own childhood experience, and to use these as a form of character development? Any child brought up in such a repressive atmosphere might indulge in anti-social behaviour (as Leslie did) or reactionary thinking (like Stephen.)

The David sisters: Mary, Anne, Lisbeth

Chapter Nine

The House of David

Shortly after leaving The Hall in August 1939 Stephen was working in the theatre, and it seems to have been a pretty tough job. Writing to Mary David, Arthur Wilkinson remarked, "If he finds it tiring I think that points to a new play. He's probably writing dialogue in between scenes." Before joining the Navy in June 1941, Victor Lucas met him in one of his moods of Russian melancholy. Arthur Wilkinson tried unsuccessfully to revive *Hamlet* in the Scala Theatre.[1]

Stephen then worked for the Metal Box Company, which he had to leave when he was called up for war service.[2] A contemporary document records him leaving Llandaff at the end of a visit to spend the rest of his 'leave' teaching in Bristol,[3] which accounts for David Campton's assertion that he taught in a Bristol School, as part of his war service!

In the early part of 1940 he collapsed, probably in Hermione's home because she rushed him into a nursing home at 3 Wilbraham Place, Sloane Street, very close to her own apartment in Kinnerton Street. He was suffering from starvation and malnutrition.

"I believe he has been very ill," Wilkie wrote to Mary David, "and he wasn't too good when I saw him." Hermione spent a fortune nursing him back to health. As he later wryly observed, if she had spent on him a quarter of what it cost in the nursing home, he'd never have been there.[4]

Whilst at Central School, Stephen's circle of friends included two sisters - one at The Hall and the other at Art school. Sympathetic twins, with totally different life patterns, Anne and Mary David were lodging in Chelsea. Anne was a student of Mark Gertler at the Westminster Technical College, and she drew and painted Stephen on several occasions.[5]

The fact was that he captivated all three sisters. The third, Lisbeth, records in her diary putting aside other business when Jo came to Llandaff, and the pity, and the great pity to see him go. Long walks... long talks. He could be the most wonderful diplomat. One day the young people were on holiday at St. David's, sitting in the garden talking of poems, and suddenly Lisbeth remarked that one of her favourites was *How odd of God to choose the Jews*. . . She had said it without thinking and there was the danger of an embarrassed silence momentarily, but Stephen put everyone at their ease instantly by dropping the remark that it had always been one of his favourites also.[6] Talking to Lisbeth on another occasion about their beliefs, he said that the history of the Jewish race had, for him, been one of the strongest arguments for God's existence.

Whilst Anne painted him, to Mary he was top person. He was obviously very fond of the entire family. His step-sister Shirley expected a permanent alliance. During one early leave from the Navy he said to Mary, "Shall we get engaged?" but she replied, "I don't think so." He sighed, and said "I'll ask you again," but he never did.[7]

The David family lived in the Lodge, a house close to Llandaff Cathedral. Their father had been a Major in the First War, and commanded an Anti-Aircraft battery in Cardiff in 1941. Near neighbours were a family called Read whose daughter Catherine married one Jack, who became well known as J.W. Lambert, Literary and Arts Editor of *The Sunday Times* and also Chairman of the Arts Council Drama Panel.

Another constant visitor was fellow student from The Hall, Beryl Dunn. Writing to Mary towards the end of the war, she observed "(Stephen) is capable of making love most excellently - but it doesn't matter because his tongue is well and truly in his cheek."[8]

The friendly and welcoming atmosphere of this household, its motley assortment of visitors and friends and the constant comings and goings, drew Stephen there often during the pre and early war years. Mrs David was a most hospitable mother, indeed she had acted as mother for a large family from the age of seventeen onwards, and in the 1940s open house was taken for granted: Margot Fonteyn slept there; John Arlott, noticing on a visit that Mary had only Sassoon's prose, recommended she get on to his poetry.

Llandaff organist W.H. Gabb (later Organist and Composer to Queen Elizabeth II) was constantly playing the grand piano, Mary noted that he and Stephen loved each other's company, each being outrageous/creative in a slightly different way. Then in the summer of 1939, when the family was staying at St David's in Pembrokeshire, Michael Joseph contacted them to discover where Stephen had got to, and what he was up to.[9] Were the Davids a normal family or an abnormal family? It was certainly the first time Stephen had experience of a caring family.

In December 1940 he was back in Llandaff, hours later than anticipated, and working hard on his pantomime script. *Cinderella*. By the 20th he had nearly finished it.[10] Rehearsals started on 22nd December and were held daily, interrupted only for a riotous party to celebrate cousin John's twenty first birthday.

Catherine Read had already left the Hall when Stephen burst into her life like a breath of fresh air, with his long legs and arms, flat dark hair falling over one eye, a wide smile which lit up his face and a rich resonant voice. Mary and he had gone to ask her to play Principal Boy in the pantomime, which they were going to perform to the troops.

Jack Lambert was on leave and attended rehearsals, impressed by Stephen's energy and enthusiasm.[11] By the end of the month when Stephen was worn out, a very under-rehearsed dress rehearsal was given for the benefit of the domestics in the afternoon of the 1st of January. Opinions varied from the not bad to enjoyable, but the first performance the following afternoon at the Fairwater Hall was a great success. The audience was composed of members of the Sunday School and other local people. Stephen gave an hilarious impression of Carmen Miranda, dancing the tango and singing *When They Begin the Beguine*.[12]

January the 2nd was one of the coldest nights for years; faint traces remained of the snow which had fallen several days earlier. There was a clear starry sky, and bright moonlight.[13] At about six o'clock, the cast assembled at the Davids' house to await pick up by the army for the evening performance. At about 6.15p.m. a call came from the Anti Aircraft Headquarters at Penylan Court to say, "We're holding the transport for the moment; we don't like the look of things."

An audience of about 150 anti-aircraft forces and ATS were assembled there, but no cast arrived. Minutes after the telephone call from the Anti Aircraft Headquarters the first full scale air raid on Cardiff rained down on Llandaff. A breathless Lisbeth phoned Penylan Court to say that a bomb had hit the Cathedral!

The raid started with incendiary bombs: Llandaff looked like an illuminated Christmas tree. All Saints Church at Llandaff North was burnt out; the Insole Estate area suffered from high explosive bombs. There were three landmines: the first, a parachute mine, touched the cathedral and exploded alongside it in the south churchyard, the second was a direct hit on the south-west corner of the quadrangle of St Michael's College, demolishing two blocks, and the third. . . did not immediately explode. When the siren went Mary's father had already sorted out the pantomime cast into various places of cover - some on the cellar steps, others in a lobby or under the dining table.

When the first bomb fell the sound was unmistakable, though it was impossible to tell what had been hit, and everyone stayed in their sheltered places. The second bomb, on hitting St Michael's College, blew in the dining-room shutters at the Lodge, (even though they were held in place with iron bars slotted into sockets,) and of course the windows, which were more or less floor to ceiling.

The shutters prevented anyone being cut by flying glass. . . the lock of the front door held, but the door splintered away and was blown open. Stephen was composed and helpful under fire, but it was very cold under the table without the windows. When the all clear sounded the cast realised that all the houses round the Green were shattered and that the Cathedral had had a direct hit. . . the roof had been blown off.[14]

As a postscript, *Cinderella* was successfully repeated on the 11th of January in the Reads' house and £11.5.0 was collected.[15] In a letter to the author in 1996 Lisbeth wrote:

> The summers of 1938 and 1939 had been golden times, and anyone who shared them was part of the family. I saw Stephen as a sort of Laurie from *Little Women*, with Anne as Meg, Mary as a combination of Jo and Beth, and me as Amy, but life became too full to notice that we didn't come to the traditional happy end.

Chapter Ten

The Cruel Sea

Stephen's war years were fulfilling. But for them he might have stayed with Metal Box and become the engineer he often said he ought to have been.[1] He was suddenly independent, and his letters from this time all testify to a growing stability and maturity.

He had joined the Royal Navy Volunteer Reserve as an ordinary seaman at HMS Raleigh on the 4th of June, 1941. He was drafted to HMS Drake on the 12th of August, and to HMS Broke, a tender to HMS Eaglet, on the 7th of November, 1941.

In 1942 he was undertaking a correspondence course in Latin. Then on the 3rd of May he went before the board:

> ... (it) consisted of an admiral, a school-master captain and one other officer; they all asked questions in turn about ships meeting head on, how anchors are secured, was I a Boy Scout?... did I know navigation?. .. but no flags. Then I retired from the room and made a rapid calculation of the number of questions answered wrongly and was summoned back into the board room by the tinkling of an odious bell; the admiral did not say "Sit down," which was the expected good news so I knew it was the expected bad news - but in the quietest voice he said "You will leave here on the 16th, spend five weeks at Lancing, two at Greenwich and then be made an officer"[2]

On the 3rd of July 1942 he was appointed Temporary Sub Lieutenant and went to HMS King Alfred for training. His first appointment after training was in August 1942 to HMS Paragon for duty with Admiral Superintendent Contract Built Ships and then to HMS Waveny upon commissioning. Between August and October of that year Ministry of Defence records are unclear. He is shown going from Waveny to Western Isles for training, a ship he says he is not very fond of, and only a month later, in November, to HMS Ryde for watch keeping duties. However his letters for November are addressed to him at HMS Lady

Shahrazard, which he is not jubilant about. It was not a very active job and not a particularly active ship.

The Lady Shahrazard was a ship to which one was appointed for courses of an anti-submarine nature, and may have been on Loch Long in Argyll where until recently there was an anti-submarine firing range. A letter dated the end of November speculates on his getting leave and seeing Mary on the way south. Wren Mary was in Greenock, a short water crossing from Loch Long.

He went to HMS Ryde on the 2nd of December. It was actually a newly commissioned paddle steamer, used to patrol the Thames approaches on anti-aircraft patrol, and was a ship which introduced newly commissioned officers to sea service. He was always the ringleader in any escapade, and Ryde allowed Stephen's sense of humour to flourish.

One of the officers in the wardroom was a rather tedious Australian given to boasting of his prowess with women. A group of fellow officers, with newly commissioned Sub. Lt. Joseph as their leader got together and invented a woman who initiated a correspondence with the Australian, Sub. Lt. John. The correspondence went on for about three months, gradually becoming more and more amorous. They slipped their letters in with the postal delivery, easily done as everything had to be censored, and so all mail went through an officers' hands.

They carefully had the woman move from Portsmouth where she had joined the WRNs, and told him in one letter, that she was moving to Chatham, where they hoped to arrange a meeting. Every time he received a letter, he used to recount small details at breakfast in the wardroom.

A Chatham WREN was organised to play the part of meeting Sub. Lt. John. At the last minute she dropped out. So Stephen produced some greasepaint, and one of the other men, Lt. King, was dressed and made up, and all were there to watch the meeting. In no time at all the ruse was discovered, and the poor Australian officer reduced to apoplexy. "You load of bastards," he called them. His fellow officers recollect Stephen joking in racing terms that he was 'out of Gingold...by Maschwitz!'[3]

His next posting was as Gunner to HMS Newport towards the end of March 1943. The ship was just what he expected and he was very happy about it. Newport was an ex-USA Lease-lend ship and not the best of seaworthy vessels for the Atlantic, having been designed for Pacific waters. Stephen slept on a camp bed in the wardroom and after one particularly heavy night of force nine gales, the petty officer steward went in to prepare breakfast, to be met with the sight of Stephen, covered in cutlery, burst jars of pickles, jams, cruets etc., amongst which he had been sick. He looked up, said, "Oh Myers, good to see you," and was soon on his feet.[4]

The ship was used on Convoy duties in the North Atlantic - anti U boat patrol and rescue. They were therefore often in and out of Scapa Flow. As the *Newbury Weekly News* reported it, at the beginning on February 1944:

> while the officers of the destroyer, HMS Newport were having dinner when the ship lay at anchor in Scottish waters... there was an ominous splash outside. It came just as they were finishing soup. The quartermaster half slithering half jumping down the ladder, burst into the wardroom. "Tish has fallen overboard!" he panted. In a flash the officers were making for the ladder. "Tish" was the ship's mascot, a seven month old puppy. She was the favourite of the ship's company and regarded as a lucky omen. First on the upper deck was Sub. Lieutenant Joseph RNVR, a 22 year old Curridge officer. By the time the First Lieutenant arrived, Joseph had stripped naked, then, with a line round his waist, he dived into the icy water. Just as Tish stopped swimming, Joseph grabbed her by the scruff of the neck and held her up. "I was only in the water about five minutes, but it seemed ages, ... I've never been so cold in my life."' [5]

Someone must have told the local paper... suddenly there was a picture of him with the mongrel on the front page of the *Evening Standard*... he'd been awarded the P.D.S.A. Medal of the Year, and the R.S.P.C.A. Silver Medal of the year... he was quite embarrassed.[6] He was none the worse for wear, and the dog was full of life as ever, but sadly, a month later when she was out walking with her owner, she died of an epileptic fit.

In March 1944 Stephen was in Greenwich on a course at HMS Drake, having the most splendid time he had ever had under the name of work. Enjoying, the wonderfully free and easy atmosphere, Christopher Wren's beautiful Painted Hall, in which they dined on some of the best food in London, he wrote to his sister:

> There are two reasons why we are given such a holiday; first is to make us realises that an officer in the Navy has an historical and aristocratic background - though the latter part is wasted on me, and the second reason is very shortly most of us will be in dreary or dreadful appointments for which we will be more willing in gratitude.[7]

On the 4th of May, 1944 he went as Gunnery Control Officer to HMS Avonvale. In most of his letters to his stepmother he respectfully sends love to the members of Copyhold, Michael's farm; occasionally he asks Shirley to ask mother if it is alright to come and stay; asks her to thank mother or father for this or that kindness. Through his sister he was punctilious, but on the first of June 1944 he wrote to his parents, to thank them for a parcel.

He had finished *Gold and Scarlet* and was hoping that Amersham Repertory might stage it. His antagonism had been worked out. His letter may have been written in an unguarded moment. He says he is writing in a ten minute gap, but its composition and length suggests an hour or more. He does say he has had no sleep during the preceding week, but we can hear him reproving his parents:

> The most objectionable thing about the Royal Navy is the tendency to regard human beings as machines running according to rules and regulations - K.R. and A.1. - any failure or breakdown is a cause worthy of punishment (also laid down in the rules!) In fact all humans fall short of any ideal standard.
>
> Punishment will bring them no nearer it; it may remove them further. Those in authority when they fail may possibly have the graciousness to apologise but cannot see that the fact that they themselves make mistakes is proof that others may also make mistakes without malicious intent worthy of punishment. Oh well, what does it boil down to in principle? The ever ignored instructions of Jesus Christ, the blatantly obvious lesson of all history. Tolerate. Tolerate all men.
>
> I like to think of mankind as slowly progressing not simply to material perfection but to something a little more mysterious than that, which we cannot expect to understand any more than Neanderthal man could have foreseen or understood parliament or X-rays. . . I suppose tolerance, like charity, begins at home. Therefore it can never be achieved.
>
> But no, even if one hates ones nearest relative there is at least no cause to hate all men. And now having talked about tolerance, charity and love (or hate to be precise) I can't see the difference between them so there's no sense in using one term to explain another. . . what a cheek I have to bore you. . . I've wasted my ten minutes. . .

Avonvale played its part in the Allied landings on the French coast, then towards the end of 1944 was on active service in Adriatic waters. Having done an anti-submarine course, he was trained in the use of radar. His Captain knew little of this new fangled device. Stephen was Gunnery Officer on a destroyer off the Dalmation coast on a mission to pick up underground workers. It might have been Sir Fitzroy MacLean who spent much of his war career organising the Yugoslav resistance.

In the sights of the radar beam Stephen's men picked up a signal for a ship which could only have been an enemy vessel. Stephen informed the Captain, who went to look at the radar screen. The Captain was uncertain, and said he'd have to be a lot nearer to the vessel to be convinced it was the enemy. Stephen knew that with radar, proximity was not essential. Time was of the essence. Avonvale might be hit, or the enemy vessel cruise out of harms way, all of which had to be explained to an old-school Captain, so that he could instruct his Gunnery Officer to give orders to fire. The sequence of orders, from the Captain down, was de rigeur. It was not permissible for the Gunnery Officer to act on his own initiative:

> The atmosphere was tense. Stephen said to his Captain "Do you want to get the ship or don't you?" "Well of course I want to." Stephen shrugged, saying to the captain, "Well in that case, fire!" Then he turned to his seaman, and instructed, "FIRE!" The seamen fired!

> The Captain said, "Mutiny, Sir," and pulled out his revolver. It was mutiny, strictly speaking. Stephen had given orders without permission.[8]

A Ministry of Defence letter reports he was:

> Awarded the Distinguished Service Cross for bravery, resolution and skill in a successful action against enemy destroyers off the Dalmation Coast – 1st /2nd November 1944 H.M.S. Avonvale.[9]

The Captain had been awarded the DSO!

In January 1945, back from the Yugoslavian coast Stephen was in hospital in Devonport where they X-rayed his stomach and did some unpleasant tests, after which he was transferred to the military hospital in Bristol. Posted to HMS Terpsichore on the 11th of March, he was again in hospital, this time in Gibraltar by 23rd, sorry to leave the first Captain in four years for whom he had any admiration.

Three days later he was complaining to Mary that he had been pronounced fit, but did not feel as if he was. Acute sea sickness had landed him there, only two months after leaving Devonport. It is unlikely that he mentioned his history of malnutrition to anyone. It is not surprising therefore that he should remark "my faith in the medical branch is shaken a little."[10]

Recommended for service to a bigger ship, he was assigned to HMS Abercrombie by the 11th of April. But big ships have a greater complement of crew and this one was not altogether a happy ship:

> Mary, I'm still no shadow of a Christian, and can find no substantial beliefs nor principles anywhere. The mysteries of religion, the theories of science, the problems of politics leave me more and more bewildered, less and less certain of anything. I'm far from finding that nice set of values which is to be my anchor...[11]

He had been promoted temporary Lieutenant on the 1st of January, but the promotion did not come through until the 22nd of April, by which time he was proudly wearing his second stripe, though disliking the ship heartily. Being Education Officer to an unwilling crew was dispiriting, but generated plenty of dynamism, so that by November he was being recommended for a full time instructors' position:

> I can write nothing now... nothing inspires me, no ambition spurs... very well, there is no harm in slipping into an unproductive mediocre plain existence - but this is denied me. Why?... I'm haunted by ghosts of past and possible selves.[12]

Then with the war over his future looked less certain and he was dealing with the resettlement of hands. Abercrombie appears to have been the catalyst which caused his personality to experience an even more serious disorder. In August he was again complaining of his weakness of going round in circles when the occasion demands a forward drive, and also of having an unquiet mind.

Until the Abercrombie Stephen had been on small ships, which are tossed about on the seas and can play havoc with all but cast iron constitutions. He had had years of under nourishment, malnutrition and chronic sea sickness, tests in Devonport, convalescence, and within months the same in Gibraltar, not enjoying the sturdiest of physical constitutions. Parental abuse, and now physical abuse.

In small ships the crew are known individually; on big ships with many hundreds of men, there is much more formality and more of the discipline he describes in that rare letter to his parents. There are also opportunities for anti-social and secret practice. A society with a low morale is a society in which the bosses, those in command at whatever level, are uninspiring, tyrannic, or decadent. His later letters from the Abercrombie begin to show the gloom which he was to fight against for several years.

The gloom may have been the anti-climax after the Adriatic experience, it may have been the insecurity of the imminence of peace and the need to consider the future, or it may have been physical abuse, which is a continuing problem aboard ship where seniority and opportunity can lead to devious practice. Of this there can be no proof, but a subsequent poem appears to point in one direction:

> I have met the monster in the secret room
> Of which they told me long ago
> Long ago I was gripped by the cold hand outstretched
> That I supposed friendly - the first deception
> When they told me the terror of the secret room.

He was an innocent and a virgin, barely aware of his own sexuality or charm. He was a junior officer being buggered by a senior. He was also being restrained by acolytes and ritually symbolically tarred, possibly in the boiler room. The assignation is simply accomplished. The Senior enters a room, points to the victim and with a toss of the head indicates he is wanted elsewhere. The victim complies. There is no alternative.

> For you must know
> It was dark, cold, dirty with black dust they smothered me
> And there was a smell attractive like tar, from a distance
> But under the nostrils, distasteful
> Overpowering, growing into the bones
> And inside which ached.

If the spirit was rebellious the flesh acquiesced. For the first time in his life he was wanted. The young man did not distinguish between love and lust - how many young people do? Who it was did not matter so much as the need to feel wanted, but he also knew he was being wrongly abused.

Whilst there is no evidence to hand that Stephen ever indulged in other homosexual activity, it is clear that this incident left him deeply scarred as he came to grips with his maturity. The tyranny of the Father was superseded by the tyranny of the Authority, the superior officer involved, the perpetrator of the act.

He could forgive his father at last, but never Authority. He had a new focus for hatred.

Power.

Stephen with Tish

Chapter Eleven

Salad Days

After the war Stephen went back to the Metal Box Company, and they said "According to our records you worked for us and left," and he replied, "I left because there was a war on. I went to join the Navy!" But the rule of the firm was inflexible. "You started with us - you left!" That was it. So he never became an engineer, although he did have reason to bless the company later.[1]

Having secured early release because of a national shortage of teachers,[2] he was teaching at Heatherdown in January, 1946. Long since closed down, it was a school for the delinquent child, to whom he tried to teach the joys of Keats. He was sent for one day by the Headmaster, and as he approached the door it crashed open. A boy flew out, pursued by the Head with a cane! After two terms he said he'd rather cart coal than teach.[3]

A bonus of the job was that he had Wednesdays off, and would meet his stepsister Shirley in London where they saw most of the Old Vic productions at the New Theatre. With Olivier and Richardson in their prime, and productions such as *Peer Gynt*, *Oedipus*, the *Henrys IV, V*, etc., this was truly a golden age in the history of British theatre.[4] However, his stomach condition had reappeared, perhaps as a result of stress at Heatherdown. Shirley wanted him to partner her to a society ball in Grosvenor House. In decline, he laid plain his credo:

> . . . I don't know how much I can blame myself as a self conscious human for my character and functions, or how much they are formed by inheritance and environment. I am in search of some truth - I'd like to find the most perfect way of living on one hand, and I'd like to find some single sincere and worthwhile expression of myself on the other. I have only learned so far that I find good things, more in humility, than riches.
>
> I detest the barriers (built so well in my own mind) that separate class from class in our society - but if I have any ambition to break those barriers, it is to go down. . . I know I suffer fiercely in high places and

among high people. . . to submit to the agony of strained behaviour without redeeming grace is quite beyond my desires. This is symptomatic of my general state of mind. . .[5]

In April 1947 he learnt that he had won a scholarship to Cambridge. Twenty years on he admitted being embarrassed to sit the examination in his Naval Uniform amongst youths years his junior.[6] Once in Cambridge the age differential was never apparent, so many similarly demobilised servicemen were catching up on their interrupted or missed education. Stephen quickly found a circle of like-minded friends, though Shirley thought most of them weird "I should know," she commented, "I married one of them."

Stephen had just gone up, and she arrived to find a note at his lodgings. ''There are 8 or 10 people coming to tea - ask Mrs Sampson for some cups and 3 packets crumpets. . .' all written down what I had to do, 'Gone to rehearsal, I'll be back as soon as I can. . .' Everyone else in the building was terrified of the housekeeper, but Stephen had charmed her." Shirley was an ingenuous teenager entertaining men in Stephen's absence. One by one they all left and Michael Savage, whom she ended up marrying, stayed on. They went to dinner, and half way through Stephen turned up, saying "Ah, there you are, thought you'd be here."[7] Michael Savage's father was an architect and had designed the interiors for Woolworths' heiress Barbara Hutton's house.

Stephen read English at Jesus College, following the shortened two year degree course that was available to ex-service students.[8] There is plenty of evidence to suggest that apart from his creative experience, his lower Second degree was earned.

For a term, he was Drama Critic of *Varsity* magazine which Stephen Garrett was editing. He organised a Scene Design competition in February 1948, and produced his own magazine, *Cambridge Writing*, published by the Young Writers Group of which he was Director in the Easter Term. *Cambridge Writing* had General, Literary and Arts editors.

It has poems from six different contributors, three stories - one by Michael O'Donnell (who became a doctor and a broadcaster) and another which reads suspiciously like Stephen in disguise, concerns a guignol puppeteer whose marionette commits suicide mysteriously mid-performance by cutting his own strings. It is then discovered that the puppeteer has died with mysterious slash marks on his flesh.

An article on Outlook for Decor by Stephen himself rails "Time after time conventional painted flats cramp the audience's imagination. The box set has become traditional. Producers, actors and audience expect it, and seem fairly satisfied however bad it is." He argues that attendance might improve if there were more experiment, including a talented use of lighting. . . highly skilful lighting in simple architectural constructions.[9]

An editorial echoes for literature the ideas he was to propound for theatre a decade further on. "Where is the new generation of English writers? Where are the novelists to debate, question, explain, praise, blame, or shock our restless times?" it asks. He was looking for new ideas, or new ways of expressing old ideas. It continues, "Art cannot be divorced from the society it serves and illuminates. This is the age of speed. . . of streamline in design. Some may prefer the hansom cab, but the aeroplane is here to stay for all that. . ."[10]

Only one edition of *Cambridge Writing* seems to have appeared, priced at two shillings and six pence, but the Young Writers Group also published two volumes of poetry – *Cambridge Verse One* and *Cambridge Verse Two*.[11]

His energy and enthusiasm during his two years earned him lasting admiration from his contemporaries. Michael Savage recalls him as volatile, extrovert, and sensitive; Richard Baker was a great admirer. . . and found him generous-hearted and genial. He was "bigger than life, exciting, exotic."[12] "One of the curious things about Stephen was that his utter dedication to theatrical things seemed to unsex him. I never knew of him being in love. He didn't have any favourites, but he would put an arm round a shoulder at the drop of a hat. He never voiced any prejudices. If he knew anything about sexual deviance he never mentioned it nor did it make his hackles rise. He had no mania or phobia, no colour bar or racial prejudice," Peter Tranchell remembers.[13]

Also in 1948 he was one of six undergraduates who produced a sixpenny report, outlining their *Project for a Cambridge University Radio Station*. The station, to be operated by undergraduates, would broadcast regular programmes in term time for a local audience. Carefully detailed, the report suggests ways of casting abroad the wealth of material produced privately and publicly by students - drama, teaching, poems, short stories, news and sport: "the news might be collected with the co-operation of the Cambridge papers, including the University paper *Varsity*." [14] As a management skills exercise it is excellent.

Of the report's editorial group, Stephen Garrett enjoyed a career as an architect before being appointed as curator of the Getty Museum in California, and David Widdicombe became a Queen's Counsellor. Office space, personnel, methods of transmission are all detailed, expenditure, together with a specimen week's programme outlining broadcasting from 8a.m. to 11p.m. History does not relate what critical reception met its publication, anticipating as it did local radio by some 40 years.

Stephen appeared in several productions. According to Richard Baker he wasn't the greatest actor in the world, being rather inclined to strike dramatic poses which had a hint of the burlesque about them,[15] and his sister earned opprobrium for laughing at his performance as a Chinaman with a pigtail in *The Lower Depths*.[16] He played Lennox in the Marlowe Society production of *Macbeth*, and *Diocletian* for the same company in a production he describes as 'quaint' in *Cambridge Writing*. Another student directed him in *Ticket of Leave Man* for the Amateur Dramatic Company.[17]

The ADC also performed his own one act play *What Happened in the Bedroom* on the 3rd of November, produced in a setting by Richard Ashton, which draped the stage with an enormous spider's web made of rope. It is an extended revue sketch, and as such is of its own time and space, appealing to an audience of cognoscenti. The action takes place at the rehearsal of a 'lost' scene from *Macbeth*. Clearly inspired by Thurber whose *Carnival* had been published in America three years earlier, the missing scene takes place in Duncan's bedroom. It replaces the Porter scene, which is an interpolation by Massinger. It reveals that Duncan was murdered by a conspiracy of Malcolm, Donalbain and Lady Duncan! When one of the characters protests that Lady Duncan doesn't appear in the play, the reply comes, "Yes she does, she's in this scene. Remember Lady McDuff only appears in one scene."[18]

As an old gentleman he was in *Fortunato* by the Alvarez Quinzero Brothers which Antony Knowles directed; they then appeared together in *Bartholomew Fair*. This was directed by George Rylands between the 11th and 15th of March 1947 and Stephen played Knock-Hum, a horse courser. Within days he was involved in his major contribution to his two years at Cambridge - the resurrection of the Footlights Dramatic Club, and its' *May Week Review*.

The re-animation of the club was brought about by Arnold Edinborough and Jonathan Routh (later of televisions' *Candid Camera* fame). Even at Cambridge Routh was inclined to be a little crazier than most: to one event he brought a horse up two flights of stairs into a dance hall. Edinborough and Routh then had a disagreement and both resigned from the committee which promptly elected D.C. (ever afterwards 'd'Arcy') Orders to be president. d'Arcy set about raising funds and bringing the club back to life. He wrote to all sorts of people requesting donations, and one came from Eric Maschwitz.[19] Stephen became the club's producer and Vice President, and Peter Tranchell whose studies had also been interrupted by the war, was elected Musical Director. He remembers:

> At our first smoking concert, when the cabaret of songs and sketches had ended, the members, some 80 strong, fell to singing rugby songs, which many had learnt in the services. Stephen and I talked of this and decided that we must provide chorus material some of which could have obscene verses for rehearsed soloists. This at least would mean we were using original lyrics and music. Thereafter I arranged for duplicated song sheets to be handed out to all members. We solemnly sang through songs, some of which were far obscener than the rugger songs we strove to do without.
>
> These home grown products were greeted with much satisfaction and merriment, and sometimes had to be repeated. I recall that Stephen contributed several items. Two come to mind: *There's An Opening For You In The Navy* (which was in response to a naval recruitment poster then posted up all over the place, which showed the rear view of a sailor lad with a cruiser framed between his open legs. This song suggested all too clearly the reason for joining the Navy [20]

There's An Opening For You

> Admirals when
> They want more men
> Post posters to proclaim it
> They offer you
> A job to do
> But tactfully fail to name it.
>
> There's an opening for you in the navy
> All the officers' cabins are double
> You don't have to keep with
> The bloke that you sleep with
> And you can't get the chaps into trouble.
> And the seamen know just what to do
> Though the hammock is not made for two
> In vain have they tried
> To squeeze side by side
> But two into one will go

For it's fine one on top one below.

Admirals when
They want more men
Announce it on a poster
And soon perhaps
You'd be the chaps
Who'll go on the admiral's rosta.

There's an opening for you in the navy
And a sailor need never be lonely
Whatever the weather
The crew pulls together
O there's all sorts of fun for men only
All the men go below when it's late
And the gunner lies down with his mate
There's nothing to fear
For the sea makes men queer
Sailors know just what to do
So be sure there's an opening for you.

...I'm a sailor myself so I know
Just how far a good sailor will go
In each port we flirt
With a nice bit of skirt
But once we're at sea we've forgot 'em
        For at heart we prefer a belle bottom. [21]

The other song, *Up The Cam!*, was interested mainly in fornication upon a punt on the river Cam. A cleaned up version appeared in the June 1948 revue.

d'Arcy: Smoking concerts were held at the Dorothy Café to enable members to try out their material. At one meeting Stephen said that there was sufficient material to justify producing a May Week revue.

Tranchell: We suddenly found that during "*May Week*" (i.e. the first two weeks of June) the theatre would be available for the Footlights to stage a Revue. It was the exam term, when many people are preoccupied with catching up on work omitted during the preceding terms. Our notice was short, some 5 weeks... a complete script had to be passed by the Lord Chamberlain... still we managed.

d'Arcy: Stephen collated the material, wrote sketches, rewrote other people's sketches - much to their disgust - cut sketches (more disgust) dealt with the props, lighting, publicity, printing, practically everything.

Tranchell: Throughout the traumas of putting the show together, producing it, etc., etc., Stephen was a saint. He was never bad tempered. He was never cross with anybody. He worked into the night without complaining. He was ceaselessly full of drive and enthusiasm.'

d'Arcy: We managed to get the use of the A.D.C. Theatre and, as the press reported 'the *Footlights* shine again' albeit for only four performances, and all sold out.'

Hermione was present to cheer everyone on, and a huge group of them went down to a party she gave at Kinnerton Mews - always playing *The Game*. Lifting the toilet seat in her house they found 'Thank God there's a Man in the House,' printed on the underside.[22] She was appearing in one of the *Sweet and Low* series at the Ambassadors Theatre, and pulled strings to have the performers invited to repeat the show on Sunday the 15th of June 1947 before an invited audience. Although Stephen did not appear in the Cambridge production he chose to do so in London (where) his performance as Carmen Miranda was hilarious.[23]

Seven of the musical numbers were written by Peter Tranchell who directed the music and played piano - one of his two assistant pianists was Richard Baker who was then at Peterhouse. Samuel French the play publishers bought several songs for publication.[24]

In March, sporting a healthy beard, Stephen attended the wedding of his step-sister Shirley to Michael Savage at Stamford Dingley. Michael Joseph had recently moved there to the Garden House once the home of novelist George Henty and before him Jonathan Swift.

The wedding took place in the church at Yattenden in Berkshire made famous for its hymnal devised by Robert Bridges. Peter Tranchell was organist and Diana, daughter of the famous cartoonist H.E. Bateman, was one of the bridesmaids. They were near neighbours and friends of Shirley. An artist in her own right, Diana helped paint the scenery for both Footlights revues and married Ken Willis who appeared in both shows.

Whilst he was sporting the beard Stephen took off for a hitch-hiking holiday in France. Peter Tranchell remembers:

'Somewhere down south, possibly Mendes, there'd been a gruesome murder. The description of a wanted man merely stated stature, apparent age, complexion, and beard. Stephen was handed, by a lorry driver, over to the police.

The police were convinced they had the murderer. After a night in the police station lock-up, Stephen suddenly produced his passport. (I never understood why he didn't do it straightaway upon arrest.) The police became extremely cross and he was lucky not to be beaten, but they released him with imprecations and gesticulations. Stephen was amused at rather than critical of French policemen.'

After the Footlights success of summer 1947, membership picked up again. The club lost the exclusive atmosphere of the pre-war period; instead they were pushing for members. The club held its first dinner for ten years, with Norman Hartnell and Jimmy Edwards as guests of honour. The revival of the club did not escape the administrator of the Arts Theatre, Norman Higgins. Knowing that revue was a commercial certainty, he offered them £100 to put on the 1948 *May Week Revue* at the Arts. (When the show indeed proved a sell-out he arranged for a hundred guinea donation from the Arts Trust and passed on a fee of twenty-five guineas from the BBC.'[25]

La Vie Cambridgienne in 1948 was an altogether more ambitious show. Music was by Peter Tranchell, with additional material from Ben Gradwell and others. Once again sketches and songs were by David Eady, Kenneth Poole, Ian Clements and Ben Gradwell; Richard Baker contributed a sketch and abandoned the second piano, and Simon Phipps wrote one number. Stephen wrote six, designed three of the settings, and again directed.

Of the performers Michael Westmore became Head of Light Entertainment at the newly formed commercial television company Associated Rediffusion. Charles Parker made a career out of radio documentary, although there were those who thought him unoriginal.[26] (He was to unsuccessfully sue Joan Littlewood and Theatre Workshop for plagiarising his script of *O What a Lovely War*.) Michael O'Donnell became a doctor, whose friendship with Frank Muir & Dennis Norden led him to a career as a radio presenter and quiz-master; whilst John Morley became a night club performer and prolific pantomime author. David Eady directed films and became Director of the British Film Finance board.

Critical praise for Stephen's production of *La Vie Cambridgienne* was united. In the *Daily Telegraph* W.A. Darlington wrote:

> Every time I was interested enough to look at my programme I seemed to see the name Stephen Joseph and I now find that this young man produced the whole show, wrote the best sketches and designed some of the scenery.[27]

> The BBC recorded several items for broadcast on the *Light Programme*. Then in July the cast, went to Alexandra Palace where they recorded a dozen or so items for TV transmission. Meeting up with her husband once again at the last night party in Cambridge, Hermione quipped to Maschwitz "Haven't we met somewhere before?".[28]

One of Stephen's few paradoxical actions in Cambridge was his determination to join the Pitt Club.

> This was very conservative, founded in 1835 for gentlemen with plenty of huntin' shootin' and fishin', but the main attraction... in those days of rationing, was the talented chef who produced delicious off-ration dishes. Stephen was duly elected, but I cannot remember him ever dining there.[29]

In his periods of depression, he could, and did astonish several of his contemporaries:

> Stephen had got interested in Theatre in the Round - he'd taken me to see a performance of plays done in this way in a tent on Midsomer Common and was convinced that this was the theatre of the future... But on the night I said goodbye to him, he came to my rooms in the roughest of clothes, covered in coal dust. "The theatre could wait" he said...[30]

> He had taken a part time job at the coal depot... heaving 2 cwt. sacks of coal. This was the dirtiest, most back breaking job he could find. I asked him why on earth?... he wanted to work with ordinary real people... do something with his hands. But the real reason I think was that he wanted to prove to himself that he was not effeminate, which is what his father always accused him of being. [31]

Michael was subject to depression; he would disappear for weeks seeing no one;[32] Hermione 'wished she could drop this witty, cynical, insincerity, just for a bit... and be herself.'[33] Here was their offspring, "wanting to connect with the working class, so he'd got a job as a coal heaver for British Rail."(

69

There's a good opening for you in the NAVY

Peter Tranchell

Chapter Twelve

Hard Times

Alan Broadhurst, Brocky, was running the theatre in Lowestoft with his second wife, the actress Vivien Wood. The company had been formed two years earlier. In a spirit of optimism many of the cast had pooled their wartime gratuities setting up the venture, only to see their personal effects go up in flames when the theatre burned down in June 1946. So they decamped to a building which had been the Garrison Theatre, but had reverted to the Sparrows Nest Pavilion. Once a popular touring date - Gracie Fields had performed there - the company had to screw back the seating which the Navy had removed.

Broadhurst managed the company through a most buoyant period in theatrical history. After the rigours of war people wanted entertainment, and in Lowestoft, as in other regional repertory theatres, this meant showing the latest West End plays. Their London runs finished, these were released for performance in the provinces. It was not every repertory company which could boast the services of Rank Starlets, like Bernadette O'Farrell nor the young Fulton McKay, let alone a renowned designer in his day, Tom Lingwood, and the young John Neville.

Within weeks of coming down from Cambridge, the coal dust was gone and Stephen spent two weeks appearing along with Fulton McKay in *Golden Boy* the Clifford Odets' play - a modern American allegory about a boxer fighting for a place in the world, as an individual.[1] The following week he directed Synge's *Playboy of the Western World* with Fulton McKay as Shawn Keogh.

Before returning to Lowestoft he was in London to direct for the Under Thirty Club which had been set up in the previous year by Oscar Quitak, Karis Mond and Hazel Vincent Wallace. These three actors at the beginning of their stage careers had looked sadly at the overcrowded profession and essayed the great odds against which young people with talent and enthusiasm had to struggle.[2] The Club staged four Sunday night shows in the West End.

Alec Guiness had helped the committee and agreed to be president, and they amassed a distinguished list of patrons, including Robert Helpmann, Sir Laurence

Olivier and Dame Sybil Thorndike. Four first time playwrights had their plays performed and over 50 artists their work seen. Sunday meetings were also arranged with well-known speakers, the first being Peter Brook, himself an excellent example of the contribution that youth can make to the theatre. One of the plays Stephen directed for them was apparently about the Bevan Boys and written by Peter Shaffer, but no details of it have come to light.

In London Stephen shared a flat at 61c Holland Park with three Cambridge friends, d'Arcy, Ben Gradwell and Michael Westmore. Their weekly rental was £2.50 - 62.5 pence per week each. Their housewarming party, well laced with theatrical guests, provoked complaints about noise from the landlord above, so Stephen immediately invited him to the party and introduced him to Hermione. He subsequently took her out to supper.[3] Stephen assumed the role of warden of the establishment and evolved an elaborate system of double-entry book-keeping which he insisted was required because of the varying nature of the residence of the four tenants. Ben Gradwell was a medical student at the Westminster Hospital and therefore away in vacations; Michael Westmore and Stephen were both trying their luck in the theatre, and d'Arcy Orders was the only one normally resident and, with a job, having a regular income. Stephen's system was designated 'Capital and Revenue.'

Stephen spent hours poring over records, before coming up with the monthly contribution from each. The experience stood him in good stead, because in later years, when d'Arcy became honorary auditor to the various companies, Stephen's records were quite professional.[4] d'Arcy remembers :

> it was during this time that Stephen felt he might be missing out of something - the opposite sex.
>
> One day, at breakfast, we were all astounded when he announced that he would be absent from the flat for an indefinite period as he had come to a satisfactory arrangement with a young lady to set up flat with her in a house in Ealing ON A TRIAL BASIS. Within a couple of days he moved out. I was later invited over for a drink and duly shown round the flat including, of course, the bedroom which contained a double bed which, even although it was nearly six p.m. showed unmistakeable signs of being slept in BY TWO PEOPLE! Within a couple of weeks, he was back in Holland Park, no mention of the incident by anyone being made.

His friendship with Peter Tranchell was to continue for some time also. They continued to correspond, and together wrote much of a musical, *Come to Codwyn*

Bay, which they hoped Oscar Quitak might stage. An innocent story, it concerns two unattached men and two similar girls, a train journey to Codwyn Bay, and a mix up over luggage,

> S: I've lost a suitcase that's small and navy blue.
> A: I have too.
> S: I'm certain to be able
>   To recognise the label
>   With a red and white design...
> A: Just like mine.
> S: I found my suitcase the moment I found you
> A: I did too... [5]

They collaborated for a time on an adaptation of *The Mayor of Casterbridge* as an opera which Tranchell wanted to enter in a competition the Arts Council was sponsoring. The winning entry was to be staged as part of the Festival of Britain but it became too grandiose and was shelved. Tranchell performed a heavily truncated version some years later.

Back in Lowestoft by the 16th of November Stephen was directing and appearing in the following week's production of *London Wall* by John van Druten. John Neville, five years his junior, had arrived for the production the week before without much enthusiasm for a mediocre comedy and not expecting to stay. When Stephen re-appeared there was an instant rapport between the two, and they tried to inspire the company. *London Wall* was the last production in the Sparrows Nest, a characterful if draughty and bitterly cold building soon to be demolished, to which the audiences went with their travelling rugs and hot water bottles.[6]

For their production of *Jane Eyre* on the 29th of November the company moved back into the newly rebuilt Playhouse Theatre. Alan Broadhurst was Mr Rochester, and St. John Rivers was played by John Neville.

Neville had also been in the Navy and at Dunkirk, and both he and Stephen shared a deep commitment to the theatre. Together they discussed productions and production methods - the problem of staging absorbed them. Each preferred the open form of staging, Neville because it "allowed an actor to communicate more freely, to serve his author more truthfully,...(with) freedom, clarity, imagination."[7]

Stephen believed that those who were working in the theatre had a serious responsibility to improve things. In a later, unfinished, autobiographical novel he wrote:

People like me are trying to force the theatre to come to grips with the twentieth century. Establish new traditions perhaps. Make mistakes certainly. We're alive aren't we? You know what is the grandest noise in the universe? The laughter of an audience in response to great comic acting. The unique signal of humanity.

If you're in the theatre you're in it. Every bit of you... if you've got any sense you'll let the actors get on with their jobs and tell them when they're good. We've ruined the theatre by taking initiative away from actors, and allowing producers to impose interpretations onto them. Actors are the great priests of the universe...[8]

Both Neville and Joseph were:

learning what weekly rep. implied. Getting the bearings of a new play on Tuesday, study its first Act on Wednesday, the second on Thursday, and the third on Friday; give two performances of the current play on Saturday, rehearse the new play on Sunday, do it on Monday, and then start again... Not all the parts and plays are worthy of this conscientious effort... yet nearly every part, however trifling, (has) some technical query; unknown to its audience, the Playhouse could be a theatre of the most earnest private experiment.[9]

Then on Sunday the 19th of December Stephen attended a performance given in the round to members of the supporters' club in the Grammar School. It was not his first acquaintance with arena presentation, but this production of *A Phoenix Too Frequent* was a different kettle of fish. It was performed by amateurs and produced by Jack Mitchley, a young man who had trained as a food chemist.

At the start of the war Mitchley was in a reserved occupation, became a conscientious objector, and then Drama Adviser in Norwich. In this guise, running weekend schools, he had discovered the appeal of walking around his actors while they were rehearsing. He decided to try performing in rehearsal conditions - with two or three rows of seating surrounding the players – Theatre in the Round. Of himself Mitchley remarked that when you have played in a theatre seating 1000 and the next night presented the same performance to an audience of 25 in a barrack room by candlelight, you discover what theatre is about.[10]

Reporting the performance, the *Lowestoft journal* described :

the audience seated 3 deep around the acting area (feeling) themselves to be personally present in the tomb. Mr. J. Mitchley pointed out it was just this feeling of intimacy which gave the arena production some advantage. In some plays it was even possible to draw the audience right into the action of the play as crowds of onlookers, which naturally brought a feeling of reality and keen personal interest, almost impossible by the picture frame tableaux of a proscenium theatre.[11]

Stephen sought Mitchley out after the performance and they spent hours talking. Whatever his previous experience of open stage productions :

> When I saw this (one), of *A Phoenix Too Frequent* in the round, I was delighted at the simplicity of the lighting and staging, and the natural and easy way the actors set about their tasks. Clearly many tiresome conventions might be abandoned and new ones seized to advantage. I enjoyed the performance immensely and returned to the repertory theatre with a bee beginning to buzz at the back of my mind.(12)

Christmas Shot opened a week later. Devised and produced by Stephen and Alan Broadhurst, it had musical items by Peter Tranchell, and several sketches from Cambridge. New ones, written for the occasion, were by Stephen, members of the cast, and by Ben Gradwell, David Eady, Colin Eccleshare and Simon Phipps. Stephen repeated his Potted *Carmen* and two of the *Codwyn Bay* numbers found their way in. His style ranged from the sentimental:

> '...I'll follow the fishing from Banff to Hull
> From the Clyde to Aberdeen
> But I've a home in Glasgow
> And Dave's from Glasgow too
> That's where we'll stay
> And live the whole year through...'

to the outrageous, *I'm Bertha the Bearded Lady* I'm Bertha the circus Queen:

> 'I once tried to fly to Australia non-stop
> But my whiskers got caught in my co-pilot's prop....
> My dreams of romance were pricked like a bubble
> It wasn't the ring or my job caused the trouble
> He left when his feelings got hurt in my stubble
> I'm Bertha ... (etc.)

Many years later Stephen recalled:

> During the time John was at Lowestoft, (with Tom Lingwood) ...the

three of us formed a sort of adventure group, trying out all sorts of personal experiments - in particular the close working of actor and scenery (not an easy task in weekly rep.) In *Power Without Glory* the whole thing was to be done "for real" this meant not facing front at all.[13]

It was not the local idea of fun. Halfway through the week the manager said to Stephen... "We've just had the biggest batch of letters in the history of the theatre - and they are all disastrous."[14]

His next major production was to be John Neville's last with the company - the one best remembered by audience and actors - Ronald Duncan's adaptation of the Cocteau play, *The Eagle has Two Heads,* about a Queen disconsolate after the death of the King and a poet who steals in to kill her but remains to protest his love. "The costumes, the dialogue, and the settings, make it one of the company's more outstanding productions..."[15] In the final scene the poet Stanlislas has to rush forward and bounds up the stairs to the Queen's side. Poison grips him. The queen falls bringing down one of the curtains, and dies. Stanislas falls backwards, rolling down the entire staircase to die at the bottom. Neville especially liked his death fall - head first down the staircase.[16]

Then he was off to an engagement with the Barry Jackson company in Birmingham. The partnership of ideas and ideals had been brief and Stephen held him in great affection thereafter.

Stephen stayed on and did four more productions but tensions had developed and he and Brocky no longer hit it off. He was unconventional where Broadhurst was conservative. Broadhurst was having problems with the local management committee, and was to leave shortly after Stephen who often appeared at rehearsals in his able-seaman's uniform.[17]

Following his new found inspiration, it was impossible for Stephen to settle back into the well-worn production method. Conventional theatre had begun to pall, but it was to take a while longer before he felt fledged enough to fully shake it off.

Then, early in 1949 something happened to mellow his father, Michael Joseph. He had been a domineering husband, a bully who treated his wife badly. He had her in tears on many occasions. Edna had become afraid of him and would do anything to placate him. She never stood up to Michael, wasn't a person to show hurt. She had no one with whom she could discuss things - anyway this was a time of social taboos.

Stephen's sister Shirley remembered, "She was eaten up with this insane jealousy, hatred, I could see it all the time as a child, and it was really, really horrid..."[18] She had vented her jealousy on Michael's two older children in return for her suspicions of Michael's infidelity. One day their youngest child, Richard, went to his mother in the hall, with a rod, some string and a pin, and asked her to bend the pin so he could go fishing. As she bent her concentration to the task, she collapsed.[19]

Edna had been nursing a carcinoma on the brain. No one suspected her behaviour or reactions may have had a pathological connection, and by the time they did, it was too late. She was taken to the best surgeon in London, ironically the same man who had operated on Leslie's tumour, but he was unable to stem the tide of the disease.

Michael hated illness; he complained to a companion:

> It is pitiful... that beautiful woman - her hair is coming out... teeth rotten... the only person she wants with her is me - I can't bear it... I'm the only person she'll have in the room...[20]

The end was mercifully speedy and Edna died in May; but even in her death Michael was unfaithful. He was in bed with Mary James and showed her two photographs saying, "I'm going to marry one of these, which one should I marry?" One was a rich Australian, the other a Right Honourable, daughter of a High Court Judge. Mary James had no hesitation. "Michael you are such a snob you will have to marry the Rt. Hon." At the time of the marriage in 1950 Stephen observed, "My mothers keep getting younger."[21] This is the story as Mary James recounted it, but Richard demurs. At the time in question Anthea's father was not a judge and so she had not yet assumed the Hon. title.

Meanwhile Stephen was in Frinton. In a very small company, such as the tiny summer theatre at Frinton on Sea the Producer may be Manager, Stage Director, Lighting Designer, Scenic Artist, and Actor as well.[22] Various writers remember that summer of 1949 in which Frinton was:

> A very weird place, no pubs, full of ex-Wing Commanders, Rear Admirals, and Nuns recovering from nervous breakdowns. It seemed... to have been frozen in time... where less successful middle class couples sent their children and nannies, to get rid of them for the summer. Pretty joyless...[23]

It was Quite unique - a time warp - Edwardian - no coaches, no pubs, one hotel. Very charming - a bleak northerly wind. A little cliff with lawns - a sign *No Picnicking on the Greensward*. The bookshop booked the tickets, and had a sign in the window which read - Richer than me you can never be - I had a mother who read to me.[24]

About as untheatrical a town as one could imagine... it was full of villas, bungalows and 1930s concrete bunkers where the *Radio Times* was contained in an embossed leather cover... Old ladies arrived in chauffeur-driven Rolls Royces, to performances of more or less chauffeur-driven plays...[25]

The theatre was a Hall, seating about 250 people.

These were weekly reps, standards low, houses small... a tight rehearsal schedule, but luxurious to those in twice-weekly rep., where they put on a play in three days flat...[26] A smart woman ran a restaurant and let the actors eat for two shillings, but she wouldn't feed the girls.[27]

John Osborne wrote to the author:

When my wife... came down for the last night I was there... my very non pro-ish landlady tried to charge me ten shillings, for her sharing the same bed. It seemed to sum up the whole place.

. . . I never made out what the under thirties were. Whether they represented anything more than the accident of age itself. I don't know! They did seem irredeemingly middle class... twin set and pearls sort of actresses who all looked like flavour of the month engagement pictures in Country Life, and sorely in need of a jolly good fuck...[28]

1949 was the first Summer that the Under Thirties ran a season in Frinton. The company lodged in the house of Henrietta Gradwell, Ben's recently widowed mother, and some of Stephen's contemporaries from Cambridge were in the company.[29] Oscar Quitak wrote :

I asked Stephen to be Art Director, which meant he made and painted all the sets... directed 3 of the plays, acted in two of them... was business manager... He and I got the highest paid salaries of the company, together with the others six members - we all received £8 per week. Stephen said, "I think I can find a housekeeper who can come and do the cooking, as long as she has her own bedroom."[30]

For a week Hermione descended on Frinton and kept house for the company, who must have lived like lords that week, because she had food hampers sent up from Harrods. Two of the plays they did were *An Inspector Calls* and *Candida* and describing the season in his book of scene painting Stephen recalled :

> The Women's Institute Hall had no dimmer board. We switched on the lights at the beginning of the play, and they stayed on until the end. But I was not content. I borrowed a switchboard from a friend who was manager of a big theatre that had just been re-equipped. It arrived just before the dress rehearsal of *An Inspector Calls* and I fell into the temptation of arranging a complicated lighting schedule to give the production a cinematic effect. There were seventy nine lighting cues. The stage manager didn't miss one; but they were not very well conceived, as you may guess. After the first night I listened in the foyer for comment - and sure enough two old ladies were discussing the production. One said "Did you notice the lights going up and down, dear?" and her friend replied "Yes, there must have been a power failure." [31]

Birds of Sadness had been put on at the request of a West End Management, who wanted to see the play on stage without the expense of a tryout. The ancient Chinese proverb has it, 'you cannot stop the birds of sadness flying around, but you can stop them nesting in your hair.'[32] A representative of Tennants came down, saw the production, and left without comment. Another play Quitak recollects Stephen directing with the company seems more like one tried out for a Sunday evening in London – *Return to Bedlam*. d'Arcy Orders audited the books, which showed the company operating a small profit of about £15.

At some point during the year Stephen was an 'extra' in the courtroom sequence of David Lean's film *Madeleine*, the daughter of an eminent and rich Glasgow architect accused of murdering her French lover. Ann Todd starred as *Madeleine*, but even his closest friends cannot recognise him under the bewhiskered make-up of the court ushers. He also walked on in *Trotty True*, a film directed by Brian Desmond Hurst, a constant visitor to Hermione's parties.[33] Before the year was out, he had also gone back to Central School, this time in a teaching capacity.

When he first went to The Hall as a pupil in 1937 the Vice Principal was Gwynneth Thurburn, who had herself been a pupil of Elsie Fogerty. In 1942 Gwynneth became Principal, a position she held until her retirement 25 years later after 48 years at the school. Gwynneth was as influential as Fogie had been. She denounced Mayfair accents for being as strangulated in their way as cockney. She preferred the rich rumbling voices from the moors and advised her pupils to be true to themselves. "People are their voices. To cure a person of a boring voice you have to cure them of being a bore first."[34]

She was also perceived by many pupils, along with Walter Hudd, Peter Copley, and other teachers, to be idealistically left, of left of centre, politically.[35] She took a close and personal interest in her students, registering every one who came under discussion in her weekly staff meetings, attended every entrance test and audition, every verse speaking test, every performance.[36] It was to 'Thurbie' Stephen went from Frinton - a safe harbour in a storm? - a medium in which to experiment? After a trial production she recognised the value of his unorthodox method, and the waywardness of his teaching, and committed herself to his development also:

> I can't remember how I came to invite him onto the staff. He came back to see us after the war and then he went to Cambridge, as a student he showed interest as a person - it wasn't that he had a great talent for acting - there was something there to be developed but I don't think we ever knew quite what... He founded the stage management course.[37]

He had advocated the introduction of a course on stage management, to include lighting, sound, building scenery, making properties and running the show. He insisted there was the need for training in these skills both for stage managers, and for actors who would often have to help with these activities in their first job.[38] The two year course developed and became firmly established later under the direction of Lawrence Hayes, but it was Stephen who set up the pilot course and steered it to establishment. Gwynneth remembered:

> He produced plays as well, may have taken a course in production, so many hours, so many weeks. History of Drama or Theatre, or something like that. We were much more flexible - you are when you are small. He would be full time for a while. He had a way of going off and getting a job with the Gas, Light and Coke Company to earn some money, and then come back. He wasn't everybody's cup of tea... Dickie Hudd (he was in charge of drama at the time) and responsible for choice of plays and appointing producers. All very friendly...thought a great deal of Stephen.[39]

Gwynneth's companion and The Hall's secretary 'Sarge' then observed:

> We could never afford to pay people very much - we had no funds. All

our staff were under-paid. All our people worked for us because they wanted to - that was really why we did so well in the world. It's terrible to say but that's a fact.[40]

One of his earliest productions mystified many students - a curious play called *The Black Maskers* by Andreyev - to some, the rehearsals were chaotic like the sort of nightmare all actors have when they are pushed onstage and don't know what you are supposed to do. All the cast were in black and masked.[41] Rehearsals were a shambles, but one actress, who carried the full length skirt of a medieval dress, her right hand covering her left which wore a full length snakeskin glove. When suddenly she said "The serpent is eating my heart," she dropped her right hand and the skirt, exposing the snake at her breast at which the entire audience gasped."[42] It was theatrical magic.

For Stephen these were two eventful years at the Hall, designing the stage management course, directing, teaching – *The Merry Wives of Windsor, The Rival Queen, The Critic*, a German expressionistic play *Gas*, in which he had everybody rushing about on a small stage. He was "a very exciting person to work with, full of energy and with a wonderful nature."[43]

When he went through the cast list of *Merry Wives* the face of one actress fell. He asked : "What is it Shirley?" and she complained, "Look what you've given me, I've only got one line." Stephen said, "My mother made her name in that part," and with Shirley Cooklin as the pageboy Stephen introduced lots of stage business such as eating an apple, etc., and taught the class not about acting, but about being. She did indeed steal the show.

Lucky Peter's Travels was done with only step ladders on the stage, put to different uses - for one scene some of the cast up aloft held branches to create a wood, and made bird noises from above. With Coriolanus he used a transverse stage with audience on two sides.

When he did the *Oresteia* in full, he said to fellow lecturer Heather Black one day, "Why don't you do a new translation of the plays?," just like that, so she did - bought all the editions available and rewrote the drama with Stephen's assistance.[44]

The play was staged conventionally, but he insisted on the actors wearing masks and cothurni - they then realised that the elevated footwear was necessary to offset the effect of the masks. With such a play, using a huge cast, and with the minimum of backstage facilities, dressing rooms below the stage and with access only by one spiral staircase - performance conditions for many of the cast were ghastly.[45]

For his production of *The Alchemist* he asked Diana Willis, Shirley's bridesmaid, to do the designs, but to her disappointment thought they were not colourful enough and didn't use them.[46]

Hermione attended many of the performances at the school, not just those directed by Stephen. The students were very impressed because of her fame and success, but smart as she looked, at least one student thought her neck never looked too clean.[47]

Then, immediately before setting out for the New World, he was engaged to direct *The Mortal Bard* by C.E. Webber at St Mary's Hall, Edinburgh, on the fringe, for the 1951 International Festival. The play was presented by Jack Rodney's London Club Theatre Group, with a minimum salary of £24 which was to be increased subject to satisfactory box office receipts to a maximum of £36, plus third class rail travel and £6 expenses for the second week of rehearsal in Edinburgh. Stephen describes the production in his book on scene painting :

> A delightful play, the action moves fluidly from one scene to another... The production budget was £5...The stage manager helped me build the set of 2 x 1 inch batten and string... The string formed an almost opaque background when the lights were on the downstage side of it, but, when the actors were lit from upstage, the string disappeared. The play was witty and ingenious, the acting full of fun and vigour.[48]

Chapter Thirteen

The New World

All the vibrant new writing after the war was coming from the United States; Arthur Miller, Clifford Odets, Tennessee Williams, Eugene O'Neill. Walter Kerr's Theatre Guild and Welles's pre-war Mercury Theatre had profiles higher than anything comparable in Britain.

As *La Vie Cambridgienne* came to an end, Stephen started writing to American Universities in search of a teaching position. Between engagements at Lowestoft, he had made the acquaintance of Gemma Fagan at the British Centre for the International Theatre Institute, then in Goodwins Court. Together they looked for a teaching exchange. He outlined his reasons for wanting to go. The chance to look at the drama first hand, estimate its contribution to the American way of life, and discover why it provided a field of study for degrees in some American, but in no British Universities.

So optimistic was Gemma Fagan that she suggested he apply to the Fulbright and the Smith-Mundt funds, to cover maintenance and travel costs. Hermione agreed to lend security of the £500 which was needed before he could be allowed a travel visa.

In his application for a grant, during the depths of the Cold War, he emphasised his concern with the need for greater understanding between the East and the West. By March 1951 he learned from the United States Information Service that from a large number of high quality applicants he had been successful.

As no teaching opportunity presented itself, Gemma Fagan suggested he seek admission to do research towards a Ph.D. To this end he was recommended to Professor Mabie in Iowa - one of the few universities to pioneer the acceptance of creative work for academic credit. It also had a large, magnificently equipped new theatre complex, and according to the brochure sought to encourage students in the fullest possible development of their capacities as people and as members of society. It sounded liberally orientated also and he was accepted by the University to do his Ph.D.

As he set out in September 1951, Gemma Fagan wrote that he seemed to be one of the incredibly few people in London who had ideas and drive and no particular political axe to grind. If Iowa did not live up to his expectation, the fun was worthwhile and the experience had a lasting value when it came to rationalising the Manchester Degree Course. He wrote:

> I was supposedly selected on the basis of theatre experience and a university degree; and none of these was at all necessary... indeed they were a stumbling block over which I fell too frequently into priggishness. Certainly if I had given more attention to the degree I would have missed some of the most enjoyable and instructive moments of my visit.

Iowa, in the middle of the great plains, is corn and cattle territory. Sioux country, it was nicknamed Hawkeye State. At that time its most famous son was Buffalo Bill Cody, today it includes Gene Wilder and Bill Bryson. Covering an area the size of England and with a population of less than three million, it is easy to understand that to a war veteran and Cambridge Graduate the city might appear backward or provincial.

He was a good 13 years older than most of the students there. Someone with his experience appearing in a university poses a threat to the staff, who, however mature, are likely to feel themselves, their positions and their authority, threatened. He might know more than them. He might see through them.

Primarily the American academic system is built up, like green shield stamps, on a points system - so many points per topic covered. A degree from an English University was of no value to these academics. Without a detailed breakdown of topics, subjects and the degree of proficiency, term by term, they could not function. Letters from the Master of Jesus College, copies of the Cambridge Diploma, his Central School Diploma, these were insignificant beside his singular shortcoming. He was unqualified for a degree within several years!

So, after many weeks of indecision and lost time, they decided they had to examine him to assess his 'credit' hours. In history from Herodotus to Toynbee, in literature from Chaucer to Eliot, in French orally, from Jean de Meung to Sartre, in translated classics, Homer to Seneca. The only comments arising from these examinations were, that he had passed, showed a talent for writing, and an inability to concentrate his interests!

He had already been told much the same thing by Professor Mabie. Having outlined his field of interest, he was warned that it was too wide for research leading to a Ph.D. There may have been method in Mabie's madness because the University had installed electronic equipment so that members of an audience could register instant reaction during any given performance. Mabie tried to coerce Stephen into a thesis on audience-response research using this equipment. Had he been compliant it may well have been his window to the Ph.D which eluded him.

Stephen's description of the course in Experimental Theatre seems to typify his opinion of what was on offer generally:

> Not much enjoyed by the students, the reading list too long and too dull, the assignments too heavy; too much dogma, too small a compass of critical theory, and an unfair treatment of original work.

Iowa did have a superb University theatre, seating 450. It was described as one of the best equipped theatres in the world, considering its size. The stage machinery, backstage space, workshops and offices were in luxurious proportions. He found it a constant pleasure, and was sad to report that in his opinion the drama department had gained its reputation before its theatre (i.e. the one did not live up to the other).

His crie de coeur was not a new one, that 'lack of material plant is a stimulus to artistry. When that stimulus is gone it is difficult to overcome the complacency that material comfort brings.' Expressed in more mundane terms, that an artist does his best work in poverty, in a garret.

As a teacher himself, he would have liked to try out his ideas on larger groups, but his offers to address students were almost entirely ignored. It was outside of Iowa that he found the opportunity of addressing meetings, speaking on Drama in Education, Contemporary British Theatre, Contemporary British Film and Elizabethan Theatre.

He was able to arrange visits to these Universities - Coe College, Illinois and Michigan - on an expenses basis. Escaping the narrow confines of Iowa were the most enjoyable and instructive events of his stay. His visit to Illinois happily coincided with a contemporary arts festival. There he was more acutely aware than in Iowa of the place of drama in education. He sat in on classes, exchanged experience with faculty members, and had enlightening discussions with the Director.

How he must have wished he could engage Professor Mabie in such dialectics. Mabie had accepted Stephen to do a Ph.D. in a year, but he had wasted so much time it was no longer possible. The sense that, for whatever reason, he was being squeezed out and denied the chance to achieve what he had been offered, is inescapable. Once more in his life authority was blighting his chances which may have contributed to the arrogance one detects in his comments that there was a lack of intellectual fibre amongst the faculty.

Mabie now suggested he stay for a second year to accomplish his Ph.D. but his grants were for a year. Upon arrival he'd had to confirm his return passage, so when it became obvious that he could not stay, he was offered a part-time assistantship. This allowed him to earn enough money to remain at the university through the summer session. He also followed the good American custom of working through college. By doing two hours each day in the union cafeteria he was able to save half his salary. He observed :

> This work brought me into contact with people whom I had not previously met. Opened my eyes to various intriguing aspects of American life that I might otherwise have missed. It provided me with a mental stimulation that I could not find where I expected it - in class...!

He was disappointed too by his active participation. He was one of two assistants on a production of *Mary Stuart*, the direction of which was frustratingly bad. It did not help that the director happened to be the man in charge of the directing Course. Then, in the chorus of *The Beggar's Opera*, he found himself constantly asked for advice, but it was a case of 'too many cooks.' There was an assistant director with a jolly talent for inventing irrelevant business, a dance lady who introduced out-of-character business, a musical director with some excellent ideas, and a director who really didn't know what was going on. They all contributed to an aimless production.

Something which gave him satisfaction was appearing as Sir Robert Morton in *The Winslow Boy*. However he was never a good study. He confided to the director, Lewin Goff, that he was anxious about learning the lines. Sir Robert is the barrister called in to defend young Dickie Winslow from a charge of stealing a five shilling postal order from a fellow cadet at Naval college. Stephen found it a difficult part to learn, especially the long interrogation scene between Sir Robert and the boy he has been called in to defend.

Each time they went through it Stephen would say afterwards, "Got it right that time," and each time Dickie would say "No!" His bacon was saved by the boy so adapting to the situation that he gave a plausible answer to whatever question was fired at him. One newspaper review commented,

Stephen Joseph strode through the part of Sir Robert Morton, famed lawyer, with a mixture of callous cynicism and restrained sentiment.

It was good training for the boy, too. In the role of Dickie Winslow was a young man by the name of Jerry Silberman. One wonders what he introduced into Terence Rattigan's rather austere melodrama for the *Iowa Citizen* to remark that, "to Mr Silberman the play owes its advantages of comic relief... which brought laughter and applause from the audience." Even the *Daily Iowan* described the play as a jugful of laughter in a jigger of tears. The year after Stephen died, Jerry Silberman found success in Hollywood. He had changed his name to Gene Wilder.

In the end Stephen had to settle for a Master's Degree. He wrote *Preparatory Notes for the Production of Twelfth Night* to recall the Original Conditions of Performance. It is a gossamer construction. On the title page Mabie has written a note wishing he had been more specific in part 3 (his most detailed section). He also comments "you are on thin ice several times in Parts 1 and 2, but surely no thinner than many others have skated before."

He presented a paper entitled *Renaissance Man,* revolving around the life of Giuliano dei Medici who was killed in the Pazzi plot aimed primarily at his brother, Lorenzo, 'Il Magnifico'. The history is interspersed with detailed cameos of life, learning and achievement in Renaissance Italy. It is his best piece of writing, and unremarked.

For his practical contribution he wrote a play entitled *What Would Mildred Have Said?* The plans for the play were laid before the Experimental Theatre Course, though the script could not be more orthodox. The plans were then criticised by fellow students and the course instructor, who also gave considerable private time to discussion.

The first draft was read by another group of students to a small audience. There was further criticism and revisions. The second draft was directed and performed onstage before an invited audience, most of whom gave written comments. After further discussion the finalised script was presented as thesis material.

Harold Schiffler, who directed the performance, has total amnesia about the play and the production. If a camel is a horse designed by a committee, it tells us much about this faculty that Stephen's play should have turned out to be so characterless and bland.

He was to return to Britain with another completed manuscript, *Murder My*

Legacy, a more interesting and better constructed play than Mildred, although suffering from overtones of melodrama.

On Wednesday the 6th of August, 1952 at 7.30 p.m. the commencement of exercises occurred at the State University of Iowa to confer Advanced Degrees, Certificates and Degrees to Chartered candidates. A Master of Fine Arts Degree was conferred on Michael Stephen Lionel Joseph, BA University of Cambridge 1948, for his dramatic art thesis, *What Would Mildred Have Said?*

In the month before his departure he was determined to make up for lost time. Meeting up with two or three other friends who had travelled out similarly, he went to Seattle where he saw plays at the University of Washington's Penthouse and Showboat Theatres. He examined these theatres and the University Playhouse. He also saw a production of *Present Laughter* performed in the round at the 'Cirque' Theatre.

In Portland, Oregon, he was shown the various stages of Reed College. Then on to Ashland to see *Henry V* done on their mock Elizabethan stage. On his way back to New York he saw Detroit's Will O'Way summer stock company, and went over several theatres belonging to the Cleveland Playhouse. He wrote :

> All these theatres were interesting and gave me the formula: A clean, well-equipped theatre will show dull acting, while inadequate equipment and untidiness are consistent with genuine entertainment from the stage.

This formula was to be Stephen's credo for the rest of his career. He does admit, though, that his formula got knocked on the head when he saw some excellent acting in New York. Eli Wallach in *The Rose Tattoo* and Charles Laughton, Agnes Moorhead and Cedric Hardwick in Shaw's *Don Juan in Hell*, then emphasised:

> The fact emerges that drama is an affair between actors and audience - stages, theatres. Directors, producers, and even authors are only of secondary importance. All else is trappings.

Chapter Fourteen

One Great Vision

Stephen's re-appearance at the Hall was eagerly awaited. He had become a legend to many[1] and when he did reappear a great cheer went up.[2] Compared to the other teachers he was very young and very sensitive. He wore strange clothes - cowboy boots and plaid shirts,[3] or corduroy trousers and big boots... workman's donkey jackets...[4]

He was not dangerous to know, although even that was contentious in a school which became firmly divided between the Stephen Joseph breed of free thinkers, and the ultra conservative Oliver Reynolds set. Fertile young minds of both camps even concocted scurrilous stories - weird, as they were wide of the mark. For example "Hermione found Stephen in bed with a guardsman and she said, 'Put that guardsman down'..." and "Oliver Reynolds and Barbara Francis (another teacher) are living together..."[5]

Stephen returned from America also full of ideas of ways in which he could help improve the course of his alma mater. Although Stephen's father considered him feckless, he was actually a very careful person and the scheme he proposed to Miss Thurburn for an advanced department he believed could justify itself financially. "There is no end to my revolutionary zeal," he told her "without wanting to tread on toes."[6] He was advocating speech therapy as a university syllabus; enlarging the student-teacher scheme; concentrating dramatic work by studying a play over a three week rehearsal period instead of spreading it over a term.

He was exciting because he was innovative, but comforting also. He gave his students space and allowed them to be themselves, to explore themselves both in terms of performance and development. He didn't have the unpleasantness or the rudeness of his contemporary John Dexter, who would ride roughshod over, and be obscenely rude to students to get his way.[7]

He was encouraging, but never doctrinaire. He gave people a chance to do things no one else would, as when he cast an insignificant lad in a romantic leading role and gave the glamorous lead to a small catarrhal Jewish girl whose misfortune was alopecia.[8] When his peers complained that this or that person wasn't right he'd whole heartedly agree, but then remind them that this was a school! It was their turn. They had come to learn, and without experience, they never would.

He treated students like human beings, had a rapport and an ability to communicate. He would become one of them and come down to their level without being patronising. He had boundless, exhausting enthusiasm and, quite rightly, expected them to do anything. He also had his mother's wit, so was never nonplussed. He always had an answer. He probably directed students better than actors, because he became nervous of people whom he suspected, wrongly, had more talent than himself.[9]

"In some ways he was a very masculine man, but in other ways he was a motherly figure. A brother and a sister. Asexual really."[10] He was always ill at ease at his mother's parties, although he nearly always took male friends with him. Not like Pandarus, but maybe as talismen, to protect himself from her scrutiny? It was possibly a reaction to her world which sent him along the road to more austere theatre.[11] Many people noticed that he was never really part of Hermione's coterie: Shirley thought them all too 'theatrical' for him.

In the winter of 1952 he directed *The Careless Husband* for the Mask and Dagger company at Leeds University. They were opening a new theatre as part of the National Union of Students Festival. Mask and Dagger was an independent group which toured each summer, run by students of The Hall. The company went North on New Year's Eve. Dances and street congas notwithstanding, the next day was spent rehearsing. If 1953 could be described as Stephen's year of trial by fire it started with just that. While Harry Landis and Shirley Jacobs went through their paces onstage they observed Stephen helping the Stage Manager Paul Massie to put out a fire in the lighting box.

The *Manchester Guardian* reviewer welcomed :

> This . . . chance of seeing (*The Careless Husband*) must be to students of the theatre . . . one of those nips from the lees of Restoration Comedy which tend to be flat indeed. An unhandy performance could make it unendurable, and lo, here we had not mere competence but elegance, players who knew how to move, as well as speak, and a producer (Stephen Joseph) whose deftness earned the imperative curtain calls of an audience which has showed itself to be far from uncritical! [12]

Not that Stephen liked directing. There was no place in his life for the orthodox "You will move from A to B donning your glasses as you go" school of production. His ideal was something like a Jackson Pollock painting where you worked from the middle of it. He preferred directing a bad new play to directing an established one.[13] He considered most trained actors over directed, and was not fond of the students who waited to be told what was expected of them. He wanted them to find their own answers - if he had to impose a solution he felt he had failed.[14]

Not that he was incapable of being authoritarian. When he directed *King Arthur* and all the students had to sing, the protests were terrible. One, who in tears said she wouldn't sing, eventually did. It was Mary Ure, and within a year she was singing on the stage in the West End opposite Paul Schofield.[15]

At the start of rehearsals the orthodox director arrives with his script, problems resolved, moves mapped out, and sound and lighting cues marked in. Stephen turned up with a pile of motor cycle magazines. His class was astonished. At the start he would be attentive, but if bored, he would pick up a magazine and read it and then another. When some brave soul asked, "Sir, when are you going to direct us?" he would remark "When you give me something to direct, I'll direct it."[16]

Responsibility for characterisation and moves were pushed onto the students. He asked questions about the scene, about the characters' motives, relationships and proximity. One girl, angered to have been told her performance was dreary, then howled her lines, gesticulated wildly. At the end of the scene she stood defiantly centre stage, breathing heavily, waiting for an explosion. Stephen said he hadn't realised she could act, after which the whole production became alive.[17]

He would remark to a class, "This fellow is one of the most versatile people in the whole place, but he's lazy,"[18] and to another, "there are several ways of playing this character, and you haven't got it yet."[19] He would float ideas - often outrageous - to spark off discussion and then sit back.[20]

If it was unkind of Bernard Shaw to observe that he who can does - he who cannot teaches - there is a germ of truth in the remark. The Hall was about to witness a trial of strengths between the Man, and the Superman. Educational establishments often bristle with people whose sensitivities are delicately balanced, or who are merciless in their contempt for their fellow teachers. While Stephen was in Iowa, Walter Hudd had retired, and his place been taken by Oliver Reynolds.

To say there was competition between these two would be to make an understatement. Oliver was meticulous. Stephen was popular. Students were split between those who loved Olly and those who loved Stephen. Jeremy Kemp remembers Reynolds as a very mysterious person in many ways, yet when he was playing in the wilds of Canada years later, he kept thinking "What would Oliver have said." Heather Black explained :

> With Reynolds they knew exactly where they were. Stephen was very charismatic and demanding, "Take this part away and do something with it," like he'd said "Go off and rewrite the *Oresteia*" - you did it. Stephen was a great anarchist - some people were drawn to that and some wanted safer waters. There was a volcanic feeling about him. Never greatly critical, he'd have ideas and get excited - a bit like a Catherine wheel throwing off sparks.[21]

Reynolds had worked under Michel St Denis at the collapsed Old Vic School. He was a very precise, meticulous, organised person. If he got a bee in his bonnet he would stick by it whoever disagreed. He had standards, but alas (the school) couldn't afford the standards he had had under St Denis. Stephen's working methods were, in Reynolds view, slapdash,[22] and his popularity among the students fuelled Reynolds dislike of him. Vera Sargeant, "Sarge," explained:

> Oliver heartily disapproved of Stephen. They were at daggers drawn - there was no love lost between them... Oliver was a great help to us, he was very strict and did a good job but I can imagine there were a lot of people who didn't care for him, he was very set in his ways. Reynolds helped set the school on a stable setting - he had a very strong quiet personality, but he was not a leader. He made friends and enemies.[23]

And Gwynneth Thurburn added :

They were two personalities that were bound to clash.[24]

What prompted Stephen to undertake a production of Purcell's *King Arthur* is anybody's guess, but direct it he did. It was performed on the 3rd of July. He always claimed it as one of his favourite works, even after the debacle. In 1953 the school probably saw it as a fitting contribution to the Coronation celebrations that year. It has a purity and musical clarity, a quintessentially English sound. In this sense it could be seen to reflect his father's desire to be English.

Fairest Isle all Isles excelling

> Seat of Pleasure and of Loves
> Venus here will choose her dwelling
> And forsake the Cyprian Groves.

Describing itself as a dramatic opera, (the text is by John Dryden), it is in fact a play, with interpolated songs, dances, symphonies and masques. It contains some of Purcell's best music, from the delicate intensity of *Fairest Isle* to the rollicking blasphemies of *Your Hay is mow'd, and your corn is reap'd*.

It also contains enough irony to appeal to an anarchic streak, "the Gods from above...pity mankind that will perish for gold..." It too is a battle, New England over Old - a battle for a new order - symbolically a battle between son and father.

When originally written and performed on the Jacobean stage, stuffed with machinery and hands to move the scenery, it was a magnificent spectacle. Describing the 1995 revival at The Royal Opera House a reviewer remarked that it relies above all "on a brilliant ensemble effort... four hours of baffling, beguiling spectacle."[25] Done under makeshift conditions on the Central stage it did not quite achieve the desired result. Where a complicated and fine attention to detail was required, it degenerated into a Hellzapoppin. It was Stephen's Achille's heel, and he fell. Ronnie Scott Dodd remembers :

> I was playing the Banks of the Thames, and my costume had been issued in absentia, so I got one costume out of sync all through the show. I sang a few notes, and had this absolute horror of knowing that everything was going wrong and not knowing why. I had rehearsed it so carefully The entire production was going wrong, not in a diffident or scared way, but in a big way.

> Arthur had decided he wasn't physically big enough so he built himself an entire chest - overlooking the fact that the chest came up to his chin - so he had no neck! There were two rostra at the back indicating a chasm over which he was about to leap, and as he indicated that he was about to call the elements, Earth and Water to rescue - he stepped forward and fell down between the two rostra. But his artificial chest prevented descent and they had to pull him out - but with absolute integrity. The artists didn't deteriorate in any way, so once he was on his feet he went to playing the role forcefully.

> The stage management had torn up newspaper to float down as snow and suspended it in nets over the stage, but it fell in great gobbets.

While it was falling the actress playing Britania, Mary Ure, had to crawl from one side of the stage to the other unseen, while Dariel rode the Waves.

There wasn't much room for her to rise from, and as she came up she was covered from head to foot with pieces of paper that had stuck to her - and fluttered off as she sang - and the actors still didn't laugh and were furious with the reaction from the audience. The more seriously the actors took it, the more the audience laughed.

Wendy Craig sang "Hither this way, this way bend ..." She was the wicked spirit tempting the army to follow her before they finally overcome her temptation. The army consisted of four students plus the King and rehearsals had gone well.

When it came to the production, she had been given a shrunken pair of tights, the crotch at her knees - so she had little legs sticking out - and she couldn't move very far because her stride was being restricted at the knee. Each time she sang "Hither this way" the army got it wrong and moved in the opposite direction...

When the crown of the wicked King fell off, it rolled round the entire stage and was picked up by Benedikt Arnason, who realised that the last thing he wanted in his hand was the crown and handed it to the person next to him, who didn't want it and handed it to the person next to him and so on, till the last man who had it realised he was going to be left onstage with it, so he handed to with his other hand to Benedikt who was about to leave the stage. It had gone all the way round the stage. Rehearsed for a month we couldn't have done it better. And of course the audience watching fell about.[26]

Patricia (Paddy) Greene added :

Because we were so serious, the more they laughed, the more awful we became, we tried harder. This was an examination.

Hermione had come to see it, and came round to see us afterwards, tears pouring down her face, "If I could take this production as it is and put it on in a London theatre it would run forever, as long as you didn't get any better."[27]

After that it was "What were you doing?" and, "Why did you give these students this awful job to do? It's ridiculous." As a matter of fact, we learned more from that than from a lot of things. So we didn't have Stephen for the third year.[28]

Before the year was over, rumours began to circulate that the school was going to take *The Careless Husband* to a Youth Festival in Bucharest in the summer vacation. The Bucharest bit turned out to be true, but in fact they were to take two short plays, and parts were available to anyone adventurous enough who could raise the nominal fare.

There was a communist organisation based on the Theatre at Stratford-atte-Bow to which student Harry Landis belonged, and which set up the trip. The Fourth World Festival of Youth organised to unite the worlds' young, was in part to celebrate the Korean War Heroes. There were a number of fellow travellers at the Hall. Gwynneth was thought to have sympathies, or to be a member of the Committee for Cultural Relations with the Soviet Union, and Peter Copley and Dickie Hudd were similarly committed.[29] The Hall's property at 52 Hyde Park Gate was rented to the Russian Embassy.

The students and staff who went were accompanied by a small team filming the trip. The renowned Walter Lassally was cameraman and Monty and Anthony Simmons were directing. The documentary they later produced, *One Great Vision*, was a record of the event. The fact that Lassally was an East German meant they had to fly to Prague as he would have found it dangerous travelling by train through East Germany.

These were the deepest years of the Cold War, and pressure was put on several members of the company not to go. Stephen wrote to Peter Taylor in the Foreign Services of the American Embassy to clarify their position. The trip could affect an actor's future chance of working in the United States. Many students were lectured on the foolhardiness of such a visit behind the Iron Curtain.[30]

The performance which was going to Eastern Europe was premiered at the Unity Theatre. The London Student Players presented two plays, one was the Mystery, *The Deluge*. The script, which used to be performed by the water drawers of the Medieval city of Chester, tells the story of Noah and the flood. Stephen played Shem, whilst Noah was Patrick Carter who had been King Arthur. Clive Goodwin played God at the top of a pair of steps. Everyone wore black leotards and tights.

The other play Stephen wrote himself. *The Key* tells the story of Harold, who goes to the theatre with his wife, Betty, and his mother-in-law. He discovers that he has lost the key to the front door of their home, and his mother-in-law is very angry. The curtain rises on a Victorian scene: Mr Roper strongly disapproves of the man his daughter Susan is in love with. The man, Jack, is an actor and Susan has a ticket for the play he is in, but Mr Roper seizes the ticket, locks Susan in the cellar and throws away the key. Harold recognises it as the one he has lost.

Mr Roper now goes to the theatre with a pistol to shoot Jack and watches the play, waiting for him to appear. This play tells a story of Shakespearien type, concerning a diplomatic marriage that is about to take place between a prince and princess who are not in love. The prince however is loved by a girl. She, disguised as a man, Sebastian, waits for him; the princess is in love with a nobleman, Grumio - enacted by Jack. The princess is to have a large dowry, treasure, contained in a chest. To prevent the marriage, Sebastian throws the key of the chest into the sea. Mr Roper recognises the key as his... so does Harold. The key has now been lost three times!

Roper tries to shoot Jack but the young man escapes and they fight. Roper boasts that Susan will die locked up in the cellar. Harold now feels guilty. His key could have released Susan. As the play approaches a chaotic climax, the theatre manager steps forward to calm down audience and actors. He explains that the plot is merely a fiction, that the key does not exist, except as a symbol, and that the meaning of the play is symbolic. If the audience is convinced of its reality, this is the symbolic reality of all drama. It provides the key to many problems of life !!!

There were plenty of news photographers at the airport to see them off. It made a good press story, but when the plane arrived in Prague, late at night, the authorities removed God!

> When we got to Prague they said, "Olive Goodwin?" And he said, "No, Clive." He obviously wasn't Olive, so they took him away in a black car, and we thought, well we won't see him again.[31]

They'd all heard about the Cheka and the KGB. The clerk at the embassy had misread the C as an O, and had printed Clive's visa on a Female visa form. They all spent an uncomfortable night sleeping on wooden slats or on the floor of a student hostel, worried, whilst Clive was accommodated in a luxury hotel. The next day was sunny and they were taken on a tour of the beautiful city and castle. They saw the empty shops, the few cars, wide streets, ill dressed people. The guide was friendly, but guarded.[32] Meanwhile, Paddy Greene said. "Clive had a marvellous time - he was driven everywhere. We kept seeing the tail end of a car with him in it, and wondered..."

Reunited with God at the station, Paddy Greene remembered that they all joined:

> this long long train with first, second, third class and steerage compartments - just for students. The Germans bagged the first class sleepers, just like it is today. We ended up in third class on more wooden slats.

They then had what felt like a four day train journey, whiling away the time playing games. In the many stops along the way, peasants lined up on the platforms with arms full of melons and gladioli saying, "Peace Forever," in different languages. When they went through a country that hadn't been bribed they went without food.

Parties of Young Pioneers in national costume would perform folk dances or be singing traditional songs on the platforms. Further into Hungary they had a marvellous meal all laid out for them at a station, and there was a gypsy band playing while they ate. Everywhere they sang the Festival song

> Everywhere the youth is singing the Freedom song Freedom Song, Freedom Song
> We rejoice to show the world that we are strong We are strong, We are strong
> We are the Youth
> And the world proclaim our song of Truth...

According to some Stephen hated it![33]

People had come from all over the world to be part of the Festival. New Zealanders, Chinese acrobats, Koreans - and they were accommodated in dormitories on separate floors for men and women. The food was very good, but the amount of meat diminished in each meal as the stay went on. They learned later that the people of Bucharest had gone without food for weeks in order to feed the students.

> At the start of the festival they were told they'd got to parade into the huge arena before the President and the thousands. "We felt like the Christians" Stephen said, "I'm not going to do it," and I said "We've got to, Stephen," and he said "Hold my hand then." All the other countries were walking with their flag proudly; I think one of us found a small Union Jack... and we struggled behind with Stephen holding my hand saying, "I can't bear it." They forgot to feed us that day! When we did our play, nobody had

seen this kind of avant-garde theatre before. These strange costumes - any actors (in the audience) were gobsmacked by it.[34]

Paddy Greene had struck up a friendship with a Polish boy and his 'Minder.' He was very blonde and she was very dark. They talked through his minder, with bits of French and German, and out of the blue the company was invited to take the production to Warsaw, so after Bucharest, they went to a wonderful holiday camp for actors in a posh part of Poland. Paddy's friend Andrzej (was it Wadja?) was there with his group of people. She continues:

> We went on a coach. They'd decked it out as if for a party. They were having a holiday there. It was the good life the communist regime was having. They were living like lords. It was wonderful, but a bit embarrassing for me, because they had garlands with my name, Paddy, all over them. And Stephen squeezed my arm and said "O God, O God, O God."
>
> This was the cream of Poland, and they did a wonderful act for us, balancing on each others shoulders, a play, one thing and another. Then they said, now you do yours... Well we rather shamefacedly did *The Key* followed by *Noah*, but they thought it was fantastic.

The company spent a week exploring Warsaw, an extremely bleak city: its windows were boarded up and rubble, shell and bullet holes were still apparent. They visited factories and also Chopin's house, where the latest recipient of the Chopin prize played for them on Chopin's piano. Meanwhile Stephen complained they were missing watching Zatopek running!

In their perambulations in Warsaw they met a very remarkable Rumanian woman, who said, "I'm going to show you where they are, because they're not supposed to be there, so you must only look when I scratch my foot. You have not been talking to me." So they were shown men with Alsatian dogs, lurking. She was desperate to get out of the country with them. Couldn't she hide in their costume skip?

All the souvenirs they'd acquired were confiscated before their return,[35] and Shirley Jacobs remembered:

> We had a lot to think about and discuss on our return journey to the West - however, that was not the last excitement. Early that morning the train came to a stop. There was a great deal of shouting and noise, and we looked out of the window and saw flames.[36]

The train we were on was machine gunned. The most amazing things happened... the morning after the shooting incident and after a long train journey, our coach was stranded in the middle of nowhere. Without the engine![37] I looked out of the window... thinking "That looks like our props basket" - and not saying anything at the time, thinking it a mere coincidence.[38]

We all said, "What the hell is this?" and I just lay on the floor in the middle of the carriage and said, "I want some tea," and they said, "Yes, get up you can have some... Along here there's a party for you..." They'd got us a table and tablecloth and we didn't know which country we were in, and we didn't understand the language, but they were sweet, and they sang to us, and they gave us food and drink, and we said, "Where are we, where are we going?" and they said, "the train will come, the train will come." We said, "why have we been unhitched?" "The train will come..." and eventually the train came and the next stop was decadent, horrible Germany, and we got out and said "O look Cornflakes," and there were street lights and things in the shops and we couldn't honestly believe we had escaped.[39]

It was three months later, and after endless letters, that the basket and its very damp contents was returned to Central School!

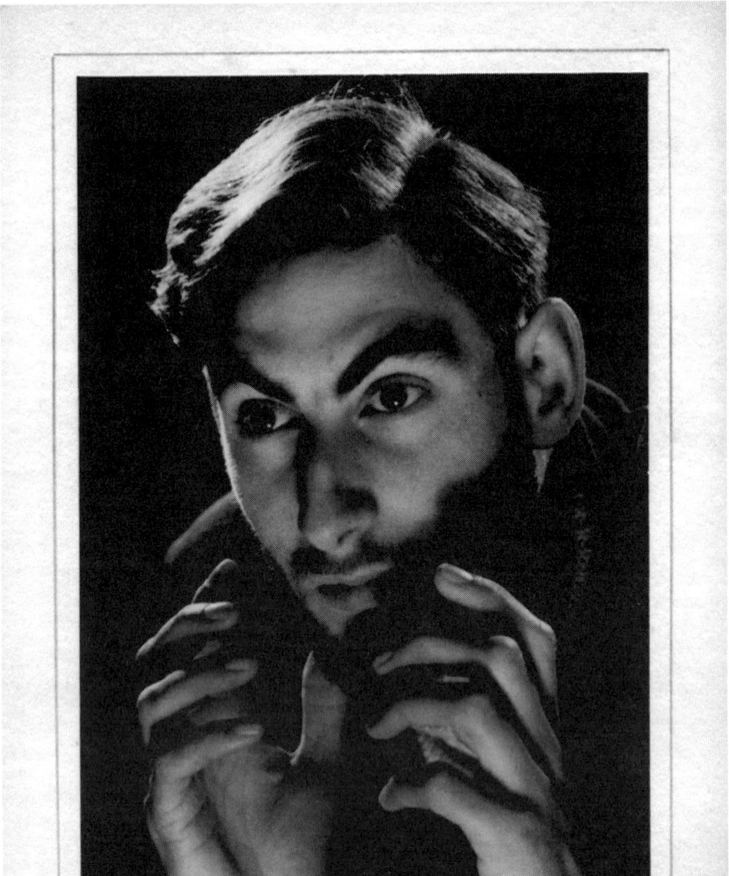

Chapter Fifteen

World's End

Stephen was going through a period of deep depression. His old friend, Hermione's colleague Gretchen Franklin, had a flat in Ashburnham Mansions, at World's End, and he rented a room from her. These were spacious flats, built to accommodate people used to living in larger houses, some had maids' rooms. Their ambience was only spoiled by a view of a nearby gasometer. Large though the rooms were, Stephens books spilled out and were piled in the hallway.

For a while he had shared a flat with Heather Black from the Hall. Splendid people though they both were, theirs was not to be a life of connubial bliss. Harry Landis claimed that Stephen was impotent. He vented his frustration in complaints about her housekeeping, her sluttish habits, the mouldy food in the refrigerator, and the untidiness, dust, chaos. None of this done in reverent care of her, rather as a means to escape his personal inability to perform. It says much about them both that she soldiered on for so long.

All the time he was manic depressive - either high as a kite or suicidal. He had terrible digestive problems, linked with the depression. He was in great pain. There were times when he was unapproachable. Then he would go off and get a job with the Ealing Council - a manual job, digging up roads.

Of course he did it for other than financial reasons. The physical expression of solidarity with the working man is documented by Tolstoy. Van Gogh sought spiritual fulfilment in field labour. Stephen needed to do manual labour and he was chastised by his mates. In his manic periods he would go on working up to the last minute when all the others had packed up and wanted to go.

Many who witnessed his distress at this time blamed Hermione, probably because she had the higher profile. Certainly she had abandoned her babies and had little affection for them, but it is worth considering whether most of the blame should not be laid at the door of his father. His taunts and jibes, physical and psychological damage, did most to emasculate his son and cause him to seek such demonstrations of ability.

He spoke of his father with no warmth, of his putting obstacles in his way. For a period of years he had analysis at St Stephen's Hospital, Chelsea.[1] He attended group therapy sessions. Four or five patients sat around, encouraged to talk about their problems. The psychiatrist at his desk busied himself with other matters and at the end of an hour collected a fiver from each.[2]

Even students at the Hall were aware that all was not well. His depressive periods hung over into college time. "We all said, well if anybody can do it, Heather can," Paddy Greene recalls. "We would all have done it because he was so lovely." Finally, and miserably, he went back briefly to d'Arcy and his pals but then to his single bed and 2,000 books in the hall at World's End.

He had directed *Lady Windermere's Fan* in the autumn of 1952, and before the end of the following academic year 1953 he did O'Casey's *Bedtime Story* for what appears to be a Finals production. He did *Pygmalion and Galatea* by W.S. Gilbert at a theatre in Russell Square with Edwin Apps and Wendy Craig in the title roles; he also directed *A Jig for a Gypsy*sy by Robertson Davies for the Questors Theatre in Ealing. The author flew from Canada to attend the first performance.

He became a member of the National Executive of the British Youth Festival Committee. Bucharest was described as one of the finest achievements in the work of the World Youth Festival. The part which young singers, dancers, actors and artists played in popularising the festival was only the beginning. It showed the important part that such activities have in building a strong youth peace movement in Britain.[3]

Gwynneth was not happy for him to be cast out of The Hall entirely. One of his many suggestions she now acted upon. In association with the British Drama League, she instituted a course of lectures on the *'Art of the Playwrite'* (sic), to be given by Stephen on Tuesday evenings at 52 Hyde Park Gate - the Russian Embassy.

To a certain extent he was following in father's footsteps, but he was inspired too by George Pierce Baker's playwriting courses at Harvard, which Eugene O'Neill had attended. Stephen knew how to write, he had seen his own plays performed at the Hall before the war, and his Masters degree from Iowa was in playwriting. Apart from his own plays and revue material, he'd prepared a filmscript synopsis for an adaptation of Hogg's *The Justified Sinner* and written an episode and outline synopsis for a radio serial based on *Henry Esmond*.

In 1956 he was credited as co-author with David Campton of a TV play, *One Fight More,* which the BBC screened and accounted experimental. Hermione called him in to be play-doctor for a script by Mel Dinelli with which she was touring the States. In her autobiography she describes it as "a wildly funny, brilliant play I wrote myself," but the two men are listed as co-authors and Stephen occasionally received royalties from *Abracadabra*. If he never wrote commercially himself, he was firmly grounded in the theory and could inspire.

The series of ten lectures per term over three terms, ran from the 6th of October, 1953 through to the following summer, and students were requested to make written applications. At 25/- per term the lectures dealt with critical theories of drama, practical techniques of established playwrights, and the relationship between the playwright, the actor and society. One of the first to enrol was Neville Hunnings, who became a lifelong friend and member of the Board of Management when Stephen set up the Studio Theatre company. The course appears to have run over two years.

In the autumn of 1953 Stephen directed three plays for the Leatherhead Repertory. Hazel Vincent Wallace was in charge, Oscar Quitak's secretary from Frinton. As part of a belt-tightening in the repertory movement Leatherhead had combined with Canterbury to perform fortnightly. This meant the company rehearsing in situ then performing for a fortnight first in the one town, then in the other.

He had three very contrasting plays to do, *The Hasty Heart*, a weepy drama set in a military hospital; Peter Ustinov's soufflé *The Love of Four Colonels*, and *A Murder Has Been Arranged*. If he didn't come up with anything very startling with any of them[4] that is probably because there is nothing very startling that one could do with three chauffeur-driven West End successes.

The crunch came when he fell asleep during one dress rehearsal. He decided that if the production wasn't live enough to keep him awake only God only knew what it would do to the audience. At which point he quit.[5]

He also did a touring production of *Seagulls over Sorrento* for H.M. Tennants. They were the leading impresarios in London. The play had had a long run in Shaftsbury Avenue with Ronald Shiner as the star. Shiner's understudy was booked to tour, especially for H.M.Forces, around the Mediterranean. They rehearsed in London, and with two members of the West End cast in the company there can have been little for him to do but carbon copy the original. He handled a very experienced cast with confidence and aplomb, and an old Cambridge acquaintance, Anthony Knowles, had a small part in the production. They opened in the Canal Zone for Christmas, and Stephen saw the production on there before flying back to London leaving them to tour to Malta.

He directed for a while for Hornchurch Repertory, one of the plays being Maugham's *Noble Spaniard*, and a director friend later accused Stephen of costing him a fortune. "When I saw your production I thought it was a winner" he complained, "When I came to produce it myself it turned out to be a complete dud."[6]

For Christmas, he was asked to do a production of *Smugglers Beware* at the Toynbee Hall in East London. Pamela Binns had been to an audition and overheard two actresses talking of one they'd attended earlier. She pricked up her ears and telephoned the Hall

> Early next day I made my way to Toynbee Hall. Stephen arrived about ten o'clock, I accosted him and asked to be allowed to audition, and a few days later he telephoned to say I'd got the lead, Henrietta. He thought the part was a bit pretty-pretty and was looking for an actress with guts... so we started rehearsing. The play, by an Australian writer, was being presented by James Thompson, a drama student whose parents owned 70,000 acres of sheep farmland in New South Wales.
>
> Then James Thompson dropped his bombshell. He told Stephen that he wanted his girlfriend to play Henrietta instead of me. Apparently he'd really put on the play as a vehicle for her, then she'd got another job which had now fallen through and she wanted to do *Smugglers Beware* after all.
>
> Stephen was furious. He was adamant that he wouldn't replace me... The management was equally insistent that I should go. Stephen showed his true metal. He sent all the cast home except me. He said, "You and I will strike. Mr Thompson will soon give way when he sees that we mean business. You are going to play Henrietta."
>
> So, for four days during rehearsal hours, Stephen and I sat in the ABC tearooms at Aldgate East, getting through innumerable buns and cups of coffee. Stephen talked entertainingly all the while, making light of long hours. At the end of four days James Thompson recognised the immovable force that was Stephen. He was afraid that he would have no production at all, and he allowed me to be reinstated as Henrietta. I played the part...

Forever after, Pamela Binns was known as "Little Miss P.B." to avoid confusion with his housekeeper, PB, whom we shall meet shortly.

Chapter Sixteen

To The Barricades

Stephen developed his credo that for around three hundred and fifty years we had had the same sort of theatre. Theatre design had been taken for granted - we had the best possible proscenium arch, or picture frame stage. Through it we observed a performance. From Ben Jonson onwards, moving scenery and stage lighting improved, until, with the advent of electricity, spectacle entertainment was what filled large auditoria - from horse races to train crashes. Even Shakespeare did not escape spectacle as people like Kean's son, Charles, had sets built which took hours to put up and performances therefore lasted five or six hours. Elsewhere horses, deer, rabbits and all forms of livestock were introduced into sylvan settings.

As a reaction to all this fine detail and historical authenticity, people like William Poel experimented with a return to simplicity. Whether building a replica of an Elizabethan playhouse upon a proscenium arch stage can quite be called simple, is open to debate.

When film took over spectacle, theatres changed from places of live entertainment to places of canned entertainment. There did not need to be any architectural innovation. The transition from proscenium theatre to film show was simple. In Britain it led to a number of theorists questioning what it was that theatre did better than film, and experiment began. Not that experimentation was without precedent in Europe!

In the 1770s Goethe wanted a larger forestage for his theatre at Weimar in order to re-establish direct *contact* between actor and audience.[1] In Meiningen's company actors were forbidden to look directly at the spectators... even a percentage of *important* speeches had to be delivered facing upstage. Reinhardt experimented on a massive scale with productions like *The Miracle* in an arena, but earlier still Appia had emphasised that the actor was the whole point and life of the theatre.

Nikolai Okhlopkov's Moscow Realist Theatre was the first modern theatre to use completely central staging. From the centre there were four walkways that ran along the four walls of the auditorium, devices designed to bring about the meeting of actor and audience so that it was impossible to separate the two. The audience was surrounded by actors just as the actors were surrounded by audience. In Maxim Gorki's *Mother*, Okhlopkov carried this so far as to have one actor hand to any spectator sitting beside the stage a loaf and a knife for him to hold.[2]

In 1898 Lugne-Poe presented *Measure for Measure* in a circus ring, on a stage little different from a sixteenth century booth stage with the audience on three sides, and earlier still in 1836 Tieck was arguing that to play Shakespeare genuinely, without distortion, we must begin with a theatre which is similar to his.[3]

A hundred years later, in 1936/7 Robert Atkins directed a short season of plays – *Henry V, Merry Wives, and Much Ado* on a stage that attempted no impossible realisation in physical terms, a stage for poetry. The stage was in the Prize Ring on Blackfriars Road, not far from where the Swan Theatre once stood.

The Ring yielded a stage thirty-four feet wide by thirty deep. The elevation of the platform by four feet combined happily with the proximity of the audience. It was a stage both intimate and removed. To the *Daily Telegraph* reviewer the novel staging at the boxing stadium gave the plays a liveliness and rightness which cannot be got else-where, and for Ivor Brown in the *Observer* the plays gained in speed, flexibility and intimacy ... soliloquies being infinitely better spoken on a platform to a surrounding audience than from behind a proscenium arch. The audience become friendly participants, not detached spectators.[4]

Around the same time in Dublin, Hilton Edwards wanted :

> a first hand knowledge of the new methods of presentation discovered by the continental experimental theatres... in spite of Appia, Craig,... and except for the work of such producers as Robert Atkins and Theodore Komisarjevsky, ... the art of the theatre has become indistinguishable from the art of the camera... The theatre has lost the individuality it once had - the stage picture must step once more out of its frame and become three dimensional, and it must live, not by its semblance of reality, but because it is reality.[5]

In the United States, Norman bel Geddes was designing innovative imaginary theatres as early as 1914,[6] and in New York Orson Welles had created a sensation with his Mercury Theatre company :

I believe in the factual theatre ... (the audience) should know they are in the theatre, and with that knowledge they may be taken to any height of which the magic of words and light is capable of taking them. This is the return to the Elizabethan and Greek theatre.[7]

Another interesting experiment of Welles' was to play his productions without an interval.

In Britain the new Elizabethan age was heralded in 1953 and brought television into thousands of homes for the first time. People rushed to buy TV sets so as to witness as it happened the spectacle of the occasion. The young Queen, her fairy tale romance, coronation, and the pageantry had the corollary effect of bringing second hand entertainment into millions of homes. It also precipitated the decline of audiences in hundreds of theatres and cinemas throughout the country. Many closed or converted to bingo halls, ironically a different sort of live entertainment, and one demanding participation from its audience.

The Arts Council Report 1954-5 records the alarming number of theatres and music halls which used to house commercial companies - closed because of falling receipts, increasing rents, and the payment of Entertainments Duty. It has to be said that of the theatres then operating, many had decidedly dubious standards.

These were the days of programme changes twice weekly, of twice nightly repertory; of touring companies playing a different venue every night, sometimes the cast having only hours in which to learn the Shakespearean role they were to perform that night. These were the days of tired reproductions of West End successes. Failed (i.e. not West End) actors could embitter a company into being lacklustre, repetition itself lead to jaded performance.

Many small theatres closed unnoticed such as Gainsborough and Southwold. Even big repertory companies had to discuss the possibility of mergers or the interchange of productions to try to reduce costs. Bristol Old Vic / Birmingham Rep / Liverpool Rep was one possibility mooted. Sheffield and Nottingham agreed to a trial season together. Salisbury and Guildford planned one for 1955. "A year full of despondency about the closing down of so many theatres..." cried *The Stage* – "Chesterfield closed! Farnham closed! Leicester Royal sold and demolished. The West of England Theatre Company forced into liquidation."

In Scotland the decline of audiences was noted; 15% at Perth, 10% at the Gateway, 12% at the Citizens. Vivien Leigh caused a furore when she stood up in the visitors gallery of the House of Lords during a debate, and cried out in protest at the proposal to pull down the St James Theatre to make way for offices. Her call did not save the theatre.

As well as apathetic attendance the Tax menace had to be faced and fought – "Because of a lethal tax that yields £2.25 million a year, theatres all over the country are being forced to close down. Famous playhouses, music repertoires, Victorian Music Halls, are putting up their shutters. Dozens of others are struggling against repeated losses," reported *The Stage*.[8]

Writing a decade later Stephen pointed out that:

> in the last fifty years about 500 theatres have closed or been pulled down... only half a dozen built to replace them. Thousands of inadequate halls have been built with enclosed stages that have unsatisfactory backstage facilities, poor sightlines and inefficient stage lighting...[9]

Not that all theatre was commercial and lightweight. In 1948 Tyrone Guthrie memorably directed The Thrie Estates on a thrust stage setting in the Assembly Hall of Edinburgh. Bernard Miles toyed with the idea of an Elizabethan setting for Shakespeare in 1953 at the Royal Exchange before deciding that he liked to have his audience in front of him. Down from Manchester, Joan Littlewood was out east at Stratford experimenting in style within a conventional building.

When Stephen was planning his first season in Scarborough London had not yet been startled by Orson Welles' *Moby Dick* on a bare stage with ropes and battens for scenery. Playgoers had not had an Angry Young Man snarl at them from the stage in Sloane Square. The angry old German 'enfant terrible' Bertolt Brecht had not yet thrust his ponderous albeit influential *Mutter Courage* onto the stage of the Palace Theatre.

On the whole experiment was confined to content rather than conditions. If there was much in the air which was intellectually vibrant, there was still difficulty in assessing what Aunt Edna's nephews and nieces wanted from the theatre, apart from the glossy sophistication of the *Reluctant Debutante* and *The Little Hut*. Were these *Salad Days* over?

In 1947, the year Stephen saw the Conesford Players in Lowestoft, Margo Jones opened her Theatre in the Round in Dallas. Her first season was ten weeks long, working on a budget of $750 per production. The first season established the policy of the company by presenting four new plays and one classic.[10] Twelve years later the company had premiered seventy six new plays, including the first performance of a Tennessee Williams play, *Summer and Smoke*, which gave her company national prominence. She is quoted as having said:

> I found out that when you have no money to do a show... you are forced to be ingenious; as a result, you can sometimes even be creative.[11]

Here was inspiration, whether conscious or not, and coincidentally the year that Margo Jones died, Stephen opened his Scarborough company. Where Theatre in the Round was low profile, he proposed to raise the sights.

Turn Right at the Crossroads

Chapter Seventeen

Thrift

For the North Riding Education Committee Stephen conducted many weekend courses and summer schools. The most significant of these was held at Scalby on the outskirts of Scarborough in a house called Wrea Head. These acting schools were organised by the education officer for the Riding, John Wood, and had started before he left the Hall. He sometimes took one of his pupils with him; Jeremy Kemp was one, and considered it a relaxed and admirable concept. When Stephen walked into a room he was noticed, but he was like a worker rather than the commercial brand of 'guv'nor'.[1]

Margaret Boden remembers Stephen expounding his theories :

> about all the best new plays coming from the States because they had so many experimental theatres, and there was nowhere in this country for new playwrights to have a showing for their work... and if only he could get a place and some actors, then he would try out the works of these new playwrights. And John Wood threw him a challenge and said, "Look if I take you to see the librarian in Scarborough, who, I'm sure will be very sympathetic, will you come along?"[2]

And as Stephen later wrote, "after a friendly and helpful talk with W.H. Smettem, the librarian, our first booking was made."[3] He also had several scripts from his playwriting course which he judged worthy of performance. "I had no money of my own, and no one else's was available for a theatre venture based entirely on new plays by unknown writers. The idea of theatre in the round was first considered for reasons of economy."[4]

So here was a season to be planned for Scarborough the following summer, without a company, management, capital, equipment or assistance. In the latter he was most fortunate. One of the course participants at Wrea Head who directed plays for the Scarborough Theatre Guild, Harry Casey, was a cousin of the *Sunday Times* critic Harold Hobson. Harry Casey was committed to the drama, and introduced Stephen to Margaret Boden, a Licentiate of the Royal Academy of Music. She was a member of the Scarborough Theatre Guild, as was her husband, Ken.

Ken Boden, an insurance inspector in the town, so pestered her about how the Guild ought to manage their affairs, that in self defence she challenged him to help them. Ken was an action man. He supported all Stephen's seasons in the Library, stepping softly round the professionals' occasional sensitivities.

Afterwards he organised the seasons himself when Stephen was no longer either willing, or able. Without Ken's determination, and dogged unflappable drive, the Scarborough seasons might never have got off the ground or prospered. (Ayckbourn kept Ken in employment until his death in 1991, despite the contempt of Alfred Bradley, who wanted him replaced by a professional manager.)

The Memorandum of Association for Studio Theatre became registered in June 1955 but there was a lot of work to do before that. Friends, acquaintances, rich and famous were canvassed to buy shares. B Shares were £1 each, and there were as many of those as anyone was likely to want! An A Share cost £10, and conferred the privilege of voting at meetings, eligibility for election to the Board, and membership. No one was allowed to hold more than one. On that point Stephen was paranoid.

Lord and Lady Ulick Browne wrote to say that they had just met the mother of Queen Elizabeth, "We told her about the £10 shares and she was thrilled at our buying a share and said she was going to send you a cheque herself."[5] If she did there is no record of it.

An uncle by marriage, Ben Levy, declined, and J.B. Priestley with oblique diplomacy suggested a meeting discussing the season after the summer. In theory he had an ally in Priestley, who in his *Art of the Dramatist* had written :

> I would write for theatre in the round, the opposite of the movies both in its cost and its art, the theatre where everything visual, except the close and vivid faces and figures of the players, is left to the imagination.[6]

There were promotional talks, and Clement Glock at the Royal Opera House wrote inviting him and Minos Volanakis to dinner to meet Alec Spearman the Member for Scarborough, and his wife Diane. "They will help in every way..."

The playwriting courses produced two of his Board members, Neville Hunnings and David Campton. Gwynneth Thurburn from the Hall, Gemma Fagan from the I.T.I., and four of his Footlights friends, the Hon. Anthony Lyttelton, brother of the more famous 'Humph', David Eady and Stephen Garrett were another three. The last was d'Arcy who had followed Hermione's advice after she saw one of his better performances:

> Hermione: May I give you some advice?
> d'Arcy: Certainly Toni.
> Hermione: If I were you I should leave the stage.
> d'Arcy: Why, Toni?
> Hermione: Because you have a marked lack of talent!

So he became an Accountant, a Board member, and their business manager.

One willing slave, Clifford Williams, just down from the Manchester Unity Theatre recalls Stephen surrounded by highly successful whiz kids:

> We all rather courted Stephen's favour. People could easily be hurt by him, because he could forget your existence. He never seemed to have enough time for one. He had charisma, was intensely interesting. He represented a flag, a rallying point, for those who wanted to do plays by writers like Strindberg, and new writers. He was a big chap. You could always stand behind him, as it were. You felt he had muscle, clout.[7]

And so we come to Renaissance man. The civil engineer who writes, draws, paints, philosophises, invents - Leonardo da Vinci. Stephen's inspiration. The subject of later lectures. His role model in achievement. Stephen running a playwriting course, planning a summer season of plays, negotiating with the Chief Fire Officer, Chief of Police, Librarian, costing out printing, publicity, raising capital, raising seating, gathering actors, acquiring rehearsal rooms and dealing with correspondence. In all these things Stephen's charm stood him in good stead.

When once he had bought his house, one of the first things he planted in his garden was Thrift, sea lavender, which grows in sparse soil and clings to the rocks around the coast. He admired its tenacity of purpose and its ability to grow and prosper in the most meagre of circumstances. Here was inspiration also.

He had four plays, an eight week season. A cast of actors and stage management was needed. Like his father, Stephen budgeted very carefully. His projected profit and loss for the first season was very close to actuality. He could pay the company £8 per week each, but some actors were married, could they live on that?

Communards!

To the Barricades was the rallying cry of the revolutionary, and Stephen was about to raise the revolutionary standard in theatrical terms. If he rented somewhere big enough to house the company, as at Frinton, it would reduce the cost of theatre digs. But a house without a housekeeper? Well, let's get one of them too. And P.B. turned up.

Norman Gold

Chapter Eighteen

P.B.

As Campton ever afterwards remarked, who but Stephen would put an advertisement for a housekeeper in *The Stage*, and who but P.B. would have read it? During her lifetime P.B. was always an enigma, hinting at past grandeur, and giving very little information either about herself or her late husband, whose memory she extolled.

Some thought she had been on the tennis circuit, others had been led to think she was a ballet dancer. Her son believed her to have Egyptian or Greek Royal blood and to have been secretly transported to Britain by yacht.

She thought all children were brats and it was not until she had been with Stephen's company for five years that she acknowledged having a son, whom she dismissed as a ne'er-do-well. Then when he had a book published, and later became director of the Bolton Octagon Theatre, she basked in reflected pride.

Her son and daughter were placed in a home at birth and did not know they had parents until they were in their teens! Summoned from their 'home' they were escorted to Victoria Station and were aware of a large lady in a huge fur coat approaching them down the platform followed by a chauffeur. A strained journey in a Rolls Royce took them to their new home, where they found that the nurse they had most disliked in their old 'home' had been engaged to be their nanny![1]

P.B.'s husband, Noel Pemberton Billing, all 6'4" of him, was often litigious. He had, most notably been a litigant in an infamous libel case in 1918. So infamous that 50 years on 'Pemberton Billing' was cockney rhyming slang for a 'shilling.' The historian Michael Kettle describes the case as :

> Basically a struggle between Billing and Bonar Law; between the . . . patriotic Independent MP . . . and the dry ascetic Tory leader, who was trying to promote undercover peace talks with the enemy.'[2]

Michael Kettle appears to be imprecise, as Lloyd George was Prime Minister at the time; however, the Christian Science movement, convinced he was about to be martyred, sent a lady to him so that he would father an heir, which he duly did. In order to get publicity for his case, his own journal *The Vigilante*, ran an article about a performance of Oscar Wilde's *Salome* suggesting depravity. Since the play was by a convicted homosexual and Maud Allen in the title was (reputedly) lesbian, he described the production as *'The Cult of the Clitoris.'* The naturalised Dutch director and Miss Allen jointly sued him for defamatory libel, as he had anticipated they would.

He claimed to have a little black book containing the names and sexual peccadillos of 47,000 German sympathisers in the British establishment which he would present at the trial. Knowing of his appetite for ladies, a female agent-provocateur was sent to seduce him, which entrapment would finish him politically. Over dinner she succumbed to his charms and disclosed to him why she had been sent.

His trial was rigged. He chose to be his own counsel for the defence, and was repeatedly rude to the judge, Lord Chief Justice Darling - a bitter enemy. One might almost believe him to have been Kenneth Grahame's inspiration for Mr. Toad. He won his case, to the cheers of a huge crowd in the street outside the court. Lord David Cecil was quoted as saying to the Prime Minister of the day, that he would rather sweep the streets than be a member of a ministry at the mercy of Billing and his crew.

A prodigious, maverick inventor with over 100 patents still in his name, he invented an unbreakable gramophone record much admired by the then king; he also designed and built a land yacht, the first motorised caravan. In one month he designed an innovative gyroplane capable of vertical, forwards, backwards and sideways flight. The patent was accepted but the machine was never built, though a very similar German one was, only a year or two later.

He bought the lease of the Royal Court Theatre and developed cinematic back projection there, designed his pocket 'compass' camera and invented windable film. He was working on the military use of the aeroplane in 1908, and foresaw the coming of the Second World War. He designed a new kind of mobile hospital including prefabricated buildings, ambulances and stacking, collapsible stretchers.

Ever an eye for a pretty lady, his first ever patent was a powder puff sewn into the middle of a handkerchief for swift and easy facial first aid. An admirer of Churchill, he conducted his business from his bed, or wore a velvet track suit in bright red blue and yellow stripes. He also, what else, sported a monocle. He was a larger than life charmer, whom P.B. first met in Australia.

She was christened Elsie Veronica Farmer. At the age of 16 her mother left her Greek parents in Cairo, where they ran a cafe or restauraunt, in order to follow her soldier lover to England and eventually marry him.[3] She was born in Streatham in south London, and at the age of 21 she married a childhood friend, the kindly and reserved Owen Jones and went with him shortly afterwards, to Australia where he took up an appointment as Chairman of the Forestry Commission for Victoria.

Five years later she was in a distressed condition following the death from meningitis of her baby son. As her husband's work had taken him away for a spell, friends suggested that she join them at the ball being given in Melbourne to celebrate the visit of the Prince of Wales . . . and somewhat reluctantly she had agreed. Billing had also needed some persuading, for he regarded such affairs as a frivolous waste of valuable working time, but he saw the occasion as a useful public relations exercise for his company.

The date of the ball in Melbourne, the 29th of August, 1929, she forever after celebrated as her true birthday, for P.B. claimed that her real life had only begun from that moment, when she was introduced to, and became enamoured of, Noel. She had clearly inherited her mother's passionate temperament, because when she heard some months later that Billing was planning to return to England, she had no hesitation in leaving her husband to join the man who had by that time become her lover.

Their fortune and lifestyle altered constantly as Billing made and lost huge sums with his inventions. P.B. was his secretary and lover, (his cook and nurse later on): within seven years they had a daughter and a son who were both sent away to be looked after. Billing had numerous affairs which he would signal by suggesting P.B. go to Harrods and do some shopping.

This was his cue for entertaining a new young lady, a situation with which P.B. was quite sanguine. Indeed, she claimed to have had several abortions during an affair with theatre owner Bronson Albery, whom she used to meet at the Savoy Hotel.[4] Then on the 6th of December, 1937 Billing came home and said to her that she had to wear something special the following day as they were going to a wedding. "Whose?" she inquired. "Ours!" came the reply. For richer for poorer, in health and in sickness, P.B. adored him.

When he died in 1948 at the age of 68, she was 50 years old and devastated to be without him. She continued to live in their yacht at Burnham on Crouch so as to have him still about her.

He left £13,000, the yacht and possessions and a trust fund set up from the income of a property he had bought a 29 year lease on - a house in Gloucester Place. According to his biographer, he was a poor judge of character and P.B. was always convinced that his accountants, who rented the top two floors of the house, were less than honest in their assessment of her income, so little did she receive, but she resolutely refused to sell the boat (an ex-Naval Motor Launch which he had converted into a home) and which must have cost her a fortune to moor.

Nine years later she was very short of money. She had never had to work for a living, but she could not afford to continue as she was; so, at the age of 59, she answered an advertisement in *The Stage* newspaper. She was one of only two or three respondents, and Stephen organised a selection committee to interview her, consisting of himself, 'Shosh' Tabor and Shirley Jacobs. P.B. was duly engaged at a salary of £5 per week to cater for the company and keep house in Scarborough.

P.B. was a very large lady, with lightly hennaed hair, and she always wore Billing's monocle on a thin black silk ribbon round her neck; she had painfully fallen arches, so that one wondered how she could progress, let alone run a house and kitchen. Her kitchen was always suspect - she called herself a slut, and said one day she would write a sluts' cookbook. She was, as a lady should be, averse to dusting, but didn't object to cooking. Her food was superb.

Her secret was that Billing loved baby food, and she cooked all her vegetables with sugar in the water and then glazed them with butter. Apart from catering in the house she made huge gateaux which were transported to the theatre where she also served coffee, scones and cakes after each performance. All her catering equipment was taken to and fro each day. P.B. worked for her money.

She was always very protective of her late husband, as if she was aware that his cause célèbre was not one which would be treated with gravity amongst the generation of young actors with whom she mixed. She transferred her hero worship to Stephen, whilst remaining alert to the foibles of mankind, and loved to gossip about sexual intrigue within the company.

Campton says Stephen found it very difficult to respond to her demonstration of affection :

He would go round periodically chuntering about P.B., "She's got to go... I can't stand it any longer." P.B., in a maternal sort of way tended to smother him, and he couldn't stand it . . . And in between going around muttering about P.B. "She'll have to go" he said at one time, "you know this is the only family I've ever really known."

We certainly did live together like a family - we ate together and went off to our rooms to work. But very often in the evening we would get together with Stephen and listen to music and for a while we did provide him with a sort of family.

Publicity brochure, 1962

Chapter Nineteen

Beside the Seaside

If this was a Hollywood screenplay, our next scene would be one of the rich and famous arriving in limousines for the opening of a glittering first night, which would ensure the success of Stephen's venture. In reality, it was to take another 40 years, and after his death, before such a scene came true, when on the 27th of April, 1996 the new Stephen Joseph Theatre in the Round opened in Scarborough.

A conversion of an art deco cinema in the centre of the town, it aptly reflects the fact that Stephen spent most of his professional career dreaming of converting buildings, but this latest is also wedded to state of the art technology, with hydraulic lifts, a sophisticated lighting grid, secondary auditorium-cum-cinema and bookshop.

The whole thing under the direction of the man Stephen most wanted to run his theatre, Alan Ayckbourn. And if we were still in Tinseltown, we would discover that Stephen and Ayckbourn were blood brothers since their respective father and mother shared favours sixty years before. When, in conversation, Mary James told Michael Joseph that she was going to have a baby, he asked in some alarm, "Is it mine?"

In 1955, the publicity brochure proudly proclaimed that Scarborough had everything for everyone, and once the Studio Theatre came to stay that was no mean boast. It had a cosmopolitan air, two bays of golden sand stretching for three miles along the coast against a backdrop of rugged cliffs, dominated by an impressive castle. The harbour was a working microcosm of its tourist attractions, the continental cargo boats jostling for position with Scottish herring boats and luxury motor cruisers tied up alongside sailing dinghies and sleek yachts.

The castle, built in 1181 and left uninhabitable by Oliver Cromwell, surrounds the remains of a Roman signal station and sits proudly above the modest house King Richard III built for himself on the harbourside. Delius' amanuensis Eric Fenby was born there as was Charles Laughton, and his brother Tom still ran the family hotel. Of its other attractions, Wood End former home of the Sitwell family, nestles comfortably on a cliffside surrounded by semi-tropical gardens, and another pilgrimage is to the final resting place of Anne Brontë in the churchyard.

In those days one of the problems of a Spa town, established as such since the seventeenth century, was the variety of demands entertainments made upon the public. The Concert Hall seated 2,000 and the Open Air Theatre, (*Oklahoma* in 1955) held 7,000: its' chorus of 200 was almost as many people as the Library Theatre might accommodate. The Arcadia specialised in Northern humour, led by such stars as Thora Hird; the Floral Hall had the *Fol de Rols* in their 28th season, the Futurist, the *Black and White Minstrels* from TV.

The Opera House had lightweight repertory from York, whilst Max Jaffa and his Orchestra filled the Grand Hall nightly at the Spa, all these offering easy undemanding pleasure after a day on the sun baked beaches, parks or sporting leisure pursuits. Writing in the *Sunday Express* in 1961 outspoken commentator John Gordon expressed a generally held view, "When the sun shines on it, there can't be a more beautiful town in Britain."

Hermione, went one better, '"Oh, it's just like the Mediterranean," she said as she caught her first glimpse of the South Bay from St. Nicholas Gardens. Arriving for the first night and staying in Tom Laughton's Royal Hotel she said, "It's perfectly wonderful . . . I think I shall stay a day or two."' And stay she did, though some members of the company thought that she seemed bored, but she did an important diplomatic job, she sparkled and flattered when speaking to influential people, she stood and performed, and her 'little Stevie' retreated into the side lines. She wore sparkling powder on her face so that she glistened as she moved.[1]

This was the year before George Devine established his company at the Royal Court in Sloane Square. For Stephen to open an experimental theatre in Scarborough was audacious enough. His choice of plays was daring and those of an enthusiast for his medium. A classic, to act as a money spinner might have been sensible. But Stephen was committed to New Writing and four new plays were what Scarborough got. The theatre opened on the 14th of July in the middle of a heatwave. The reviews were respectable and interested. The northern critics who attended brought no massive preconceptions with them, nor did the audiences which were prepared to accept what was on offer and to judge it on its merits.

Circle of Love opened the season, written by Eleanor Glaser, who produced for an amateur group in Leamington Spa and dictated into a tape machine while she ironed. The play is about a possessive mother, the awakening of love in her son, and the love which her husband develops for a widowed novelist during a French holiday. Stephen's production was admirable, "one feels like an eavesdropper at an intense domestic drama... the audience is made to feel very much a part of the proceedings and, judging by their response, they liked it that way," commented the *Yorkshire Evening News*.[2]

The Guardian reviewer warned that "the chief virtue is also the chief danger. Not a gesture of insincerity in the writing or the acting can get by. In the hands of anything much short of genius on both sides, this will surely mean a great deal of realistic triviality on *Mrs Dale* lines..."[3] He was prophesying the trend in much post-television drama in the eighties and nineties.

The second production, *Prentice Pillar*, was a play of jealousies set in and around Rosslyn just south and east of Edinburgh, in the small chapel where the pillar of the apprentice is to be found. Superbly carved, the master mason was so jealous of the work of his apprentice, its technique and beauty, that he killed the boy. The story hinges around the idea that love is impossible without hate, forgiveness without evil-doing. Stephen had directed the author's first play at the 'Q' Theatre in London, where it won a playwriting competition organised by Jack de Leon, an actors' agent, who ran the theatre and lived on Kew Green across the bridge from the theatre. Among his judges were Clive Brook and Kenneth Tynan.

Stephen invited Tyrone Guthrie to direct the play, but he was not free for over a year, and in his letter of regrets he remarks:

> Arena style doesn't daunt me at all, provided one doesn't have to inflict it on Sheridan or Congreve or even Pinero. But if live theatre is to survive we'd better all learn to do without a lot of facilities that aren't really indispensable and concentrate on the ONE thing that is indispensable - lively and imaginative acting.'[4]

The Arts Council had refused to give *Prentice Pillar* a grant for new writing claiming that the poetic costume drama based on a medieval legend was too obscure.[5] Written by Ruth Dixon in the days when the debate raged upon the rectitude of capital punishment, the *Stage* reviewer noted a certain: "topicality in the notion of the murderer allowed to go free to bear his conscience. If he were killed, the blood of his victim would be transferred to the hands of the executioner."[6]

It was a risky play to do with English actors in a town half of whose holiday makers came from Scotland. One of the actors asked Stephen how he was doing in rehearsal? "I can't understand a word you're saying, but it doesn't matter, it adds character."[7]

Whilst rehearsing his third production, Stephen was a worried man. The *News Chronicle* on 28th of July recorded the sunniest July for 50 years, and at the seaside, when it is hot, the last thing holiday makers want to do is leave the beach too soon, or sit in a theatre at night, unless they have already booked their tickets.

In a theatre seating only 250, a less than half-full house spelled disaster. The season, too, had started under funded. He had been promised £500 from a friend, Dorothy Alison, who at the last minute, could not fulfil her promise. Ever a careful man with a budget, he had calculated earnings for a half full attendance. The best audience so far had been only 75 people, so that the average was falling well below his projections.

Stephen was anxious enough to write to Uncle Lionel and to Hermione. Her response was bleak. The Bank of England had frozen her capital - she was technically living in New York but still a UK citizen, and the amount of money any individual was allowed to take out of the country at this time was a derisory £25. She was about to open at the Café de Paris but did not know how much of that money she would be allowed to keep:

> not that I particularly think the weather has made any difference, as from what I saw of the holiday-makers who come to Scarborough it is not the sort of place to start Theatre in the Round. If you remember, when I came up for the weekend it was very hot, but the night I went to see the *Fol de Rols* it was absolutely packed. I think next time you do an experiment like this Oxford, Cambridge, Harrogate or Bristol is the place. I really do think English seaside places are the last resort for culture.[8]

Hardly encouraging in a crisis! She did go on to say she was having lunch with Michael the following week:

> Maybe I can talk him into doing something - he seems very interested in your career and we had a long chat about you on the phone. I may say he couldn't have been nicer in the things he said about you.[9]

Uncle Lionel was rather more cheerful:

New ventures are almost invariably uphill work. Given the right spirit, talent and material - plus the ability to absorb financial hurdles there is no reason why the venture should prove anything but successful.

On 16th of August, Uncle Lionel sent a cheque for £200, which he probably never expected to see again.

What Hermione doesn't appear to have known is that Michael had already come to an understanding with his son. Faced with a request from Stephen for financial assistance in starting his company, Michael had been calculating. A discreet enough six months after the death of Edna, in January 1950, he married his secretary, who later became the Hon. Anthea Hodson, with whom he had been living at the time of Edna's death. He had bought a farm for Shirley, which she and her husband ran, near Sudbury. He had another two children by Anthea, who, when once she took over the reins, became an even better publisher than Michael. It was perhaps with some prescience therefore that, presented with the problem of burgeoning responsibilities, he should come to an accommodation with Hermione's two children who could be bought off cheaply.

He proposed to Stephen that both he and Leslie would each receive a gift of £500 which would be their full and final settlement. They could expect no further legacy from his estate upon his death. Stephen agreed. It is unclear whether Leslie was asked for an opinion. Two years later when Michael died he had bequeathed his farm, worth £20,000 plus £20,000 to Shirley, the rest of his capital, approx. £16,000 to Richard, and 'Top Hat' Insurance policies and the business to Anthea. (see references)

A note of caution must be exercised here, as there is an enigmatic note among Stephen's papers referring to Preferential Shares in Michael Joseph Ltd. Although almost no evidence has come to light, Stephen and Leslie received in addition an annual dividend from their fathers' company. (In a moment of distress Leslie's widow remembers him selling theirs for £6/700.)

But at the end of July 1955 things looked very serious indeed. After only two weeks of operation, the company had succeeded in attracting less than half the audience they needed to pay their way.

The Library's committee was deeply considerate. Mr Smettem was in his last year before retirement, and therefore more laid back or reckless than his successor became, and was keen to see the operation flourish. He agreed that the £20 per week which they had originally asked for could be transmuted into £100 for the eight week season.[10] It was a generous move, but more was needed.

"We came to Scarborough from London pale and drooping and are now wonderfully suntanned. But the brilliant weather has kept audiences away." Tonight he will have to decide whether he must call a halt to his theatrical presentation and give the corporation two weeks notice of his intention to close down, Stephen told *The Times*.[11]

Not that it was a decision which Stephen took: ever the democrat, he put the decision to his company.

They had been recruited almost exclusively from post graduate students of the Hall; indeed Kara Aldridge had been a fellow student with Stephen before the war. By coincidence she had also been at Grammar School with another member of the company, Morris Perry.

John Sherlock and Shirley Jacobs were both ex students as was ASM Charles Lewsen and the stage manager Margaret Tabor, known as Shosh. She and Ralph Nossek organised a bar at the digs in Castle Road known as Shosh's Arms. They bought the booze wholesale with Tom Laughton's assistance ("O yes, yes, of course, you're in brother Charlie's business.") In her opinion :

> I don't think any of us had any feeling that we were engaged in anything either momentous or mould breaking, or anything that would evolve as it did, into something permanent. To us it was just a job until we went into proper theatre.[12]

David Campton was equally prosaic about living conditions in Scarborough:

> For Stephen there was a Shangri-la, which was the working class kitchen, which had never really existed, or existed by accident: and there was Stephen's picture of the working class kitchen almost exemplified at the house he rented over the antique shop, Reginald's in Castle Road. He decided that these were ideal squalid working class rooms and like a working class father he would shave in front of the kitchen mirror. It never occurred to him that a working class father shaved in front of the kitchen mirror because there was no bathroom! He only did it once - PB threw him out - half shaved actually, she was not having him shave in her kitchen. That was his working class never-never land.[13]

In Castle Road there was a good deal of bed-swapping, as wives and children came and went. Kara Aldridge had her child with her all the time, and PB hated brats so it is not surprising that Campton should observe that the last thing actors want is to live together after having been working together. They cannot have been unaware of the perilous situation the company was in however, when Stephen called them all together and put it to them. They could struggle on a little longer and hope for an improvement in the situation, or put up the shutters. "I can't pay you any more. We've got to decide if we go on or not."[14]

They had committed themselves for the season, and would be unlikely to find any other work if they threw in the towel, and Stephen had the most engaging and seductive personality, so they decided to soldier on. Then the weather broke and the houses started to fill up and the season was secured.

In a sympathetic editorial *The Stage* leader writer described:

> audiences treated as intelligent men and women, capable of listening to and hanging on to the words of the actors... they are colourful words... imprinting vivid images upon the mind of the listener, and spoken by capable players intent upon creating living characters... Theatre in the Round productions rely almost entirely upon the spoken word for their effect. They are becoming increasingly popular with audiences who go to the theatre to think rather than to look and relax.'[15]

These considerations were not echoed by some correspondents in the newspapers. One lady complained that it was not the policy of new plays, nor the performances of the actors, but that she would prefer to see them on stage at the Opera House. A gentleman remarked that watching a drawing room without flocked wallpaper was like going into a restaurant, being served raw vegetables, and being told to imagine the cooking. But amongst the audiences the detractors were few, and the general feeling was summed up by a writer who observed that:

> In an age pampered by the artificial luxuriance of scenic spectacle, it is refreshing to find this new form of art, which appeals to the inner and deeper feelings, and in this lies its chief claim to superiority.[16]

David Campton had been on two BDL courses in London, and at the last minute decided to go to a playwriting one being held in January 1955. Students were advised that they could send in a script for the tutor's assessment and Stephen's only comment was, "I'm starting a season in Scarborough this summer, can I use your script?"

The play concerned a modern St George who has devoted his attentions to birds, animals and reptiles, but suddenly brings into his home a young, almost juvenile delinquent girl... however she has burgled the house next door and has also run away from her old father. Where audiences received the play uncritically, reviewers felt it showed promise more than achievement. At the start of rehearsals business problems were pressing, so with the audience situation settled down and the company starting to earn box office money, Stephen said to John Sherlock, "Can you take over this production, I'm busy."

Comfortably reviewing the third production, Campton's *Dragons are Dangerous*, the critic noted, "struggling financially they may be, slipshod they certainly are not."[17]

The fourth and probably most adventurous play was *Turn Right at the Crossroads*, a modern morality about a young countryman with a gift for talking. He leaves his herd of goats, goes down into the city, becomes first a preacher and then a business man; next the leader of a futuristic state under the manipulation of another business fellow. Ultimately having taken the wrong turning at each of life's crossroads, he realises the true use for his flair for leadership and persuasion. Its author Joan 'Jurneman' Winch had seen Morris Perry sunbathing earlier in the season, and was so inspired she wrote in an extra scene showing him bare chested.

The Guardian admitted: "it has a monolithic strength, like talking statues. Its pattern is of human shapes and shadows, of void and gesture. . . one came away slightly stunned but undoubtedly stimulated."[18]

It was a nerve wrackingly busy eight weeks in which, as was his wont, Stephen taught John Sherlock and other members of the company to drive. He mounted an exhibition of Theatres in the Round both in America and on the continent - towards which the Arts Council contributed £100.

The company also gave afternoon performances over four successive weeks at Wallace's Cayton Bay Holiday Camp, about ten miles South, on the coast. "Holidays are jolly days, Wally days are Jolly Days." Their manager, Mr Wallis had booked a circus, which had cancelled, and would Stephen go instead?

> I pointed out that round or not, our plays were no substitute for a circus and would probably have little appeal to a holiday-camp crowd. Never mind, this was an emergency, and besides the entertainment was only an insurance against rain. If the weather was fine no one would come anyhow. So we agreed.[19]

It was a situation not without precedent. Theatre Workshop played there for a week in their tent in 1950 with their production of *Uranium 235*. They had played to the audience who were the radio and film generation. It is unlikely that more than a handful of them had ever been in a theatre before, so why should they miss the French windows...[20]

Stephen had recommended to Morris Perry that he train like an athlete to cope with his long speeches in *Turn Right at the Crossroads*s, which he did, and the holiday-camp audience admired his physical skill. By the end of the summer it had been another useful experiment, and one which earned a further £40 to cover expenses, and in a sense introduced Stephen to the possibility of touring from Scarborough three years later.

At the end of the financial year the loss on the season had been rather less than anticipated, and if all his funding had been available it would have been even more successful. The 'books' show a 27% loss of £599.

Back in London Stephen's landlady Gretchen Franklin was visiting her next door neighbour, the actor Anthony Marlow, then appearing in *Sailor Beware*. He confided that he was moving, as he'd bought a house.

"What's going to happen to this flat?"
"Well, we want to sell the lease."
"Hang on a minute."
She raced next door to where Stephen, mercifully, was, and told him, and he went in and said,
"How much?" and then,
"I'll buy it."

So Gretchen got rid of the 2,000 books spilling out into her hall.

Margaret Rawlings - *Phèdre*

Chapter Twenty

Mahatma Gandhi

Stephen had also landed himself a job with the newly formed Independent Television company, Associated Rediffusion. His old Footlights chum and former fellow flatmate, Michael Westmore held the Position of Head of Light Entertainments, which also had a brief for the juvenile slot. The Directors of A.R. had decided that to properly fulfil their franchise, they should be competing with the BBC's children's programmes. Westmore needed directors and offered Stephen a job.

Aimed at the Teen audience, Westmore tried to approach each day as a different age and sex slot. There was *Calling All Boys*, and *Calling All Girls*, another day might be a Quiz and Film day. Stephen was taken on to direct *Venture,* an odd sort of programme, one third old Douglas Fairbanks films, one third was Space Travel, essentially elementary astronomy, and there was a section called Sports, or Sportsview, in which well known personalities would come along. Danny Blanchflower might tell his audience how to kick a ball, someone else did fencing, and so on. For most of the time Alun Owen was link man.

Stephen's lot was always to be working in a situation where his activity was under-funded.[1] He invented a sort of Diorama which could be slowly wound on behind the performers to give the impression of movement. He took John Sherlock with him into the Department, and then telephoned David Campton in Leicester.

> There's a job going in A.R. in the programme I'm doing - writing linking material - would you like it?

Campton, was a Grammar school-boy and in class used to sit next to Richard Attenborough. He was in a nice, cosy, super-annuated job with the East Midlands Gas Board and replied that he would think about it. There he was at the top of his grade, and with one play having been performed. The next day Stephen phoned again,

> I've spoken to Michael Westmore, and you've got the job !

One of the things he took with him was his contributions to the superannuation, roughly £500. The pay was the same at £15 per week.

Since then, with occasional diversions into acting and directing most notably in Scarborough, Campton has continued to write - over 100 stage plays written or commissioned, radio and TV scripts. Items have appeared in West End revues. He won the 1977 Japan Prize and is regularly performed in amateur festivals. Leicester Haymarket have produced two of his adaptations, including *Frankenstein* in their studio theatre. Roland Joffe asked him to write *Timesneeze* which he directed at the Young Vic. It being one of three plays in the repertoire of the first season.[2]

When Campton arrived at Rediffusion the company was experiencing teething troubles and kept axing people. After a year of running the department advertising wasn't being attracted in sufficient quantity, so there were lots of redundancies. The first thing staff did each day was to read the notice board. The latest casualty list told them if they had an office to go to. Westmore said he would have protected Stephen, who didn't get fired because he kept resigning. Night after night he would go home in despair.[3] However with a second Scarborough season imminent he let his initial contract expire and with it Campton's expired also. Stephen always knew he was going to leave - he wanted to go wild with television but no one would let him, so he came to despise the medium.[4]

His new flat at World's End was very large, so Campton rented a room. He also engaged P.B. to be permanent house keeper-cum-caterer, shutting up her motor torpedo boat to moulder at Burnham. He went through many dark periods during his five years or so in Ashburnham Mansions. Faynia Jeffery remembers his bedroom with only a hammock suspended in it, and being told to paint the flat entirely black.[5]

> Stephen was subject to deep depression, up and down constantly - instead of taking a job supply teaching or directing between seasons he would take a job selling paraffin, or another time heaving coal. He sometimes came home in black despair, and P.B. would take one look at him and know whether to be welcoming or distant. He experimented with his haircuts - he had his hair cut to a short bristle, and I said to P.B. "Whatever you do don't comment on it," and when he came into the kitchen she screamed - and the next time we saw him he'd shaved his head. One of the original skinheads.[6]

To be operating successfully in Scarborough was one thing, but to be taken seriously in the theatre one has to be critically accepted in that Father and Mother of British cities, London, therefore he established a base at the

Mahatma Gandhi Hall in Tavistock Square. He had met a young Greek Director who was visiting Britain under the wing of the British Council - Minos Volanakis- and Stephen invited Minos to be Director of Productions for the Club operations. Volanakis was a very amusing young man full of self confidence, who said, "I'll put it on its feet for you." Owen Hale became honorary secretary. Their first production was on the 20th of November - three one act plays by Luigi Pirandello under the title *Three Disturbing Meetings*. Nossek and Perry were joined by Alfie Burke, Paddy Greene and by Wolfe Morris who was appearing in *The Teahouse of the August Moon*. *The Stage* liked the 'unusually well considered direction ... of which ingenious lighting was a feature.'

It could have been, it should have been, No! It was, the most energetic provoking and experimental company which had been mounted in London up to that time. Through 30 performances the company showed 12 new full length plays as well as presenting little known or new works by recognised European and American authors. Working on a shoestring budget, the actors who took part gifted their services and have had the tenacity to maintain their position in the 'business.' Apart from the Scarborough players and those already mentioned, Ian Holm, Gwen Nelson, Barry Foster, Wilfred Brambell, Richard Pasco and Michael Balfour were among the many.

Amongst the directors, there were Clifford Williams, Gerard Glaister, David de Keyser, Richard Pilbrow, and Campbell Allan. They even underwrote the losses where there were any. Disconcertingly it never became possible to consolidate the achievements and strength of the company into any permanently acceptable form. The miracle is that they achieved what they did without funding.

When Eugene O'Neill complained that there were no big men in experimental theatre he was meaning influential names. Stephen was never big as O'Neill meant it, but he was no doubt inspired by O'Neill who also said, "Theatre should give us what the church no longer gives us – a meaning."

Apart from new plays, he was putting on the world's avant-garde classics. From the States, Steinbeck and Saroyan; from France Adamov, Giradoux (which the Royal Court mounted the following year) and Tardieu; German expressionism and Spanish eroticism, Dostoevski and a new Brazilian author. Eleven new writers had one or more of their works performed, and there were provoking classics from Priestley, Chekov, Pirandello, Henry James and of course the *Phedre* of Racine.

Then Stephen would do odd things, like inviting journalists and authors to a press conference, only to serve nothing but tea and cakes, when everyone knows that in journalism respect is earned by the amount of alcohol supplied. A teetotaller himself, it never occurred to Stephen that he need ingratiate himself with the press and therefore the coverage he received was minimal.

The Stage commented on plays well suited to this form of presentation and *The Times*, after a review describing flawless maquillage and an actor "whose back is compellingly articulate," then quibbled over imperfections of presentation not yet wiped out. Alan Dent complained that the trouble was "he never felt he was in a theatre at all." One critic said that it was a good way of presenting plays cheaply, but not a good way of presenting plays; however the critics were not necessarily reflecting public opinion.

One enthusiast wrote of coming away from the Mahatma Gandhi Hall feeling like St Paul on the Damascus Road. "I had always thought that Theatre in the Round was dead mutton but I had in fact never seen any. To see is to believe."[7]

Jo Hodgkinson, the Drama Director of the Arts Council, was a Lancastrian, born in 1905. He had managed an Old Vic tour during the war and became Regional Director of the Council's Manchester office before taking over as Drama Director in London. Unusually for such a position, he was not public school, but had been to Liverpool University and taught in Liverpool and at the Toynbee Hall in London.

He was a thorough going diplomat, charming and reasonable, never committed himself in print, and conducted all his business at first hand leaving any machinations to be dealt with behind the scenes, out of sight and unchronicalled. Clifford Williams joked that he was awfully nice, had a lovely face but was a real charlatan. Jo was married, but he and his wife Winnie were childless so they fostered, and sustained their friends. Jo and Stephen probably met at the Toynbee Hall.[8] For several years Stephen was one of those younger men with whom Jo and Winnie developed a close relationship, they entertained each other and exchanged Christmas presents. Although at that point of life where age is insignificant in personal relations, there can be little doubt that, 16 years older than Stephen, there was something filial in Jo's attitude towards him. Equally it is probable that Stephen transferred his respect and affection to the older man as a surrogate son might.

Much as Jo admired Stephen, he came to disapprove of his dedication to what some of his department members considered third rate theatre. Although there was a close bond, in none of their correspondence can one detect evidence of real warmth, and if subconsciously Stephen replaced Michael with Jo, he was to be let down by the surrogate father as badly as he felt let down all his life by his own father.

Performing new plays was one thing, finding them another and as Allan Prior describes it:

> soon came the crunch, as Stephen, with immense charm corralled a number of writers to drinks at the Flat and outlined the delights awaiting us if we would write for the Round. I was myself looking for something that paid. Plainly Theatre in the Round was not it. The lack of funds was something Stephen did not elaborate upon. It hung in the air, nonetheless, for all to see... It occurred to me that Stephen had inherited some of his father's great ability to find people of talent and to direct them... All entranced by this charismatic and amiable man.[9]

Writing from the BBC the Head of Drama TV, Michael Barry owed that "Many of us have been conscious with interest of the plucky work you have been doing..." but in the theatre admiration is not sustenance. The Club operation made an operating loss of only £63 in its first year, but in the second, with a more ambitious programme, monthly performances, rehearsal rooms to hire and printing and mailing shots the loss had risen by another £600.

Without private backing, without Arts Council support, it was not a situation the company could continue to sustain. Friend or no, Jo Hodgkinson failed to respond to requests for assistance in taking over more suitable premises. Neither Clapham nor Fulham nor the Warwick Road could be afforded, and so Stephen was forced to withdraw from London altogether, but not before he took Racine under his wing.

There was a close friendship between Hermione and the actress Margaret Rawlings. In a light moment d'Arcy called her husband Sir Roxby Cox of Metal Box (he was Chairman), some called her Lady Barlow, but to the theatregoing public she was Miss Margaret Rawlings, and had a fine string of theatrical triumphs behind her. She was one of Britain's leading classical actresses, had been brought up in Japan until the age of 14 where she had been sent to a French convent twice a week, and so became something of a French scholar. A very rich lady, when in London she had a penthouse flat in the Dorchester and a Rolls Royce called Bertie. It had a flash-up sign which showed 'Thank You' as it passed another car.

Miss Rawlings nursed a burning desire to play *Phedre* upon the English stage. At first she didn't like the idea of Theatre in the Round. She and Stephen had an interview with Harold Hobson, and he admitted he did not like to take a seat and look at the knees of the people opposite, to which Stephen's answer would have been, "If the acting is good enough you won't notice the knees."

Stephen had written earlier in the year to Hobson, over unfavourable reviews, to which the venerated critic had replied:

> Surely you must see that you pose to me a problem which can be solved only in one way. If a theatre manager on the one hand wishes a critic to attend his performance and on the other asserts that all his notices do is to put him out of business, this in most cases admits of a single solution.[10]

Stephen's side of the correspondence is not extant, but only a week later Hobson was replying

> What splendid examples of resolute good temper we are displaying towards each other! Whatever else it may be I am sure this correspondence is an admirable character building exercise and that we shall both emerge from it finer and better men. . . I hope that my notice will not finish off the Theatre in the Round. . . After all there must be quite a number of people in London who will go to plays simply because I don't like them.[11]

Reverting to Sundays only and over two weekends, on the 10th and 17th of November, the company presented *Phedre*. Probably one of the most ambitious productions to date. Under the leadership of Margaret Rawlings', Stephen was able to bring together a fine team, with Michael Aldridge as Theseus, Keith Baxter as Hippolytus, Gerald Harper, Ann Sears, Helena Pickard, Enid Lorrimer and Anne Taylor completing the cast. Many shared Margaret Rawling's original dislike of the medium whereas Michael Aldridge disagreed with Stephen's insistence on the form, but became a great admirer. Keith Baxter remembers:

> Racine's work was not often done in England. We had a muscular translation that didn't attempt to copy the Alexandrine verse-structure of the original; we spoke a kind of iambic pentameter. We played it as we play Shakespeare, robustly. The French cultural attache was amazed when Theseus struck Hippolytus across the face. "In France, actors playing Racine never touch each other."

The production costs were kept to an absolute minimum, almost a bare minimum. So scanty was Keith Baxter's costume (a sort of loincloth) his mother complained of its immodesty when he sent it back to Wales for washing. The set was a bench.[12] They used the least horrible of the available translations, one made in 1890, but its language was Victorian, and the actors and actresses made many faces at the first reading. . . The first laugh at rehearsal was on Thermenes' line, "You have been seldom seen with wild delight urging the rapid car along the Strand," which conjured up in all their minds the picture of a young man in a sports car in a traffic block somewhere near the Savoy. Margaret Rawlings complained:

> "Every day someone came up to me at rehearsals and said 'You've made your part better - could you do this bit for me'. . . After a week or two I had to give up rewriting. There is a limit to the new lines that can be learned just before a first night."[13]

Not that all the company were keen on the young protégé Margaret Rawlings had brought with her to direct. Some referred too him as 'one of Margaret's boys.' Stephen had to make sure he was on hand to placate and guide, as when he suggested to her that she need not project, but play her performance between her and the other character. "Stephen brought it to me and brought it out of me" and inspired them all. Stephen affectionately recalls the performance in his book on Theatre in the Round:

> *Phedre...* also benefited from the good work of an outstanding young actor... who played Hippolytus. In a small theatre the audience can usually sense precisely what is going on in an actor's mind, and when, as in theatre in the round, there are few technical tricks with which an actor can dazzle the public, his concentration and imagination are astonishingly exposed. On this score Keith Baxter gave a deeply moving performance. ...
>
> The confidante in a classical French tragedy usually has to do a lot of listening - when the heroine is holding forth for dozens of couplets at a time, half the audience is watching the confidante. Constance Lorne gave a totally unselfish performance but filled the part with a complete and charming personality, a person who somehow reflected (as a confidante should) all the thoughts and emotions of her companion.'[14]

Whilst *The Times* review is equally appreciative:

> Because the action is not action according to the conventions now prevailing in the theatre there is advantage in doing the play unconventionally... Where trickery and make-believe have no part in the presentation the whole attention of the audience is concentrated where it should be, on what the characters are saying. If they do not say

it in French the actors can hope to make good some part of this deficiency only by sincerity and loyalty to the spirit of the text. In this respect, the entire company, from Miss Margaret Rawlings in the largest part, to Miss Ann Taylor in the smallest, was exemplary.'[15]

Maverick as ever, Alan Dent observed that when the great Edwige Feuillère played the part she was said to be as exciting as a great house on fire at dead of night:

> Why does Margaret Rawlings in this part seem merely like a gardener's smoky bonfire at dusk in an English garden? Probably because Racine in English is as unsatisfying as Shakespeare in French. All the same, a few splendid sparks right at the edge are in Miss Rawlings' conflagration. These make the whole experiment worth seeing.[16]

But it was the Sunday reviews that caught the interest of the theatre crowd as Keith Baxter describes it:

> At that time there was an amusing rivalry between Harold Hobson (*The Sunday Times*) and Kenneth Tynan (*The Observer*). Hobson was an ardent Francophile and had recently raved over Edwige Feuillère's work in Racine. Accordingly, Tynan couldn't resist baiting his rival when he wrote of Margaret Rawlings "so powerful is Miss Rawlings in the role that Mme Feuillère would be lucky is she were asked to creep on as the maid."[17]

Whatever his alarm at the discourtesy shown in a French classic, the French Ambassador wrote "Your production was so good and the notices I read so appreciative that I sincerely hope the play will be put on again."And Miss Rawlings agreed that she wanted to repeat them, and so it was arranged that the following year, 1958, they should play for two weeks at the Mahatma Gandhi Hall and then tour a week each to Birmingham, Leicester and Scarborough.

Apart from Rawlings, only Sears and Baxter were available to tour, and Bernard Horsfall replaced Michael Aldridge. The Arts Council was asked to underwrite the venture, but if they failed Miss Rawlings herself was prepared to guarantee against loss to the tune of £850. To cover immediate expenses and prevent embarrassment Stephen had to borrow a further £150 from Uncle Lionel.

. Following the first night in February Stephen wrote to Rawlings:

> So far the critics have given us space but not much other help. *The*

Times alone has come out wholeheartedly in our favour... Help or not, I have not felt much respect for any of the reviews. It seems to me that you are paying the price for your courage to join in an experiment... I am much too thrilled and grateful for your fine work to feel anything like depressed! It may not be Racine... but your performance is unique. .. and the entertainment is genuinely good.[18]

It is interesting to note that Scarborough, the smallest theatre and smallest town, generated the highest income on the tour. Birmingham, where the company was unknown, built up over the week, London was a disappointment, though Leicester played to 90% capacity. Only £500 was required to offset the losses.

The penultimate production by the company in London was David Campton's *Lunatic View* directed by Stephen himself. It was the first production he had done which had been written by the author entirely for performance in the round. Properly speaking it was thematically four one act plays, always difficult to sell to an audience, and the beginning of a fruitful relationship in which Campton's fertile imagination would be triggered by a chance Stephen remark.

Stephen would just come out with "I've got a splendid idea for a play." It was an almost continuous process, so I'm never quite sure whether the idea started with me or with (him). Sometimes it would start in a tiny tiny way - for instance one idea which he kept urging me to write, was about this clergyman who collected grasses for his hobby (Keble-Martin *Concise Flora and Fauna*) and he was finding the strangest mutations in his grasses, which he couldn't categorise any longer: and then I added to it, and he's not even noticing that strange things are happening to his family. That particular play became *Mutatis Mutandis*, which is about a couple who have a weird mutant baby... [19]

A Smell of Burning was written after a breakfast conversation in Ashburnham Mansions when Campton and Stephen were sitting looking out of the window at the gasometer only yards away. In the play the Jones's are seated at the breakfast table unaware of what is happening in the world around them, and that their house is on fire. These four playlets could correctly be described as apocalyptic allegories for what was happening in the world outside, and sadly, even the audiences, many of them, did not appreciate the point. Allan Prior remembers seeing his friend's play, in which most of the characters wore brown paper bags on their heads!

This was in the last of the four plays, *Then,* inspired by Stephen's fury at the critics carping criticisms of not being able to see the actors faces in the round. Stephen said to Campton one day, "Write a play where people have their faces covered." 1956 was in the middle of the Aldermaston period - intellectuals railed against the nuclear armaments industry. Following nuclear experiments it had been discovered by government scientists that a wooden hut would be blown to smithereens in a blast, but whitewashed on the outside it might withstand an explosion. Similarly, glass windows would not shatter if covered in paper. *Then* carries on from a nuclear attack, in which two survivors, still alive because they were wearing paper bags on their heads, ponder on whether it is safe to remove them. . .

It says much for the striking impression the play made on the audience that in talking about the production the most memorable aspect is that 'everyone' wore paper bags, when it was the last and briefest play, for only two actors! Stephen had great faith in *Lunatic View*, so much so he made a point of inviting his father to a performance. Michael went with Shirley. To her embarrassment, he kept making spiteful, cutting remarks :

> It was the worst thing I've ever had to sit through with father, when nothing less than Noel Coward was going to satisfy him. . . . people were sitting around on benches in Piccadilly, or Eros with paper bags on their heads. . . his remarks in the silences. . .[20]

Campton's success in these works was to write very funny dialogue around thought provoking ideas. They appealed to the young audiences more than to the entrenched -

> I hold Campton in the greatest respect, but I have found that there is a vast difference between his superb realistic dialogue. . . and the lack of discipline in the short plays. . . I feel that an author who escapes into fantasy deliberately avoids the measuring stick of realism... If you could persuade him to write me an honest, realistic play about some vital social or personal issue of our day. . .[21]

What more vital social issue of that day could exceed the nuclear one, even today, is difficult to imagine.

The last play of the autumn season was *I have been here Before*, Priestley's famous time play which then went on to tour. The programme note plans for an exciting series of Sunday shows in the New Year of 1958. Writing to T.C. Worsley at the *New Statesman* Stephen observed :

> We have staged over thirty plays... so *The Times* writes about Theatre in the Round in Milan. *The Daily Telegraph* writes about Theatre in the Round in America. And the press in general whenever short of topics writes about the lack of experimental theatre in this country

Worsley had asked Stephen to let him know if his notice had any effect on the audience attendance

> What makes a difference is not your notice, but the fact that after *The Times* and *Sunday Times*, you. . . *The Tribune*, besides *Truth* all talked about the play. Copies of the *New Statesman* were brought into the theatre. . . by members of the audience anxious to make sure we were the theatre under discussion. . .If the earlier performances had been as well attended (as the last two) we should not now be looking vainly for gold to pay our losses.[22]

Stephen never discovered the crock at the end of the rainbow, and so the Club performances came to an end after a performance of the aptly titled *Who Cares?* at the Chenil Galleries, Chelsea in June, immediately before the third Scarborough season.

Philip Clifford, Rosamund Dickson, Stanley Page, David Jarrett, Alan Ayckbourn, Hazel Burt, with David Campton - *Four Minute Warning*

John Rees, Shirley Jacobs - *Wuthering Heights*

Chapter Twenty One

Scarborough

I sat this evening beneath the cragged and ruined castle . . . the sea, seething with anger . . . the sun barely glanced through the clouds all day . . . its rays were only faint shafts. Rain came, and, had lightning followed, then possibly the perfect overture would have been composed by the elements for . . . *Wuthering Heights*.

A Yorkshire notable who contributed hugely to the success of the company and whom we should not overlook, has to be Desmond Pratt. His newspaper reviews and enthusiastic support went a long way towards attracting an audience.

> We sat in a square looking down or across a pool of light . . . watching Heathcliff and Cathy . . . This production is theatrical excitement at its highest.
>
> Pratt had absorbed Stephen's enthusiasm by osmosis, it was infectious. His companies warmed to it, and so did the audiences.
>
> To this kind of theatrical presentation . . . I am now a convert."

To keep the Club operation going in London and to maintain the Scarborough season there was nothing for it but to get a job to subsidise them. Money had to be earned to pay the bills. For his second season the Arts Council gave him a grant of £250, which was increased to £500 in year three, then doubled in 1959.

His need to deliver coal at this time was pragmatic. It paid better and was more easily obtained than lecturing might be. He graduated to hawking pink paraffin, then to a gin factory in Hammersmith. He could pick up a job for a few months and drop it more easily than he might lecturing. It was also relatively mindless, and gave him the opportunity to occupy his thoughts in resolving problems.

When Hermione learned what he was doing she was horrified, and instructed her agents to send her most recently accumulated repeat fees to her son so that he might quit his common labour. He was no doubt grateful to receive the cheque, but £64 was not the fortune required, so it did not alter his resolve. On one occasion an amazed Chelsea resident, having tipped her coalman two shillings, told her nephew, "I had my coal delivered by your boss."

The nephew was Alan Ayckbourn who had joined the company as Stage Manager for its second Summer season. Ayckbourn's father had been leader of the London Symphony Orchestra and his mother a writer of short stories which found a market in *Woman's Own, Woman* etc. Known as Lolly, she wrote under the name of Mary James, and her childrens' stories were published by Michael Joseph.

Ayckbourn was educated at Haileybury whose most famous son at that time was probably Rudyard Kipling. John Morrell, the journalist and Beirut hostage, was a later pupil. Ayckbourn's first job after school was with Donald Wolfit for a three week season in Edinburgh. He became a student actor at Worthing before being offered a job as ASM at Leatherhead Repertory by Hazel Vincent Wallace. The Stage Manager there was Rodney Woods, and when Woods took the job of managing the Scarborough season he invited Ayckbourn to join him.

Minos Volonakis saw Ayckbourn in Scarborough and asked him to join the company in Oxford where he was then in partnership with Frank Hauser. Apart from that brief spell at the Playhouse, Ayckbourn devoted almost ten years to Stephen's company.

When as the new stage manager, Alan Ayckbourn went to meet Stephen for the first time in Ashburnham Mansions, he said, "I think my mother lives here." She was actually renting a room on the floor below.

Lolly was going through a difficult period and was waitress in a Lyons Corner House. Stephen used to go with three or four of the cast . . "Let's go to see Lolly, and have a coffee." She suspected his motives and may have been right to do so. Lolly was having to come to terms with having no Michael. Unaware of any background history, P.B. said, "Invite her to tea," and when she came Stephen was very polite.

1957 was a year in which realities had to be faced. The Arts Council grant was solely for use in Scarborough. The showcase productions at the Mahatma Gandhi Hall, even though the actors gave their services, were becoming more expensive to mount.

One of Stephen's Company Directors was the Hon. Antony Lyttelton, whose father-in-law happened to be Chairman of the Pilgrim Trust. Lyttelton had sounded out his in-law and now indicated that it might be worth while to apply to the Trust for a grant.

Losses for the 1956 season brought the accumulated deficit to £867. The Club performances in London added another £200 to that figure. Leaving the season in the hands of a Manager and Director had left him time to be in London to plan the public performances at the Mahatma Gandhi Hall. They were his biggest gamble and added a further loss on the books of almost £1200.

The third season opened with Clive Goodwin's production of *The Glass Menagerie*. Goodwin had been a student at The Hall, a leading intellectual and one of the editors of *Encore*, but in practice it was not only Stephen who considered the production not as good as it should be. It relied too much on technical aids and not enough on acting. However, most audiences liked it, and when the company performed the play at the Cayton Bay Holiday Camp a man went up to Ayckbourn at the end and put a bag of money in his hand. He and his chums had been so distressed at the plight of the girl with the club foot in the play that they had had a whip round and collected money for her! The cast had high tea on the proceeds.

Attendances were improving, as the Full House notices showed. Scarborough was warming to Theatre in the Round, and the Theatre Guild were suggesting a permanent stay in the town. The Mayor was keen. Whilst the Librarian made earnest noises he claimed other uses for the concert hall in the winter. So Stephen was asked to present proposals for a permanent operation elsewhere. It became an almost biennial request.

As a preliminary, a three week winter season was booked for 1957 and the touring operation of the company firmly established.

Writing in March 1958, Jo Hodgkinson commiserated on the death of Stephen's father. The ACGB gave Stephen an outright grant of £500 for the purposes of exploring and hopefully solving the problem of finding a permanent home for the company.

Some aspects of Stephen's policies attracted publicity. His was one of the first companies to play the National Anthem only at the beginning and end of each season, not at every performance as was usual. Another was his insistence that a drama gained maximum intensity if played straight through without an interval, and that was always his policy, even when the play was *Hamlet*. By so doing he encouraged the audience to take coffee and cakes afterwards, with the chance to mix informally with members of the company. His other mostly unremarked policy was that he never charged the audience for his programmes, nor sought sponsorship by asking businesses to advertise in them. They were part of the public service he wanted the theatre to be.

He was convinced that theatre, as it existed in the 1950s, was on the point of collapse. It was overweight, far too complex and expensive, far too subsidised and untrue to its times. The way forward was to have scores of little Theatres in the Round, one attached to each major or medium-sized public library. A resident company of actors would keep the repertoire of great plays alive in it . . . and new drama introduced - just as the books part next door housed the classics and new writing.[1] Theatre was a basic need for everyone and should be available to everyone, as is the National Health service, as it was in classical Greece.[2]

It was a very revolutionary concept in the late '50s, as still is the idea that theatre is one of the vital organs of the society in which it exists. "Place yourself in the '50s," Stephen might say, "and what are our beliefs? We have none. The slate is clean. Therefore the theatre should be . . . an empty working space . . . simplicity is paramount . . . we will probe our instincts, through drama, and start discovering a direction again."[3]

It was a philosophy which generated a great loyalty within the company, actors returning time and again to work for the ideal. Ayckbourn felt inspired also. Between seasons he wrote to Stephen: "What is needed most of all at the moment, is a more or less permanent acting group. That is why . . . I would like to stay with you, rather than try my luck in the more commercial grind . . . I lay myself before you as a foundation stone of permanence."[4]

Another budding writer who joined the company as an actor was Ian Curteis who absorbed Stephen's philosophy during rehearsals and breaks. To Stephen theatre was as important within the community as politics, football or the church, because it was a sounding-board for what was happening to all human beings outside it.

He believed that to place actors (or politicians) on a platform (stage) transformed them into idols (gods), and therefore the shape of the theatre and the physical relationship between drama and its audience always mirrored the society in which it existed. Thus the Greek amphitheatre reflected the structure and beliefs of Athens under Pericles – he used to insist "it is best to have the acting area on the floor level and to raise the seating... this reduces the actors to the role of human beings. There is plenty of room overhead for whatever Gods there may be."[5]

A further example, he argued, was the apron stage in Elizabethan theatre, at a time of thrusting confidence. The Italian renaissance theatre was for the Duke and lesser nobility while each level of the huge and complex nineteenth century theatres, like the Paris Opera with its tiers of seats, reflected and accommodated one slice of society: stalls for the upper classes, Royal circle for nobility, upper circle for the bourgeois and gallery for the working class.

He would carry radicalism into his direction. He would, in a conventional sense, refuse to direct - he'd say "You do it, you discover how your actions towards each other on stage illuminate the text. To have a dominating director is to live in a society which tells you what to do." He was the very opposite of a puppet master - the text was not words, of course, but a web of interaction of character. There were no rules, except to try to discard what had been taught so badly in the treadmill of weekly repertory.[6]

Where Stephen's method of presenting plays began to be accepted he tried to change the ritual of script dominated drama also. In January 1958 he wrote to the Lord Chamberlain submitting a synopsis for a planned public improvisation. The story line was a very simple one of a widower who dominates his daughter, is a TV addict, and wins the football pools. That allows her to go off with her boyfriend because her father doesn't notice the difference between her and his new housekeeper.

Once more Stephen was banging his head against a brick wall, and not one he could topple on his own. Much as the Lord Chamberlain looked kindly on the honourable tradition of Commedia dell'Arte, and would have liked to accommodate it, his hands were tied. "The Comptroller," his office explained "has no power whatever to dispense with a Statute . . . he is legally bound to demand from you the full dialogue and descriptions of allied action of any play you propose to stage . . ."[7] Once again it was a case of being ten years ahead of his time.

Never an enthusiast where Stephen's company was concerned, the Arts Council Adviser who saw a double-bill was both uncompromising and remarkably flattering:

> *Halfway to Heaven* . . . is a worthless piece . . . it was badly played, and a very poor advertisement for any kind of theatre. *Alas, Poor Fred* was very good, most interesting . . . the cast of two are excellent . . . I was astonished how well this play went down although Stephen Joseph told me that they had had more responsive audiences . . . This is the first time that I have been at all convinced that Theatre in the Round might

have something to offer that they could not get in a conventional building."[8]

For the 1959 season Ayckbourn's mother Lolly took a house in Scarborough. Sundays were fun days in Lolly's house, and the company would often sit around joking, playing games, going off on weird flights of fancy, with Ayckbourn making funny tapes, sending up the whole season, impersonating the other actors and doing all the voices. At this time he was writing very gloomy, serious plays so that those tape recordings foreshadowed his later comedies.[9] Stephen was inclined to drop in, to want to be part of the fun, and to share in the jollity as it might have been in Kinnerton Mews (Hermione's house). Lolly thought he was trying to be centre-stage and didn't approve. He must have sensed her criticism because it was the last occasion when he was inclined to join the company socially. They were roughly the same age, but walking out one day he told her he would have liked her to marry his father.

Lolly was one of the candidates P.B. liked to speculate he might become attached to, so she undoubtedly did not know of Lolly's Josephian connection. It is interesting to speculate if, privately, Stephen himself ever wondered whether, by chance, he and Ayckbourn might be related.

Ayckbourn had been brought up in a house where his mother wrote constantly; he himself had written a play at school and as an ASM at the Oxford Playhouse with Ian Curteis, used to scribble his early works in the wings between performances.[10] He was complaining to Stephen about one of his roles when he was told, "If you want a better part, you'd better write one for yourself. Write a play, I'll do it, if it's any good."[11] Ayckbourn recollects the catalystic play as being *Bell Book and Candle* but that season had been announced in advance and there are only six weeks between the two productions. A more plausible account will be examined later.

Ayckbourn's first play, *The Square Cat* was directed by Stephen, who had inherited his father's skill of editing and could be ruthless. Ayckbourn recalls, "He read it very quickly. My impression always was that he flipped the scripts through with his thumb . . . and was able to tell you immediately what was wrong with it."[12]

"Alan Ayckbourn . . . gives his best performance of the season. Dona Martyn backs him up with first class acting . . . and William Elmhirst is a tonic as (her) son."[13] The season finished above 60% capacity - no mean achievement given glorious weather.

1960 was a season of repeats, most of the plays having been seen at The Library before. *Prentice Pillar* gave way to *Wuthering Heights*, then followed Ayckbourn's second play, *Love After All*. Each had been successful in its season as originally produced, but Jo Hodgkinson was eager for Scarborough to be more mainstream. He judged theatre by West End standards and was not always sensitive to what Stephen was trying to achieve with his company. So he persuaded Stephen to take on a new young director he was trying to promote. The grant was increased to accommodate the extra salary, but by the time these first three plays were on, the budget had been eaten up, and Stephen had argued with the two men running the season. Both had solid CVs, but both were steeped in mainstream theatre.

> I failed to get my manager up to scratch and sacked him before we opened... Further misunderstandings . . .got so complex that I finally asked (the director) to leave . . . (his) productions are now a lively reminder to me that the Theatre in the Round demands special talents, and that a small theatre is different from a large one, . . . a good producer can make a good play boring. This last fact is underlined by the farce which was very funny when produced by Clifford Williams, is now only vaguely amusing . . . tho (sic) I must admit it is brilliantly directed[14]

It was an unusually tough policy decision and several actors considered their position in the company. One actress left, and Stephen wondered if anyone else would. Campton remembers him saying "Ayckbourn will go. I'm sure Ayckbourn will go." He was being unusually neurotic.

He was usually very gentle, very kindly, as Ian Curteis remembers:

> To actors when they were getting it wrong, were using a bit of stage-trickery, like a double-take, he would put his arm round the shoulders and tell the actor how well it was coming on, how much good stuff was emerging - but there was the little matter of - well, would you think me unkind if I said something that looked like a double-take? Now that isn't letting this thing happen by itself, but imposing a rather outdated and stale trick on that moment, to get a laugh . . .

> You see these buttons on this jacket sleeve? They've long since lost their purpose over a hundred years ago, but you still find tailors insist of sewing them on for decoration. That's what you're doing, sewing on useless buttons. But this is 1958. Clear your mind. Just do it naturally . . . [15]

A View From the Brink was three short plays from David Campton to demonstrate the lunacies of the Cold War, war in general, and the after-effects of nuclear war. The first is a duologue between two diplomats; in the next the successfully returning soldier is reduced to a boasting wounded wreck, and in the last the proud father has to inform his wife of the effects of radiation on their post-nuclear baby.

> Mr Joseph . . . has managed to show that his theatre is never more successful than when it is showing off this type of subtle farce. It gives the pace a fluidity which the orthodox proscenium arch frustrates . . .[16]

In 1962 Stephen found his dream house. At 119 Longwestgate he fell in love with an old rectory which the Church Commissioners were selling. It was to cost £500, and he was not sure he could raise the money, so asked d'Arcy to join him as part-owner. In the event he bought it on his own, and on his having done so Hermione gifted him £500 towards renovations, at the same time giving Leslie a similar sum.

With the summer season's plays into production, and with the assistance on his stage management, he enjoyed ripping out damp and decaying lath and plaster walls from the basement, and planning his garden. His first plant was a single sunflower and Hermione brought a majolica tondo of Virgin and Child for the outside wall. The ample size and modest early Victorian style of the rooms, together with his all-white decoration reflected his simple meditative ethic.

The only ground floor room with a window onto the street was the dining room, which Shirley and her husband decorated as their gift, and it was the only room to have curtains.

With his committment to Scarborough also as a home, there was a fresh movement towards a permanent theatre. The Mayor was enthusiastic and friendly, and once again the question of a permanent home was optimistically raised. The Mayor, Councillors, Aldermen, the Borough Engineer, the Deputy Treasurer and the Director of Libraries met with Stephen in July to discuss the possibility of building a permanent theatre. The council had already agreed in principle to an Arts Centre but were now concerned that local amateurs had no suitably sized accommodation at reasonable cost.

Stephen was asked to draw up rough sketches of a suitable building with the Borough Engineer. Mervyn Edwards, the librarian, wrote to the ACGB in August for discussions. Jo Hodgkinson was in Scarborough within a month; Stephen organised an informal Sunday morning meeting for discussion and to sound Jo out about the formation of a Trust to run the theatre. Even at this early stage Stephen considered the formation of a local Theatre Trust an essential pre-requisite to the launching of a 'local' theatre. Bearing this in mind, it might be asked why he did not do so later in Stoke on Trent, but that question must hang in the air. Sad to record also, the driving force behind these steps towards a permanent theatre in Scarborough was the Mayor, who died unexpectedly, and in the event the necessary dynamic died with him.

Desmond Pratt sneaked in on two of the productions for the 1961 season during the Hull Arts Festival the week before. He reflected on the growth of experiment and the revolution which was beginning to take place in the British Theatre. Tyrone Guthrie's work in Edinburgh and Canada had inspired the shape and size of the new Chichester Theatre. The Questors in Ealing and the Pembroke Theatre in Croydon were influenced by Arena staging whilst the Congress Theatre, Eastbourne and the Mermaid in London were attempts to break the bounds of proscenium theatre.

The Pembroke management had asked Stephen to run the theatre in Croydon. There is no indication anywhere of why he chose not to, but the likely explanation is that he felt the pressure for a commercial programme in Croydon, and one over which he would not have total control. Innovators must create their own space for development and not be ruled by committees.

The second British Drama League in the round Festival was being held after the professional season in Scarborough with teams from as far afield as Southampton, Bradford and Greenock, where there was a vibrant amateur theatre, several of whose members later became professional. William Bryden was one such. "The future has obvious glories, for not only can the movement grow internally, it can offer to the commercial theatre a new stream of actors and writers."[17]

Earlier on Stephen had directed the newest Ayckbourn play, *Standing Room Only*. Stephen wanted Ayckbourn to write a play about overpopulation. "He outlined his plot, which was set on Venus, where the population was now expanding... so I set it in Shaftsbury Avenue in a bus."[18] The bus was of course stranded in the ultimate traffic jam, and the city had been gridlocked for years.

As *The Stage* was unable to send a critic, Joan Macalpine the Company Manager wrote an anonymous and glowing review for the play, "Will no management drive this bus into Shaftsbury Avenue?" she asked, and West End manager Peter Bridge rushed to Scarborough and was so delighted with what he saw, bought an option. Stephen felt very chirpy, "We have just sold one of our brand new plays to a London manager. It is not my favourite play, not my favourite manager but the author's very good," he wrote to his mother.[19]

A year later the Library's committee was still discussing the possibility of a new theatre, or of the council taking over responsibility for the company. Mervyn Edwards, the Librarian, was publicly anxious that the company would continue its work in Scarborough, though in private was sparing with his assistance. It appears he would rather they were elsewhere in the town. He probably reckoned that the company was by now too high profile to dismiss, but did not want the nuisance of it in his building, nor want the responsibility of its demise laid at his door.

Writing to Jo in September, Stephen committed to paper what Jo might have preferred to be only an allusion. Perhaps Stephen was too sensitive:

> It seems to me that we are doing one or two things of very real importance to the theatre, presenting new plays, exploiting new methods of presentation . . . I find it difficult to believe, as you hinted, that the Arts Council is prepared to ditch this.

Jo's response was suitably diplomatic, and told him he was talking nonsense, and knew it. "I shall do everything I can to encourage Scarborough the moment Mervyn Edwards gives the signal," he wrote. But Mervyn Edwards never gave signals. Only damp squids.

Stephen was delighted with the building of the new Chichester Theatre. It, as it were, legitimised experiment on a big scale, but he had his reservations which he shared with Mary David:

> It is undoubtedly a very exciting building indeed. It seems to me to be the most important theatre to have been built in this country since the war . . . However, acoustics are undoubtedly bad, and, in my opinion, the theatre is too big . . ."[20]

His letter goes on to explore terminology, which he was to influence, because to the uninitiated any form of open stage was Theatre in the Round. Due to his insistence, terms like end-stage, thrust or arena stage, distinguished Theatre in the Round from other forms of experiment. He repeated for Mary's benefit:

> It is important that theatre is becoming a more meaningful art . . . new

stages are helpful when they come into the auditorium . . . the enclosed stage presented a remote drama. The open stage can present a drama that belongs to the audience . . ."

An intriguing coincidence is that when Mary David from Llandaff married, she became Mary James, the name by which Lolly wrote.

Leslie, Stephen, Margaret, Hermione

Skatch Stephen Joseph

The Yorkshire Post - 10 June 1961

Chapter Twenty Two

Makeshift

What in heaven's name takes place at 41 Fitzroy Square and who will be sponsoring your visit there?

Following the third Scarborough season Stephen took his biggest risk and applied for a public performance licence at the Mahatma Gandhi Hall. Two of the productions he planned to present were part of the summer operation and therefore without production expenses. Both were new plays. Jo was not a happy man when he put two and two together. With consummate innocence Stephen's next letter was thanking him for his Christmas gift. Hoffnung's *Acoustics* was great fun and just the ticket for a quiet moment in the front-of-house manager's life.

Touring was for Stephen a necessary evangelism, a way of taking revolutionary theatre to theatreless towns and to hopefully encourage one of them to offer a permanent home to his company. Scarborough's good intentions were to rumble on for ten years or more, but there was rarely optimism that they would provide a permanent home, only a forlorn hope. They wouldn't say yes and they wouldn't say no.

Touring meant packing after a Saturday night performance, driving through the night to set up anew hundreds of miles away for a show the following evening. A sufficiently large audience had to be raised on seating rostra all around an acting area - the stage. Scaffolding had been used for the first seasons in the Library , but it was time consuming to erect and expensive to hire. Therefore collapsible seating rostrums were needed: also lighting equipment and lorries to carry them. It was here that the Pilgrim Trust came in. They were a charitable body, with funds.

Even by the 50's standards what Stephen asked for was a modest amount, £900 for equipment to form a touring unit, £3,000 for the acquisition of permanent theatre premises and £250 per annum to be able to re-establish his playwriting courses. Where he was being too realistic in his application for funds he also over rated his Arts Council support, quoting them as enthusiastic sponsors.

The Rt. Hon. Lord Kilmaine CBE of the Pilgrim Trust checked out their enthusiasm by writing to the Secretary General of the Arts Council, Sir William Emrys Williams. When Jo Hodgkinson was asked to give guidance to the Secretary General he only recommended the application of the funding for the touring units. Stephen never knew the extent to which he had been stabbed in the back by his friend.

To be fair, in his reply to the Pilgrim Trust with his endorsement of the touring project, Sir William Emrys Williams said he had a strong impression that Theatre in the Round might attract a new kind of audience to drama.

> When there is a short season of this interesting oddity next in London I will let you know, for it really is an experience not to be missed. Having said all this I must also say that it is an extemporary form of drama, a make do and mend affair and I do not see any great dramatist being born out of this makeshift.[1]

He went further and said he saw no point in helping Stephen acquire a home for what was essentially a mobile operation. The fact that the company was not yet mobile and did not want to be was disregarded by virtue of Jo Hodgkinson's recommendation. After such qualified approval it is surprising to find Lord Kilmaine saying, "How refreshing it is to know that there is a bold and original experiment which you can whole-heartedly commend."[2] So Stephen was awarded the £900, bought two three ton lorries and wooden seating rostra and began five years of touring to theatreless cities.

Over the five touring years a pattern gradually emerged, three or four weeks in Scarborough at Christmas and the New Year in Newcastle under Lyme. Around these fixed dates others were added or ditched. Hemel Hempstead received two visits, and Dartington Hall became an annual treat. Other venues were explored: the Hull Arts Festival was a generous week's host, as was the new Questors Theatre in Ealing.

In their first winter season at The Library, he had chosen his material well, the first production of plays being written specially for the round by David Campton. He was an also an actor with the company, and one who understood his arena like a Roman lion. In the writing of the four plays which form *A Lunatic View,* Campton more than made the flesh creep. 'His jokes are grim (and funny) but never cruel, his fantasies have a hint of seriousness as well as mere humour,' commented the *Manchester Guardian*.[3]

Never a staunch friend of the Studio Theatre, Dick Linklater at the Arts Council wrote to suggest *The Lunatic View* as a participating production in a season of new plays George Devine was mounting at the Royal Court. Devine could be described as a conservative experimenter, like Bernard Miles at the Mermaid. He did not want to experiment with form, but innovate intellectually with style and change the direction of boulevard theatre, He wanted plays which had not been seen elsewhere, and did not admire these plays, nor this form of theatrical experiment.

Nor in the event did Leicester, where the reception of Phedre had augured well. Perhaps Stephen should have noticed the sub-text, when at a civic reception the Mayor said, "I like theatre. I'm looking forward to *Ruddigore* next week."! The company returned twice and Stephen spent a lot of time looking at unsuitable halls, but even in September 1958 he considered the city a disappointment. Then with Richard Leacroft working on a scheme for a flexible theatre and the Director of Education turning his department upside down for the company, he became reasonably hopeful for a while that Leicester might give him a permanent theatre. In a letter to Jo he philosophied:

> We have ventured into Leicester . . . like cautious explorers in a treacherous forest, or like the Israelite spies among the Philistines. How is it that one of the richest cities in the world has no professional company of its own to stage plays? . . .[4]

His first four week stay in Leicester was a model of realistic expectation, the company attracting the size of audience he had budgeted for, but it convinced him he needed a guarantee against loss for a future visit.

In planning for his second, only six months later, the chairman of the Theatre Committee, Philip Collin, was cautious. He was uneasy about the proposed programme, didn't like Stephen's leading actress, Dona Martyn, and was unhappy that she was to return. In fact, whilst the audiences were good and Stephen was optimistic the committee of opinion moulders was not. They only wanted to back a winner and did not want the failure of having to underwrite an unsuccessful tour, one that might antagonise local opinion which would perceive theatre as a loss-maker.[5]

Visiting Leicester as an observer, Dick Linklater confessed he was not yet a convert to Theatre in the Round. However he stayed the night with Collins who was Warden of Vaughan College and was shown slides of Leacroft's model for converting a building owned by the Education Committee into a flexible theatre. This he described as imaginative, practical and inexpensive to carry out. So impressed was he that he asked Collins to bring the slides to show Sir William Emerys Williams and Jo Hodgkinson at the Arts Council.[6]

Stephen's diplomacy was hard-pressed in Leicester. There was ever an air of combatativeness. Collins wanted an improved standard of acting without offering any money to guarantee the season or enlarge the company. They also wanted a classic and Stephen smarted. He asked them to suggest one for four men and two women. What is more, for their next visit they were having to play in different halls during the three weeks they were there. Not the best situation in which to develop a rapport or build an audience.

The local newspaper seems to sum up the general air of intellectual superiority displayed towards the company. Of Ring of Roses, written by local author David Campton the *Leicester Mercury* described it as a breach-of-promise comedy. Nor did it stop there:

> *The Birthday Party* by Harold Pinter is one of the most bizarre modern plays I have seen... Mr Joseph assured me... the play is an experience just as much as looking at an abstract painting... Oh dear me. Not very long ago the stage was littered with psychiatrists' couches. Then it was French dustbins. Now it's experiences... If this is the modern form of laughter then I prefer the man slipping on the banana skin.[7]

The company fared little better in Birmingham where their reception had been warm. Quite why Stephen went to Birmingham is unclear, as it could hardly be described as a theatreless city. The Barry Jackson Repertory Company were well established, as was its touring date. Presumably, as England's second city it was deemed large and eclectic enough to support an experimental cause. Also after *Phedre* he no doubt expected to return to a city which welcomed his venture.

In the event they experienced the worst week's business they had ever had, caused in part by snow. Ironically too, their press reception was the best ever:

> Among the major benefits of the dedicated Theatre in the Round company, blowing like a fresh breeze through the tinsel and gauze of pantomime... is the chance of seeing in two successive weeks the work of two of the younger generation of playwrights.[8]

Campton had just been awarded an Arts Council bursary, and Stephen was preparing to give Harold Pinter the highest ever royalty his company had paid. When Pinter's *The Birthday Party* closed in London after less than a week of performances, Stephen asked the agents if he might include it in his touring season. The agent told Pinter of Stephen's intention and the author wrote asking if he could produce the play. Pinter had been a student at Central School for a term while Stephen was teaching there. The Halls secretary Sarge said he had left due to inadequate funding. She thought he too drove a lorry for a while to make ends meet although Pinter disputes this. In his letter Pinter says, "All I've done recently is write a radio play for the Third . . . but on the whole life ain't easy. Between ourselves I don't think it was ever intended to be."[9]

Nor was it easy for the poor stage management, having to organise the moves between venues, load and unload, set up and strike and drive ancient vehicles which had been tested almost beyond the point of endurance before Stephen bought them. His manager Joan Macalpine wrote poetically:

> The van is an old police van, so constructed that the back doors will only open if a lever is pulled by the driver, who is protected by wire netting. It has a few idiosyncrasies - the left hand trafficator goes out if banged and the right hand trafficator comes back if you wind the window up and down - but it is friendly . . . [10]

For two years running the company went to Southampton, which had grandiose schemes being canvassed by Hugh Hunt for an open stage in the Hampshire area. Stephen tried to go one better and applied for permission to erect a geodesic dome to house the company. The geodesic dome was an innovatory form of architecture by the American architect Buckminster Fuller. It was a light structural framework of polygons which were then covered by an impervious membrane, and would have been an exciting shape in which to play theatre in the round. Sadly British planning authorities did not consider it a safe form of building. (It is interesting to note that the later Manchester Royal Exchange Theatre was housed in an almost identical structure).

All the halls Stephen looked at had bookings which precluded a completely free week. Even in the Chantry Hall which he settled upon, the company had to vacate for a whist drive every Monday, and whilst reviews were good the audiences were poor. In the middle of one performance a clergyman walked straight across the acting area, and then said in a loud clear voice outside the hall, "There's a group of actors rehearsing in the dark...!" Small wonder Stephen kept popping dyspepsia pills in his mouth to aid his digestion.

David Jarrett, Rosamund Dickson, Alan Ayckbourn
Little Brother, Little Sister

Chapter Twenty Three

A Long Long Trail

Where the ethos of the amateur in Essex and the Faculty in Leicestershire was antipathetic to avant guardism, there was no such feeling of exclusion in the Potteries.

With a catchment area of about 500,000 people, the Potteries is in fact six towns centred around Stoke on Trent. It was heavily grimy, as might be expected where so many fire kilns had for years spewed smoke and soot into the atmosphere. The housing red brick, industrial terraces, with a languor bred of necessity and social inability to control the environment. For the most part plants and trees do not thrive in acid atmospheres which breeds a rather sharp sort of human animal also.

Immediately to the west and therefore upwind, was the more ancient market town of Newcastle under Lyme. Rivalry between Arnold Bennett's five towns and Newcastle ran strong. The Brampton Park acts as a natural boundary, a status symbol dividing Stoke on Trent from Newcastle under Lyme, the more expansive, decorous town. Although the artisan housing is similar, the private houses and public buildings displayed a more conscious air of stucco and decoration. Newcastle's image had an atmosphere of Georgian expansiveness beside its Victorian industrial neighbours. Its municipal hall with columned facade, reflected the town's quiet self-satisfaction and confidence.

In the eighteenth century there had been a flourishing Theatre Royal in Newcastle. Within its century of existence it had declined into a warehouse, then become a cinema but was now deserted. Professional dramatic entertainment had moved to Stoke and Hanley, and the last of the theatres in the area was now a bingo hall.

Stephen first earmarked Newcastle in March 1958. The Treasurer there, Charles Lister, was an enthusiast who himself wanted to see a civic theatre established and to consider a sample visit with a view to finding them a permanent home if the company was acceptable to the audiences.[1] The Municipal Hall was happy to play host to the company at the beginning of 1959, and the council to consider giving financial assistance, after the visit. "I imagine they want to be sure the entertainment has been worthwhile," Stephen wrote to Jo.[2]

He had wanted to present *Heartbreak House*, Shaw's flagship for bravura performances, but his Arts Council grant was inadequate. This forced him to settle on four plays, each of which concentrated the audiences' awareness on the drama and the versatility of a company intent upon an exploration of human relationships. Six young actors, like the facets of a brilliant, reflecting aspects of family life. Strindberg's *Easter* opened the season, a strong straightforward drama of a family struggling against misfortune, the innocent suffering for the guilty. *Martine* by Jean Jacques Bernard is a delicate play which seeks after perfection of form and depth of insight into human nature. In Kataev's 1930 comedy *Squaring the Circle*, there are a surprising number of jokes at the expense of the Soviet regime, where two young men sharing a room in a lodging house decide to marry without telling each other.

The four week season finished conventionally with a bright new comedy by David Campton, *Ring of Roses*. It had enough flashes of brilliance and a farcical finale to send the audience home on a boisterous note. 'Theatre Group on the Crest of a Wave" proclaimed the *Evening Sentinel*. "In more senses than one it is a happy ending for this truly brilliant little company . . . they have wooed and won the theatre public of North Staffordshire."

The *Guardian* praised the young actors for their enthusiasm and sense of timing. This cup of tea was very much a brew for Newcastle. The day after their four-week run Charles Lister sent a progress report to Jo Hodgkinson who was keenly interested to have confirmed what he had been told:

> Newcastle is easily the most promising place we have visited. It is worth more our labours than Scarborough - where we are extension of the public shelter system - or Leicester, where . . . the committee really is a group of wafflers."[3]

"A great hulking brute flung himself by my side on my bus yesterday morning. It was Stephen Joseph on his way to give me a report about his company." For the moment Jo was feeling pleased. Writing to Lister he commented, "Stephen tells me that you have been talking about the possibility of further visits and of creating a more permanent auditorium for the company in a year's time . . ."[4]

Their second season of plays was more eclectic but revived the excitement of the first. Newcastle gripped the edge of its seat for Campton's stage adaptation of *Frankenstein* in *Gift of Fire*. The season had doubled in length and *The Evening Sentinel* expressed surprise that the acting worked, particularly William Elmhirst, Barry Boys and Dona Martyn. She was in her second season with the company and a great favourite of Stephen's as an actress, one who "radiates sex-appeal through a paper bag." She used to go off privately to meditate, and on one memorable occasion she chose a quiet room in which to lie in the dark. When he switched the lights on in his Parlour, the Mayor was surprised to discover a naked actress lying on the floor.

Once again reviewers commented on the brilliant lighting plot in Stephen's productions. They also thought Campton's *Lunatic View* the maddest, most original piece of theatre ever seen in North Staffordshire. Its dialogue crackling with non-sequiturs and mutual incomprehension, its dark humour presaging a group of plays which came to be generically known as comedies of menace.

Then, with Ayckbourn out of the company, ostensibly to do his National Service, Stephen presented Barry Boys in the role Ayckbourn had written for himself, as *The Square Cat*. 'This is a lightweight evening which will please most light weight playgoers."

After five years in Scarborough and two in Newcastle under Lyme both towns were now discussing permanent plans. "I think the (Scarborough) corporation would be prepared to consider a theatre in the round, incorporated in the proposed new civic centre . . . I am suggesting (to Newcastle) something similar to the Scarborough one," Stephen wrote to Jo.

Stephen pointed out that for only an extra penny on the Rates, each town might have a custom built theatre. Local government had the powers to levy up to five pence in the pound for cultural use, but none did so. At that time Britain was almost bottom of the league table for public spending on the arts - 0.575 pence per head of population. Even Turkey spent 0.9 where spending in France was 2.6, in Finland 4.3 and in East Germany 12.6p. He planned to call such a building The Penny Theatre and Charles Lister was discussing possible sites for a new building.

A year later, as the company opened their third season of plays at the Municipal Hall, the *Guardian* announced that the Newcastle under Lyme Town Council was prepared to spend £40,000 towards the cost of the first civic Theatre in the Round in the country.

One of the plays the company brought with them was *Four Minute Warning*, the latest David Campton collection. In the previous Newcastle season Stephen had been disturbed by Barry Boys' physical beauty. At breakfast one morning he had said to Campton, "Write me a play in which Barry Boys is ugly." Then as an afterthought, had added, "Make him a woman, too." So came into being *Little Brother Little Sister*, perhaps his most provocative play, but Boys had left the company before it went on..

After the first company read-through Stephen took the script, and spent five minutes looking at it, after which he took the actors through it, making heavy cuts which must have removed a third of its playing time, to the groans of the actors who saw their parts diminish. His editing was impeccable. It became one of Campton's most popular plays and the *Manchester Guardian* liked its bitter astringency. So strongly worded was *The Guardian* review that the Home Office sent a Colonel from intelligence to report on its seditious nature. Subversion was afoot elsewhere also.

It became apparent that not everyone in Newcastle was unanimous about building a theatre. The Chairman of the Finance Committee had recommended the scheme and averted attempts to get it blocked or delayed The council was proposing to sell the valuable Municipal Hall site which boasted not much more than a glorious staircase, as well as the derelict Roxy Cinema. The money raised by these sales and the resultant savings on maintenance could fund the new building, which had grown to be a £99,000 civic go-ahead. They were going to add another hall which could be used for orthodox presentation and Stephen undertook to raise £40,000 in addition.

Stephen's friend from Cambridge, Stephen Garrett ARIBA, was responsible for the design and had prepared sketch drawings. He now threw himself into design modifications, but urged, "Diplomacy. Suggest you are careful to avoid danger of Little Scheme grows into Big Scheme: approval not given: whole scheme dropped. You want a theatre, halls or no halls."

The site in the Brampton Park was to contain three related spaces - the custom built auditorium in-the-round: generous space for refreshments and a second hall, suitable for informal end-staging, cinema, rehearsal and for the use of local amateurs. In addition, good backstage facilities, supplying the needs of a working theatre, construction, storage and maintenance, were to be provided.

This theatre would strive to reflect the tastes and talents of the neighbourhood, not be a second-hand shop window for productions seen to better advantage in London.

> The unique industries of the Potteries, the nearby training colleges and the fresh tradition of Keele University should be influences that will help the theatre develop along individual lines . . . offer entertainment that belongs to its environment. Such a local flavour will not mean that the theatre will only be of interest to a few people; the very fact that the work is original should result in audiences being attracted from a very wide area.[5]

Jo sincerely hoped his Secretary General would warmly recommend the scheme to Lord Kilmaine of the Pilgrim Trust.

> The overall cost figure is not, in our view, unreasonable for a specially designed building of this character . . . (the projected Nottingham theatre was costed at £350,000) . . . Stephen Garrett was appointed architect to the Company some considerable time ago . . . we know him well, and like him, and believe him to be the man for the job . . . We are therefore wholeheartedly behind the whole venture.[6]

Kilmaine reflected he had helped the company with a paltry £900 earlier but would certainly feel justified in putting an appeal for a contribution on a considerable scale before his trustees.[7] Then he read in The Times that Newcastle were making a grant of £99,000 and wrote to Stephen wondering whether a contribution from the Pilgrim Trust was necessary after all.[8] He also wrote to the Arts Council for their guidance.

> True that the Borough Council increased its original vote from £40,000 to £99,000 for this scheme, the reason for the increase is that the Borough Council has decided it would like to attach an Arts Centre to the theatre. They have asked the architect to make substantial enlargement to his plans . . . it will exceed £99,000. Joseph has undertaken to provide the rest by his own efforts. Already a promise of £5,000 from the Elmhirsts . . . (We) suggest you defer a decision . . . and make your contribution, if your trust is so inclined, towards the final gap, if any.[9]

By any standards this was a low down stab in the back. Jo had negated the £40,000 Stephen had publicly promised to raise (without naming them) from the Pilgrim Trust.

No fight is won without skirmish. Alan Iliffe was Chairman of the North Staffordshire Drama Association. He wrote twice to the Town Clerk expressing his disquiet. There were 33 dramatic societies in the area who were, it seems, disappointed and alarmed that the council was proposing a theatre for the exclusive use of Theatre in the Round. He foresaw difficulties of drawing an all year audience and fighting his corner observed that professional theatre was a purely passive recreation whilst amateur companies gave continuous opportunity for active participation.

Stephen carefully drafted the Town Clerk's reply. He pointed out that no irrevocable decisions had been taken. He drew Iliffe's attention to the secondary hall which would be suitable for and available to amateurs, its purpose being to fulfil the function at that time served by the Municipal Hall. Considering that the cost of building a theatre in Germany was £2000 per seat, Newcastle was getting a bargain. By holding 1,000 people between the two halls it ought to be costing more than two million pounds. Many amateur companies were assisting professional theatre and vice versa, and it was to obviate such criticism that the Town Council had embarked on an enlarged project.

Margaret Rawlings was delighted with the scheme and wrote promising a donation when the time came, but six months later she returned, this time to the attack after she had seen his estimated figures and wrote: "I see that your leading actresses are to be paid nearly £3 less than your leading actors. This is something I personally and Equity can never agree with..."[10]

Another lady who was not pleased was a Mrs Gartside who had done much, and let everyone know it, to assist Stephen in his first seasons in the town. Stephen visited her diplomatically to thank her for what she had achieved and, in view of the time she had been involved, to let her know he would try to do without her services that year. When she arrived at the theatre early to bend Jo's ear, she was furious to find herself uninvited to a Civic Reception. Her two page letter of complaint mirrored much of Iliffe's concern, and Jo begged her to stay calm and sane, and offered to come and talk to her federation later on.

The Times special reporter commented fulsomely on the situation:

> One of Britain's most enterprising and elusive theatre companies may at last be on the point of finding a permanent home . . . The policy of the company has always been extraordinarily adventurous, and they have made rather a speciality of finding their own playwrights . . . If Newcastle manages to capture the Studio Theatre Company for its own it will be singularly fortunate in its choice."

The reporter was reviewing *Four Minute Warning* and commenting on Newcastle's proposed £99,000 building. "Plans have been drawn up, the money is available, and now all that is needed is planning permission."[11]

When the council applied to the appropriate Ministry for formal permission to raise the sum on money by loan, their request was deferred and they were asked to apply again two years later

> The government, which stated earlier this year that it cannot afford to build a National Theatre has announced that instead it will help provincial theatre. Accordingly, when the borough council of Newcastle under Lyme applied to the Minister of Housing and Local Government for permission to raise the capital by loan, in order to build the civic theatre, permission was refused.[12]

> "My own experience of Newcastle under Lyme together with what I know about the Nottingham project" (where his old pal John Neville was in charge) "makes me boil with rage at the behaviour of local councils in relation to theatre. Theatre schemes are used for political manoeuvring, for personal axe-grinding and . . . councils seem absolutely incapable of making any decision unless it also has the power to reverse every decision it makes. "[13]

Stephen proposed to attempt to get the theatre built in Newcastle even though it meant having to deal with people he did not trust and who could not be trusted. He knew the Town Clerk . . . had cavilled that although a site had been earmarked for the building, nothing had been set aside for access to it. "This is real *Alice in Wonderland* stuff."

His comments at the same time on the Scarborough proposal are equally brisk. The council had once again unsurprisingly turned down the idea of permanence. Not, he said, that he expected them to take any useful action:

> However, the local secretary of the British Drama League (Ken Boden) is a man of drive and energy and he's going to try and work towards a sort of civic theatre except that he will build it. The fascinating thing is that the moment he begins to make any real progress and command any public attention from the press; members of the council entertainments committee will rush to jump on the bandwagon. If he builds a theatre they will want all the credit. If he asks for their help now, they will say yes and do nothing.[14]

For the moment there was impasse, but a critical decision Stephen took that summer was to recommend that his company manager seek further experience in a larger organisation. So at the end of the summer Joan Macalpine left and went to work in Leatherhead with Hazel Vincent Wallace, one time founder of the Under 30's Theatre Group. Once she was settled in at Leatherhead, Macalpine introduced in the Round productions in a secondary space there.

Two years before, in 1959, Stephen had received a letter from a young man called Peter Cheeseman who was serving a three year Short Service Commission in the Royal Air Force. He had a B.A. degree and a post graduate Diploma in Education from the University of Sheffield, and some teaching experience. At school he had produced several one act plays and revues and whilst at University he directed Bridie, Priestley, and Tournier as well as the *Electra* of Sophocles and *King Lear*.

In writing, he had introductions from Geoffrey Ost at the Sheffield Playhouse and Professor Empson who had prepared his *Lear* text. Nothing came of his application, but two years later in August 1961 he resigned as the then Manager of Derby Playhouse and wrote to Stephen again. They met. Stephen pointed out that he could only offer £10 per week in a company not in continuous operation. He expected his manager to do the unusual for his position, from cleaning ashtrays to driving a three ton lorry. As for his directing, Stephen wrote to him:

> I am trying very hard to develop a particular attitude to presentation where the emphasis is put on creative acting. I like the producer to encourage the actors as imaginative workmen, doing a job in which each must be sensitive to his own role and also to the role of the other actors . . . I like to try and think of rehearsal time as practice time when a number of possibilities can be allowed for, final choice being taken by the actors in the face of the audience . . . this is the creative moment that the audience recognises as more exciting than anything in film or TV . . . The main attraction of this job might be the real scope for someone who wants a considerable degree of freedom and plenty of responsibility. The main limitations are financial and the dogma arising from my own personal vision of what I want the company to be"[15]

After the meeting Peter Cheeseman was engaged to start work in September. Stephen was particularly concerned that he help to build up audiences in Scarborough, Newcastle and elsewhere, repeating "I also hope you will help me in the business of getting a permanent theatre built in Newcastle and possibly Scarborough as well." The threat of £10 per week was a good way of frightening off all but the dedicated or determined, and in fact the salary was fixed at £15 and the engagement as a years work.

Chapter Twenty Four

The Potteries

Even before application had been made to the Government for loan sanction Newcastle Borough Council were beginning to hedge around its commitment to the new theatre by suggesting it would give a New Theatre Trust £20,000 subject to loan permission after that Trust had themselves raised £40,000.[1] The situation seemed so volatile that Lord Kilmaine again wrote to the Secretary General wondering whether the company should not just stick to touring. The poor man had got quite the wrong end of the stick and thought Theatre in the Round meant travelling around the country.[2]

Stephen's analysis appears to have been based on a correct assessment – some people were out to scuttle the scheme. He began to give his mind to converting a building in Newcastle where the company might establish a permanent presence, pending the new theatre being built.

Linklater in an Arts Council memo informed the Secretary General that the Town Clerk was stating that his council had never made an offer of £99,000, even though the sum had been made public and never denied.[3] The Arts Council were not inclined to recommend that the Pilgrim Trust support an appeal towards a converted building. One has to assume that the recommendation of the Secretary General was made after consultation with Jo Hodgkinson. Jo wanted a new building, or no Theatre in the Round. One can sympathise with the opinion of Lord Kilmaine. The Newcastle Council had led the theatre people up the garden path by giving the impression that they were prepared to foot the bill.[4]

Now Cheeseman came into his own. His original contract with the Studio Theatre finished at an end in March. There was enough time for him to assess alternative plans. By June he had found and Stephen agreed on, a suitable building, so Stephen must have agreed to extend his contract also. The building Cheeseman found already had a lessor but one who had gone bankrupt and the owner wanted to sell the building. It was also not in Newcastle, but a mere quarter of a mile away, however, technically in Stoke on Trent. Stephen felt he was at a crossroads. "A theatre of our own, temporary or permanent, has now become so important to me that either we get it . . . or I propose to abandon the company altogether . . ."[5]

It was no doubt intended to force the Arts Council's hand, and it was a miscalculation. Jo was going to offer no money with which to convert a temporary building, even though the idea of a permanent one a quarter of a mile away was fast becoming no more than a pipe-dream. By the end of June Stephen had instructed solicitors to proceed with the assignation of the lease of the Victoria Theatre.

In between negotiations and fund raising Stephen took advantage of an offer of a Fellowship in the new Drama Department at Manchester University. It may have influenced Jo's decision not to give any money to the Stoke venture, because he confessed to Stephen that he had known of the application and supported it:

> I have done this with enthusiasm because I think you are just the person who ought to be there, not that I want to push you into an academic backwater, far from it. But I do know how much tortuous frustration you have endured in the last few months and I do not see why it should go on. [6]

To the author they seem like crocodile tears. Jo would have been happy for Theatre in the Round to close down. After his eight years of running makeshift theatre it cannot only have been Cheeseman's enthusiasm at finding the Victoria which convinced Stephen to go ahead. He had always been determined to take whatever steps necessary to set down a permanent base. There have been many exemplary companies who toured Britain and Ireland under varying conditions, but to achieve his mission required the strength which comes with establishment.

His conviction that Newcastle would build the Brampton Theatre once it saw the fruits of success in Stoke was at this remove flawed, but at the time it was possible to believe as he put it, that "They will only back a winner which has actually won the race."[7]

By the end of July 1962 Charles Lister was of the opinion that the Newcastle scheme was as good as dead. Local amateur opposition had killed the goose even before it had started laying. Iliffe's arguments were unsound: as he correctly pointed out, amateur drama is a participatory activity. What he failed to observe is that amateur actors are not well known for their support of professional repertory. The chairman of the Finance Committee put it bluntly if blindly, saying "there is little support for the theatre from quarters where one would expect to find it - local amateurs. . ."[8] There can be no doubt that success breeds success, and that by killing the professional option the amateurs diminished their own chances.

At the beginning of August Cheeseman was announcing a rough and ready ceremony in the Victoria. The Mayors of Stoke and Hanley were invited, as well as representatives from other charities and the Arts Council. The occasion was to receive a cheque of £700 from the Midland Executive of *ABC Television* towards the cost of conversion. Significantly the Mayor of Newcastle was not on the guest list.

Newcastle under Lyme had been toying with the idea of a theatre since 1945 and as the *Guardian* naughtily expressed it, there had been little to show but the same good intentions in new clothes.[9] Stephen was committed to proving that Theatre in the Round was the mentally extending avenue along which the drama must advance in the sixties. He was trying to raise £5,000 to convert the premises and needed a further £5,000 to complete the conversion a year down the line.

The opening of the Victoria was fixed as the 9th of October, and Stephen expected the Arts Council to contribute the £10,000 they had earmarked for the Newcastle project, but wily as ever, they were not going to part with the money, because the Brampton scheme was not yet, technically, dead. It was clear that the 'Vic' would have to look to itself.

The Arts Council was not among the listed sixty six donors who helped to make possible getting the theatre conversion off the ground. Past company members were in evidence, the most high profile being William Elmhirst and Margaret Rawlings. *ABC TV* and *Granada TV*, faculty members, Merseyside Unity and Keele Players, all contributed to the successful raising of £5,000. As Stephen noted in his release, "We cannot consider the Victoria Theatre now as an interim project, but must look upon it as the actual theatre that must serve the Potteries for as long as possible:

> This is a brave attempt to set forth bravely a story about which there are bound to be misgivings . . . The Studio Theatre company has been presenting plays at the municipal hall . . . these productions have been outstandingly successful, because the company is still going - although it has never been anything so deliriously triumphant as a black entry on the balance sheet."

The Vic opened on the 9th of October with *The Birds and the Well-wishers* by W F Norfolk. At a press party after the first night, Stanley Page, the oldest member of the company had to shake hands with the youngest supporter. He was suddenly conscious of Stephen in the background, alone and totally ignored.

The press and supporters were surrounding Cheeseman, whose opening production it was. Stephen Joseph had struggled, starved, done menial labour to pay the bills through ten years of pioneering for this moment, and was now ignored and overlooked. He gave Page one of his wry smiles, said "It's a funny old world," and left the foyer. His creation had been taken from him. He was little more than a name.

Reporting on the company six weeks later, Linklater thought it stronger that it had been before although there were one or two less than adequate performances and no outstanding ones. What was more, although it was playing to 30% audiences, it did not look likely that it would improve upon that - at least in the short term.

> There is in fact, a first class financial crisis here, partly because the Gulbenkian will not allow them to use the £2,000 offered for touring and hasn't even given them the money yet, which they had hoped to use as security against a bank overdraft."[10]

Linklater correctly assessed the need to get local directors onto the Board of the company. "It is going to be difficult to persuade University and other local people to fight for, and really care about, its future unless they are involved in it," he observed. It was a subject he felt should be discussed, but of discussions there are no notes, and nor is there any suggestion, anywhere, that the proposition was put to Stephen.

Joseph was still the name to be reckoned with. It was upon his reputation that funds were made available to convert the Victoria Theatre. As Chairman this was still his company, one he was responsible for, had steered this far, and until or unless a local Trust was formed to take over from Studio Theatre, it was Stephen Joseph and his Directors who were responsible to the Arts Council and for its debts and liabilities. Not his company's employees.

Chapter Twenty Five

Catching On

Within three months of the Victoria opening in Stoke on Trent, the Traverse Theatre was opened in Edinburgh by a man who had, until shortly before, been Stephen's stage manager. Through two years, until the spring of 1962, Terry Lane stage-managed two summer seasons and two winter tours.

He had assisted Stephen on his production of *Victoria Regina*, his chief recollection of which was having to make artificial primroses for the Disraeli scene *His Favourite Flower*. He then directed *A Stranger in the Family*, and at the end of the 1962 winter tour left Stephen's company and went back reluctantly but inspired, into mainstream theatre in Pitlochry.

With that company was an actor called John Malcolm, who left Pitlochry mid-season, and found himself in Edinburgh, performing to superb reviews on The Fringe during the Festival. In mid-September Lane received a phone call from Malcolm, who had heard of a building in Edinburgh which was free and would make a good theatre. The two men met in Glasgow where Malcolm was working at the Citizens, and together with Rosamund Dickson, who was also in the Pitlochry company, drove through to Edinburgh to look at 15 James Court. The building was the property of Tom Mitchell, a man who owned half of Workington according to the local telephone operator of the day.

There was no one about when the three went to look at the building, but the property was unsecured so they gained access at the push of a door to what became the Traverse Theatre, a room sixty feet by fourteen, with an equal sized area immediately above, and with a part sunken half basement below.

Lane was a practical man, had experience of carpentry, and had helped Stephen re-structure his old house in Scarborough. He had studied art and also had experience of technical drawings and of laying out stage sets, so taking measurements and making ground plans came easily. John Malcolm wanted to start a theatre and wanted Lane to join him in the enterprise.

The three parted with a promise that Lane would prepare plans and send them to Malcolm. There were two weeks remaining of the Pitlochry season, and with the example of Theatre in the Round and the intimacy of Pitlochry as his inspiration he drew up plans for a stage which crossed the centre of the auditorium. A stage which traversed the room.

It was not a large room, and this was to be a professional company. Having chatted with Kenneth Ireland in Pitlochry and seen what profits were available from the sale of good meals, he prescribed a manifesto which demanded the use of the whole building, the basement as dressing rooms, the first floor as auditorium, and the room above as restaurant. With the example of touring in the round, and P.B.s coffee and cakes he had enough experience both to know what was required and how to go about it. So they did.

At the end of the Pitlochry season he returned to London and within a week had a telegram from Malcolm calling him back to Scotland. He arrived mid October and they set on the 2nd of January, 1963 as their opening date. They met for the first time the landlord, Tom Mitchell, who was a willing benefactor in all but cash. These two young men were keen, dedicated, appeared to him to know what they were about, and he left them alone to get on with it. It was not quite what either had expected. Both had assumed, or blindly hoped, he would help with the cost, but when the subject was broached he merely said, "If you want a can of paint or such, let me know and I'll see."

So they got on with it. Malcolm was going to act and do some productions, Lane direct and stage manage. They acquired wood from a woodyard in Leith on extended credit and Lane set to and built seating ramps. They ordered spotlights, cable and dimmers from Strand Electric and Lane wired them up following his experience with Stephen. Malcolm found and was given tip-up seats from a disussed cinema opposite John Knox house in the Royal Mile, and together they liaised with the local authorities, (Police, Fire, etc).

From the fireman they discovered they could not open a theatre in those premises! There were inadequate exit facilities. Bye-laws did not extend to a club operation, however, but from the police they discovered they could not set up a club. In England you could have Proprietorial Clubs and Private Members Clubs. Not in Scotland. In Edinburgh they would have to establish a Private Members Club. So they did. There was no alternative.

There were advantages to running a club. Neither of these men had means, they were establishing a theatre without any money or backing and being, some would say, reckless, when they ordered equipment with no obvious means of paying for it. By setting up a club, with membership pegged at one guinea, the members' subscriptions would 'pay' for the cost of the operation. They were optimists!

The manner in which they gathered their committee of management and the first year of operation has been set out elsewhere by Terry Lane, it only remains in this context to show that the theatre opened on the 2nd of January, 1963, almost exactly three months after the Victoria Theatre in Stoke on Trent. Both theatres came into being as a direct result of the inspiration of Stephen Joseph. If the Traverse attracted more attention in its first year than the 'Vic' did that was partly due to a sensational stabbing accident on the second night, but also no more than might be expected from a new venture in the premier Festival city of Europe, Scotlands' Athens of the North: Edinburgh.

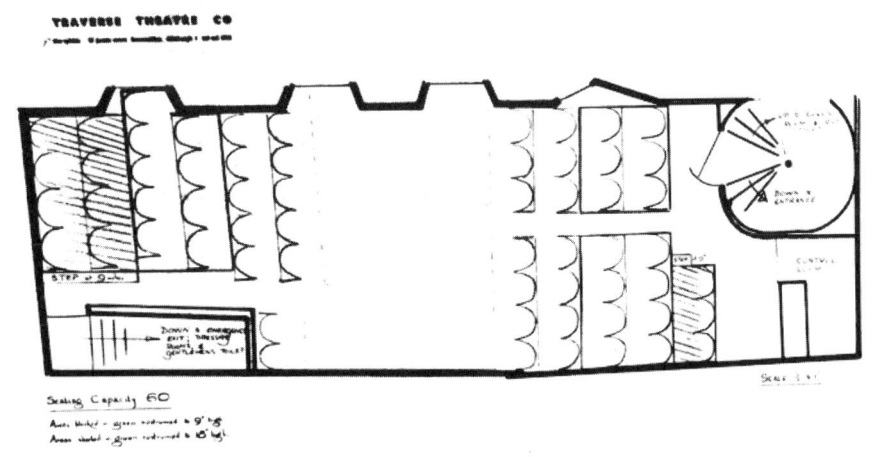

Original plan (1962) - Terry Lane

By getting the right publicity, pursuing a deliberately high profile policy, by luck and the right direction, the theatre made respectable and raised the profile of experimental alternative theatre. Both theatres have survived the test of time. In Edinburgh political chicanery got rid of Malcolm after two months and Lane after little more than a year. In Stoke on Trent something similar got rid of Stephen, but it was to take four years.

It was clear that the Arts Council were not going to fund Stoke on Trent to anything like what was needed so Scarborough became a political pawn. Stoke needed all the money it could get, so the Scarborough seasons became play safe under new management. In 1963 they received no Arts Council support. Stephen had written to Jo warning him that without more resources the Studio Theatre would have to abandon Scarborough in order to keep Stoke afloat. Jo was unmoved, only expressing his sorrow that the company had had to take this disappointing and disquieting step.[1] He must have had a moment's grace when he thought he had heard the last of the town.

When Campton wrote four days later under a new company banner as Theatre in the Round Ltd asking for an Arts Council grant, Jo checked the move by saying they had applied too late and his committee had turned the application down flat. Suddenly, after eight years of assisting Scarborough, he was suggesting to Campton that this was a case where the local authority should be entirely assisting the funding of the season.[2] Campton was at least able to shame face the Arts Council by pointing out that the Limited company had been formed six years earlier, even if it had not as yet functioned.[3]

Campton directed the 1963 season in Scarborough, the year after Stoke opened, with a balanced mixture of West End and avant-garde plays. An old collegiate friend of Stephen's from Iowa, Lewin Goff, was in Europe and directed *Affairs of State*, a play he described as a travesty of American politics.

Stephen directed two Strindberg plays, under the generic title of *Beasts*, in a production the *Scarborough Evening News* considered masterly and staggering, a presentation of brilliant theatre at its best, the kind of observation which puts lie to those who protest he was not a good director. He also did Campton's new play *Comeback*. It was a play he privately considered "stretched so far as to be weak, but the dialogue and characters better than most." Under his direction it not only proved to be a smash hit production but also one on which Donald Albery bought a West End option.

At the end of the season he produced a Confidential memo assessing the situation and wondered whether the 1963 season would be the last. It is difficult not to read the Memo as other than political manoeuvring. In 1962 Stephen sold the lease of his London flat to Robert Fyfe and bought an old rectory in Scarborough. He had asked d'Arcy to buy half the house with him, but d'Arcy was advised that half ownership would present problems so declined. The house was, therefore a major gamble for Stephen. It is difficult to believe he would have given up Scarborough altogether, but it was clearly going to be a fight to the death.

An analysis of the figures shows that the '63 season only broke even by several members of the company waiving wages due to them, David Jarrett, David Campton, Stephen himself, Ken Boden and Lewin Goff; sums ranging from £30 to £280. These fees were added to charges waived by Studio Theatre for the hire of equipment, so it is possible to construe the figures as a manoeuvre ploy, and why not? In commerce the movement of capital between companies is not at all unusual.

In October '63 the local authority had already guaranteed a figure of £575, for the following year, when Linklater wrote that a special meeting of the Drama Panel sub-committee had met and decided the company needed £1500 to see them through the 1964 season. His sub-committee, having agreed to that necessity, would provide half the figure provided the Library committee matched it.[4] For the moment they had been check-mated, and it was no wonder that Stephen began to realise the duplicity of friends in high places! It is perhaps significant that Jo was ill at the end of the summer.

With Campton's experience of business law, it was clearly going to be necessary to start another game of chess. So for 1964 the management was transformed into the Scarborough Theatre Trust, with local trustees the most important of whom was Ken Boden. Maurice Plows, an interested and keen bank manager in the town was another, and Alfred Bradley, head of radio drama for the BBC in Leeds joined Campton and Joseph. These Trustees set-to to mastermind the seasons.

The formation of the trust was not just a sound political move, it was a recognition of Ken Boden's work with the company. As the local paper put it:

> he is possibly the most active man in Scarborough so far as drama is concerned... secretary of the local branch of the British Drama League and has helped with the running of the professional company since they first started coming to The Library.[5]

They had a rush to get the company registered as a charity in time, and the season had opened before the Trust was fully established. "We want to make the future of Theatre in the Round more secure in Scarborough and we see this as one way of doing it," reported the *Scarborough Evening News*.[6]

Stephen was not only working full time at Manchester, these were years when he also wrote several books on theatre, so when he learned that Terry Lane had been squeezed out of Edinburgh he offered him the 1964 season to direct. He himself wanted to be responsible only for the new Campton play. Ken Boden was being a cornerstone to the company. He had a scheme to sell 'bricks' at one shilling a time in the foyer at the library. In fact he had organised 130 enthusiasts to sell them all over Scarborough, in his efforts to turn a pipe dream into a reality. He said, "The dream to build a new £50,000 theatre in Scarborough seems to get more tangible every day . . ."[7]

Stephen had prepared another plan, which was on view, to give the town a revolutionary theatre at the British Drama League bargain price of £50,000. It would come close to his fish and chip theatre which he had talked to the papers about the previous year. One of the main features of the theatre would be a long coffee bar, with a glass wall overlooking the auditorium, with relayed sound. Boden was quoted as expecting it to take ten years before the project got off the ground,[8] but only a week later the newspaper was wondering if the company would be back the following year.

That Stephen was losing patience, both with the Arts Council and the town council cannot be doubted. The cause of this will be made clear by examining the Arts Council attitude in Stoke on Trent in the next chapter.

The Library's committee would never commit themselves more than a few months in advance, and the Chairman would not guarantee the committee to take action the following year, or the year after. It is difficult not to believe that if Mr. Edwards had been more positive, so would his committee have been.

> It would be easy enough to over-estimate the value of this particular form of theatre. . . but at the same time it would be just as easy to underrate it. This season for instance has given the best play of any produced in the town in the form of *The Tiger and the Horse* - if you missed it you missed a wonderful experience... (the Library theatre) deserves a secured future.[9]

Stephen was never to find that security, as his letter to Campton indicates.

> Splendid idiocy in Scarborough. They won't pay more than the Arts Council has paid. So of over £570 to come they will only give us £375 at present. I have written the rudest letter ever to the Borough Treasurer. Don't be surprised if our next summer season is in Lowestoft.[10]

Perhaps prudence is the order of the day in public finance, but it hardly makes for adventurous planning, or expansion where public performance is concerned. What is more they only gave the money once the season was over and had been audited - in today's climate the interest on the overdraft alone would make such a working process inoperable.

Chapter Twenty Six

The Fellow

After the heartbreak of the Newcastle under Lyme project Stephen turned his attention to teaching. It was not a sudden or unconsidered option.

We have seen the zest with which he threw himself into the impoverished academic scene in Iowa. He had often made suggestions to improve the curriculum at Central School and to tie it more closely to the University of London. Introducing him to readers in 1955, the editors of *Encore* described his hobby as theatre and his hobby-horse as University Drama departments

In the late '50s, in a speech to the Institute of Advanced Architects, Stephen said "the study of drama at a university should not be conducted as a vocational training; the drama presents opportunities for learning and learning is in itself a preparation for life."[1]

His playwriting courses did not finish when he left The Hall, rather they continued elsewhere - for the Wansfell Playwriting course in New Wanstead, with the British Drama League in London, and over several seasons at Wrea Head in Scarborough. His lecturing activity was prodigious.

Realistically assessing the possibility that he might never achieve his objective in Britain, he made several attempts to find a teaching position in an American University Drama department. Then whilst the Newcastle saga was dragging its heels he happened to be at a function, one of whose diners was Hugh Hunt. Hunt had the Chair of Drama in the newly established department in Manchester. He was looking for someone to take on a Fellowship and offered Stephen the job. Of the other applicants Hunt had considered for the post, he remarked that he might just have taken on a few of them as students.[2]

Hunt had directed at the Maddermarket in Norwich and the Abbey Theatre in Dublin. He had a varied wartime career, in the Guards, the Royal Rifle Corps and Intelligence. He had spent five years in Bristol as the first director of the Bristol Old Vic, then another five with the Old Vic in London. He took the company from its wartime quarters at the New Theatre back into the newly reopened Waterloo Road premises. His career seems to have run in five year cycles, for that is the time he spent as the founder director of the Elizabethan Theatre Trust in Sydney. He was as much a pioneer in his own way as was his brother, the mountaineer who first scaled Everest.

He was a shy and austere man, who rarely smiled.[3] In 1961 he became Professor of Drama at Manchester University, a position founded and funded by Sydney Bernstein of *Granada Television* whose studios were in the city. It was only the second British University to establish a Drama department and the only one to offer a BA solely in Drama. There was an informality between teacher and pupil - almost a kibbutz atmosphere - envied by other departments.[4]

One of the conditions of its foundation was the establishment of a Fellowship to give a working practitioner from the theatre a sabbatical year to teach and study.[5] Hunt had been given the job of supervising the rebuilding of the University Theatre and wanted a Fellow who could be on the spot to advise on day to day matters. Therefore Stephen had little to do with under-graduates in his Fellowship year.

Hunt, a product of Marlborough and Magdalen, a methodical and conservative man[6] lacking personal charisma, clearly recognised his talents were as an adept Colonial Administrator[7] but understood the need for flamboyance in the department. Perhaps he even came to feel peeved that his staff were more highly prized by the undergraduates than he. When John Heilpern wrote an article on the Department for *The Observer* it was Stephen and his students who were photographed. (They were astonished when he entered for the press wearing a tie, gown and mortar board instead of his viyella shirt, policeman's trousers and thick belt.)

Hunt never considered himself an educational theorist, but gathered round him distinguished minds and practitioners, who could argue, research and teach theatre in ways which he seldom seemed to really understand or agree with. Stephen once remarked that Hunt was the sort of officer type who might say "Follow me men," and they would![8] Hunt echoed Stephen's opinion on the future of drama within a university, saying "Drama isn't only a discipline of the head, but of the heart and body. The trouble with drama schools is that they starve the intellect . . . we try to enrich people's lives."[9]

Since their credo for being was so similar Hunt and Stephen should have got on well, and often did, but they also had violent disagreements. In fact both men were shy and socially inadequate, but Stephen was the more articulate. Hunt had a distinguished directorial portmanteau and was in authority, but he really wasn't an authority.[10]

He considered that the function of the Drama Department was to provide an intelligent audience for the future. The idea that they might do their own plays, write them or produce them had not occurred to him.[11] In the past Stephen had been openly critical of the moribund productions at the Old Vic, criticism of which Hunt was presumably aware. It led to an uneasy truce between the two, with some occasional contempt.

Stephen's habit of putting an arm around a person while he spoke to them upset Hunt, who was an old fashioned patronage figure. He felt safe in an ordered environment, worked everything out on paper in advance, and to the derision of many students, would bring out his chess set, and demonstrate how to map out a production by using chess men. Stephen used to say that a good director was someone who knew how to make a cup of tea. [12] He liked the Diploma course to have rough edges, and rough edges embarrassed Hunt.

With his wicked sense of humour he often egged on or abetted student pranks. One was to lock the two doors to Hunt's office from the outside whilst Hunt was within. Another was to brief two students to ask irritating questions when Peter Brook arrived to give a series of lectures, which were later published as *The Empty Space*. Stephen positioned them on either side of Brook in an attempt to phase him. Mike Weller on one side interjected and giggled, while Mike Stott opposite asked about the purgative qualities of Greek tragedy, and how tragedy had declined with the invention of chemical purgatives. (Stephen knew that Brook's family money came from Brook-Lax, medicinal products, used to ensure regular bowel movement.) Amused by the whole thing Brook helped Stott to his first writing job after university with the R.S.C. and wanted to help Weller also.[13]

In Stephen's first year the Department held its second Theatre Week, the theme being *Actor and Architect*. Five or six eminent guest lectures, by people like architect and designer Sean Kenny, author Richard Southern and director Sir Tyrone Guthrie were followed by a Brains Trust. Stephen gathered the lectures and edited them into book form. In the introduction Stephen points out that most of our human nature is stunted, and much of our educational system geared to turning the imaginative human being into a mindless animal.

After his year as a Fellow, Stephen was taken on as a Lecturer, his area of responsibility was to the new Diploma students who were doing post-graduate work. His approach was to small groups taking theatrical adventures. One of his first decisions was to dump institutional furniture. He designed and had made a round table for his room: his stand for equality. In his seminars they were all questing for knowledge and no one appeared to dominate while he got the group of students hammering at arguments which might be philosophical, political, spiritual or whatever.

His reading list for the course ranged over such works as *Myth and Ritual in Dance, Game and Rhyme, The Drama of Savage People, Aristotle's Poetics. The Genesis of Tragedy,* and *The God of the Witches:* quite apart from Toynbee's *History* and *The Golden Bough.*

"No theory could adequately account for the vitality of Aristophanic comedy, the Medieval mysteries, Shakespearean drama or such modern plays as the Brechtian epic and the Theatre of the Absurd . . . a wholly adequate dramaturgical theory must rely . . . essentially . . . on histrionic considerations..."[14]

He wanted to dump much of the syllabus and to make the course become more practical. He never bothered to set essays and some staff felt this disadvantaged the students, but then they had the advantage of him, and anyone who was in his tutorial group was buoyant. He never restricted the time or the subject. It didn't matter to him if they knew anything, it mattered only that they knew how to find out.

As a raw, young, academic lecturer Peter Thomson considered it a unique course with revolutionary potential; an exciting vision in its time and one which could have become a monument, academically, the University equivalent of Neil's *Summerhill*, and it never became thoroughly institutionalised, in part because it too relied on personal charisma, and Stephen did not live long enough to establish its firm foundation. It was doing what a drama school ought to have done, and for a while Sydney Bernstein investigated the idea of establishing an acting school attached to the Drama Department.[15] Stephen had the task of examining what was on offer in other drama schools in Britain, whilst Director Michael Elliot looked at the European method.

It is unclear why Bernstein did not go ahead with the idea, but it was one Stephen approved of. He was also on the lookout for a Drama Chair to be established at York and his ideal would have been to become Professor there. He was never happy with the hard-faced humourlessness of the Mancunian, and found Manchester a dirty, sordid, and uncomfortable city. A foundation in York, with the Scarborough summer seasons nearby, was his pipe-dream.

Stephen was not without his detractors. Politically correct students disliked the fact that he appeared to have no method. They wanted to be told what to think but Stephen had thoroughly absorbed Bernard Shaw's dictum: "what is certain is that if you teach a man anything he will never learn it."[16] Instead he would say, "I don't know - find out for yourself." Nor was he clubbable with them, as were other lecturers. He never joined them in the bar, nor indulged in small talk but would move from abstract philosophy to the practical consideration of the right kind of nail to use in a rostrum.

No other member of staff could cope with the breadth of his response. Tradition frustrated him, but he could wax lyrical about unworkable eighteenth century plays and be enthusiastic about the Hippodrama. He contested that the theatre which did old plays was a museum, not a living theatre. One moment he was behaving as if he was in a late nineteenth century scholarly debating society, and the next he was painting scenery.[17]

Although he believed in the necessity of the war through which he had fought, he was not a combatant in life, not unscrupulous. He preferred to encourage personality growth based on the principles of self discovery, and commended Krishnamurti to his students. He knew that power corrupts and was more concerned to help the development of others' self-awareness than establish himself as a power base. He was provocative and liked being provocative, but not being provoked.

Senior in the department was John Prudhoe. A German scholar, who had very fixed ideas of what theatre was; he loved Germany and Germanic drama: according to Stott *Hannele's Himmelfahrt* was a highlight and he loved a good *Sturm and Drang*. He also published the very worst Goethe translations.[18] He would appear to have indulged in all the decadence one associates with the Third Reich. An overt homosexual queen he was a large man, and into body beautiful, with dyed blond hair and face make-up.

He considered himself the 'academic' lecturer, and as the Senior Lecturer was responsible for the final marking of student results. Prudhoe had rather shocked Stephen by remarking that he had all his next year's lectures written, when Stephen seldom knew what his lecture was going to be about until he started to give it.[19]

The academic world tends to cover its inadequacies and anxieties by sounding very bitter and being extremely aggressive. In staff meetings therefore Stephen was laid back. "I don't know why we study plays at all!" he would say, "Anyone can read plays." He considered they should be doing things the students couldn't do. "We should be looking at anthropology, at architecture, history, sociology."

Or while staff were jointly agonising over degree results, "Why don't we post the results first, and then invite those who disagree with our assessment to sit the exam . . . ?"

To the young lecturer it was totally sensible, but to Prudhoe the class system was meat and drink and he enjoyed the power of the marking system from which Stephen shrank. Rarely would Stephen cross swords with him even when it would have been to the advantage of one of his prized pupils. At least one student had to go to the professor to complain of a personal vendetta.[20] Peter Thomson asserts that as second marker Stephen left Prudhoe's marks unchanged, however unfair, but on one occasion at least, when Prudhoe reported a student as unsatisfactory, Stephen endorsed him as an excellent one. He also complained in private that Hunt was unaware of the ability of any of the students in his charge.

To be fair, Hunt and Prudhoe had found themselves disadvantaged. They had misunderstood the entry requirements for the course, and admitted students who almost certainly were unqualified and shouldn't have been there. Stott was one such, who realised he had got in on that misunderstanding. Then at the end of the second year the pass marks had to be massaged: it could not have been seen for too many students to fail.

In 1964 Stephen's production of *The Devils* went to a Student Festival in Parma, where it received a riotous reception. On one of their sightseeing trips the local tour guide remembered Prudhoe from the previous year and insisted that he leave the coach before he would set off. It wasn't only Stephen who was offended by the man.

For Stephen the trip was a delight.

> I will try to recollect some thoughts that passed through my mind during part of a bus journey - the part before we sang, memorably at the invitation of the professor, *Land of Hope and Glory* after a surfeit of *Rule Brittania* and muscatel wine.
>
> That visit to the thermal baths was a hint. We mocked the placid patients, breathing in sulphur fumes . . . Later, when we had feasted in an Albergo (where Verdi was born, you know) and then in another Albergo (a superior good pull-up - why are they so awful in England? . . . the AA star system is not bad but doesn't descend low enough to embrace 90% of Britain's eating places), and had sat through (was it marathon *Hamlet*) . . . the hell-like fumes seemed positively inviting.

But I fell in love with a little theatre at Sabbioneta. Influence of Palladio, yes . . . but it was not the influence that struck me so much as the huge originality of the thing. Into this little room had been stacked a complete theatre, completely reflecting its age - influence and unique creative genius combined . . . a superb mixture; three dimensional pillars and painted pillars, statues and drawn figures, perspective contrived in three dimensions and in two. In the Middle Ages the finest achievements of art were gestures in the face of an intractable world. In Italy's renaissance, artists seem to have been capable of creating a world, a magnificent, colourful, deceptive world in which moved princes and courtiers.

Nowadays, no world is safe from the finger that might press a button, and our art is fragmentary and esoteric. If the renaissance world of art omitted the working man, don't kid yourself we're doing much better . . .

Why did I fall for Sabbioneta? Is there some relevance in this theatre for the mid-twentieth century? Or is the appeal simply one of a superb harmony between the theatre and its own age? . . . [21]

One other lecturer in the department caused Stephen to be even more miserable than he was over the financial problems at Stoke. He was a very devious person who had been a monk and enjoyed very intense relationships with students which were about power. Stephen could never cope with that kind of mysterious deviousness because he recognised his inability to deal with scheming people, and it angered him. He was always a pragmatist and recognised when his arguments would fall on stony ground, and that in those circumstances argument was a waste of energy, so he got on with his small groups taking theatrical adventure.

It was typical of him to produce Marlowe in the quatercentenary year of Shakespeare's birth. Stephen's innocence of his effect on people was obvious when in a staff meeting Hunt insisted on a particular piece of casting for *Edward II*. Stephen gave a huge mocking belly-laugh "Oh Hugh, come on, you want to make it 5th rate instead of 6th!" To Stephen, Marlowe was an underrated comedy writer, and he produced his *Edward II* at a furious pace. He forced his students to make their own discoveries. For him actors weren't puppets, destined to obey the director. The director was the guide, someone to pose questions and perhaps open doors in the mind. This production was to be the students' *Edward II*, not Stephen's. Hunt considered the production remarkable.[22]

While rehearsals went on, the Lutheran Church, trapped within a circle of contemporary university buildings, was being converted into a studio for the Drama department. Stephen considered the conversion one of his biggest battles with the authorities, who wanted the studio to have a light, airy atmosphere in keeping with contemporary philosophy - let in all the light you can but be unable to see anything. In this, his studio space, he began and continued to insist on point after point. No windows. this was a workshop. Black walls for concentration on the acting. Adequate lighting grid, and so on. The only concession to public display was to be the performances.

Whereas he fought for the Lutheran Church conversion he merely advised on the University Theatre. There had been a hall on the site belonging to the university, the Arthur Worthington, which was used by various amateur drama groups. It had to come down and so the University Grants Commission had to fund a replacement. These were the days when, whilst the government was concerned about the problem of leisure, it insisted that university theatres had to be funded privately. Where replacements were concerned the rule had to be broken.

In designing the theatre the architects consulted the potential users. The amateur actors wanted a properly equipped stage, and the musical comedy people an orchestra pit. Nobody mentioned dressing rooms, workshop or storage space and then when the drama department was founded no premises were provided. So the Professor of Drama took over the clients' responsibilities and, within a limited budget, Stephen negotiated modifications with the architects. He considered it an administrative triumph, but with reservations.

> . . .the auditorium feels exciting . . . however, most people who come into the theatre are so used to low standards . . . that many of the shortcomings . . . (will) pass unnoticed.[23]

He considered the siting in a little known side street, to be poor, and the booking office so badly placed as to inhibit access to the theatre in the event of a show being a success. The foyer was sizeable but the upstairs bar too small to cope with the demands to be made on it during an interval. Whilst it was possible to get at the stage lights in the grid, once there the technician could not see where or how he was focusing the spotlight; even more wickedly Stephen reckoned that to get the proper proportions on the stage would require, roughly speaking, actors three feet tall. The whole building, whilst not unpleasant, had been sited in a fundamentally dead environment, and looked like a superior bicycle-shed. It was also dwarfed by adjacent buildings ironically housing the Department of Architecture. He was being deliberately provocative in order to encourage debate, and as ever the challenge was not taken up.

For the opening production in the new theatre Stephen delighted the new academic staff member Peter Thomson, not only by having heard of Dion Boucicault, but by proposing *The Shaughraun*. Hunt went along with the suggestion, but the play was too anarchic for him, revolving as it does around a roguish poacher, so suggested Stephen direct it.

Most of the rehearsals were taken by Richard Rothrock but however unwillingly, Stephen's hand on the helm steered the production to a triumphantly comic first night. His observations on direction procedure are illuminating, and perhaps intended as guidelines for Rothrock:

1 Open mind. Don't read the play. Listen to and watch the actors.
2 Independent exercises in physical range control, imaginative expression.
3 Never tell the actor how to say a line, where or how to move. Advise when asked, enlarge don't limit, say it five different ways.
4 Seven full dress rehearsals.

So favourably received was what some considered a creaky old melodrama, that Hunt directed it himself to great acclaim at the Abbey Theatre in Dublin, shortly after Stephen's death. With the RSC revival of *London Assurance* soon after and the publication of two plays by Oxford and three by Dolmen Press, Boucicault had been rediscovered.

> We must re-state the value of practical work . . . If inadequate skills are brought to practical work, the actual phenomenon of theatre will be misunderstood. This is a question of balance, but it is possible that a department of drama will actually allow students to learn entirely erroneously the art they are supposedly studying . . . This does not mean that students have to be *trained* . . . the student who is particularly good at practical work should be given full credit for it.[24]

Stephen had been arguing for some time that drama should be in the faculty of Science because it needed special laboratories, namely studios; . . . because drama and science mean that people do things - experiment, observe, experience. Literature, he insisted, was not enough and drama was more important than universities gave credit for.[25]

It was four years later and Stephen was still having to argue his ground with Hunt. He wrote, "If we accept that the drama course must be academic in (a) limited sense, then let us stop being hypocrites and be consistent - we must abandon *all* practical work." Poor Hunt. He was an academic and answerable to the University for his results. If there was short-sightedness it was in part an the establishment one. Stephen continued

> A performance without proper skills will be academically ... misleading, no more than a bean-feast in the dorm after lights out ... Yet we must remember that universities have allowed courses in chemistry and physics, architecture and medicine, in which practical work is not only done, but is the backbone of the course.

When asking rhetorically, can practical work be examined, his answer was an emphatic yes, and he went on to demonstrate in what way. As his notes on practical work were written in April 1966 while he was on leave from the university, it is likely that they also fell on stony ground, and if the course remained largely text-based, perhaps it was because, as Hunt observed, Stephen had, "That rare skill among theatre practitioners of being able to ally academic work with practical work," He was, in a sense, the error who proved Shaw's rule. He could, and did, and taught.

One of the underdogs of dramatic philosophy whom Stephen championed was a man called Ferdinand Brunetière whose *Law of the Drama* was published in 1893. Stephen first met it in America and maintained that there were few American playwrights who had not been influenced by it. He made his own translation in 1958 and used it as an introduction to a new dramaturgical theory with his diploma students.

Brunetière proposes that when a nation achieves an identifiable will of its own and rejoices in the exercise of power, drama reaches its highest peak and produces masterpieces.

> The amount of *will* measures and determines ... the value of a play ... *will* is king in the world of action, and therefore in history. *Will* gives power, and power is lost only when the *will* loses strength or fails. This is why people admire the rise of a man of *will*, no matter what his objective ... men of action - Richelieu, Conde, Frederick, Napoleon - have always been fond of the theatre.[26]

It is a fascinating contradiction that Stephen Joseph, who so hated power that he declared himself an anarchist, should embrace drama which, according to Brunetière, is about the exercise of power. Brunetière goes on to identify the crisis in the theatre as lying in the decline of *will* . . ."we are becoming weak winded . . . we are allowing ourselves to drift." In the opinion of the author, that was exactly the situation the British theatre was in when Stephen started his Theatre in the Round company in 1955. Successive governments had removed 'will' from people. Faced with the threat of nuclear extinction, nations of people threw away their will, and allowed themselves to drift.

It was against such drift that Stephen championed the nuclear parables of David Campton, and the freedom of expression of his other writers, like Ayckbourn. In Manchester, he championed individualism in theatre. He was not always successful. He quoted one of his failures in a programme note:

> These classes would have been more useful if they had not been so firmly based on a particular and personal conception of theatre. I am disappointed at the lack of progress I have made.

But then immediately afterwards, he was able to quote, also anonymously, a champion:

> Searching improvisations,
> Major talks by J,
> Make our Studio Sessions.
> The week's MOST INSPIRING DAY!
>
> Whether our efforts to use the Studio . . . have been successful remains to be seen. . . it is difficult to judge what we have learnt, we have certainly grown in appreciation of one another, and we have become aware of the need for self-discipline . . . [27]

Stephen had long admired the cycle of Cornish Mystery plays. Joan Macalpine had done a translation of them for him, which he had always hoped would be put on at the Vic in Stoke on Trent. So in 1965 he asked undergraduate Roland Joffe to adapt *Sylvester H'an Drhagon*, a Cornish Interlude often included in the cycle. Joffe directed his own play *How Private Solid Left the Army*, and Stephen, *Sylvester*, in a promenade double-bill production in the Studio.

Joffe was full of ideas for the production, especially the end:

> Which I visualise as a procession, utilising every level of the studio, thereby forming a pattern of colour and movement, the whole thing after all, is very much a dance with words, [28]

surely one of the first experiments in promenade performances to be held in Britain. Stephen hugely admired the students who later performed the play walkabout, in Manchester's Piccadilly, the dragon appearing from the bowels of the earth - in this case the Gents toilet!

Tony Robinson - *Big Soft Nelly*

Chapter Twenty Seven

Trouble Brewing

Stephen had been instrumental in forming the Association of British Theatre Technicians (ABTT) in 1961. A small group including Fred Bentham of Strand Electric, architects Sean Kenny and Peter Moro, and Richard Pilbrow of Theatre Projects were among those inviting attendance to a meeting in March. Stephen gave a talk about the possible aims of such an association; aims which were important enough for Peter Hall to attend the first meeting.

The ABTT wanted to raise levels of awareness, to advocate efficient standards for the planning, building or re-building of theatres, (which had begun), and to stress the importance of the proper installation of stage equipment. The newly formed ABTT then hosted the third biennial congress of the International Association of Theatre Technicians. Fifty-six delegates from 15 countries attended. In the Chair was Norman Marshall, and Peter Hall introduced the conference.

Stephen edited a report of the proceedings in a booklet called *Adaptable Theatres* and thereafter became the editor of the ABTT Bulletin, an eight page news sheet sent to members.[1]

So many poorly designed civic projects were in the offing that two years later Stephen was proposing setting up the Society of Theatre Consultants. Some wondered if there were enough people qualified to advise on all aspects of theatre design. Stephen could see no reason why the Society should be anything other than a success except for two things - "Firstly theatre people seem unwilling to trust each other. Secondly they talk too much."[2] Richard Pilbrow of Theatre Projects wondered "how many more clubs we are going to have to join," but later admitted he had been wrong, and Stephen right.

Actor and Architect, which he edited, was published by the Manchester University presses in 1964. The *Toronto Telegraph*, considered the book a 'time-wasting irrelevance' citing the lecture by Dr. Richard Southern as a supreme parody of how the simplest thing can be complicated if you study it hard enough.[3]

Stephen's *Story of the Playhouse in England* which he also illustrated appeared in 1963. Although Campton is credited, he claims he wrote three quarters of it. Certainly one of Stephen's letters refers to the book they were writing together and it is one which is most fluid and easy to read. The *Guardian* reviewer considered it brilliant, succinct, and well illustrated.[4] The book is dedicated to his last stepmother, Anthea, whose publishing house originally mooted it, before passing it to Barrie and Rockliff.

Together with *Scene Painting and Design* from Pitman the following year, these are two books more or less geared to the institutional market. Stephen's experience as a scenic artist made him eminently suitable to write such a practical work. In the introduction Sean Kenny says it is people like Stephen who give the theatre its life blood and vitality. He comments: "They ask questions - even about the Emperor's new clothes."

Barrie and Rockliff also commissioned him to write *Theatre in the Round* which was published shortly after his death in 1967 and dedicated to William Elmhirst. He was acknowledging a personal friendship as well as gratitude for the Elmhirsts' professional support. In part it is a survey of theatres presenting in the round performance, but is also a sentimental journey in which he recalls some of his favourite performances and incidences in his own company. More importantly it is a practical text for designing, lighting, directing and acting in the round. The section covering these aspects could be published as a manual by itself.

His last book *New Theatre Forms* was also published posthumously in 1968 in Pitmans' Theatre & Stage Series. Written at a time of renaissance in civic interest where theatres were being discussed and designed he points out that when cultural organisations say they can't afford a theatre, what they mean is that they cannot afford a marble monument

> A civic theatre ... is looked on as a trump card in a game between rival communities, and there is a belief that provided the front of the theatre is trumpery no other expenditure need be considered."

As in so many of his observations it is the cry of the worker, not of the people who commission the structure or the architect, who also wants his edifice to be remarkable at street level.

The degree of awareness had been raised, and where local authorities were planning civic theatres, the Arts Council was insisting upon their obtaining advice from the ABTT and the Society of Theatre Consultants before they could be considered for public funding.

Stephen's comments to the research assistant of the *Architects' Journal* ruffled the feathers of one or two important architects who considered his observations discouraging. His opinions on stage lighting are typical:

> I have actually seen a play appallingly lit - and then been told by the producer that they stayed up until 5 a.m. doing it. I could have lit the production in ten minutes - just as inefficiently, and possibly even quite adequately.[5]

For the summer of 1965 Stephen undertook another experiment in marketing his Scarborough company. He took with him three students from Manchester. One was to have been Roland Joffe, but at the last minute he happened to be passing a ship, asked if they needed hands, and signed on then and there. The students' job was firstly to go around the towns' hotels, guest houses, shops and factories, telling people about the theatre and about the plays which were being performed, then to be in the foyer to recognise and greet those people and chat to them. 1965 proved to be the most heavily attended of all his seasons at The Library.

He also staged a play by one of his students, Mike Stott who had stage managed in the university theatre and in the Library, and wrote a play about the First War spy, *Mata Hari*. When he read it, Stephen said, "I'll do it, but there is only one scene it in that works. Do you know which scene that is?" With the title role as bait, he was also able to lure a return to the company of Dona Martyn.

Also returning for the summer were David Jarrett who had been *Hamlet*, Peter King, and Pam Craig whose most recent work had been with Alfred Bradley for BBC Leeds. She had been brought into the company by Terry Lane for whom she worked at the Traverse, and was to work later in Stoke on Trent. Stephen also brought a group of students, some of whom began professional careers that season. Hunt's daughter Caroline was one; as Caroline Bone she later joined Paddy Greene and Pam Craig in *The Archers*. Another was actor Terence Wilton, and also Claire Venables, an undergraduate who gained her degree from Manchester before being taken into the Department as a lecturer. There were those who thought Stephen rather intimidated by her intellect, but if that was so he would hardly have taken her into the company. She certainly felt intimidated by him as box-office assistant.

Alfred Bradley attended most of the seasons in Scarborough as well as allowing students from Manchester to be inducted into broadcasting methods in Leeds.

In 1965 he directed the Scarborough company for the first time, three short plays by Alan Plater, David Mercer and Henry Livings. Eileen Derbyshire appeared in the season as did Livings who discovered the flip side to Stephen's charm and intelligence, which he considered a built-in failure generator:

> The half had been called on the opening night, and the stage director came round to wish us luck and to tell us he was off on the London train for a job interview; he gave us a cheery wave and disappeared into the night before we'd got our mouths to close again. The stand-in to the stage director had got to work the lighting board, and muffed both lighting cues in the first play. She was a charming Cypriot girl who had never worked a lighting board before. I found Stephen in the interval, affable as ever, and told him what I thought of his managerial skills. Next time I saw him, he'd crammed his vast frame into the lighting bridge and was working the lighting plot himself. I suppose he was too nice a man to refuse his Stage Director permission to abandon us, perhaps it never occurred to him that he could refuse.[6]

It was in this season that Ayckbourn's first big success, *Relatively Speaking*, was performed under the title of *Meet my Father*. The Arts Council Drama Assistant who saw the play dismissed it as cliche-ridden.[7] Jo was sending him to build up closer liaison with provincial theatres, and told Stephen, "I should make the most of it if I were you because you have had most to complain about in this respect in the past and by Jove, how you have complained."[8] The Assistant questioned whether Stephen should be the Chairman of the Scarborough Theatre Trust and thought Scarborough's Theatre in the Round very square.

Stephen directed Ayckbourn's play and Campton's *Cock and Bull Story*, together with Stott's *Mata Hari*. But all was not well in Scarborough that season. The library committee had a Concert Hall, an Exhibition Hall and a Council Chamber above the library, which they did nothing with. But neither did they want to have the Theatre in the Round there. It would have been the simplest conversion in history, but Mr Edwards was not Mr Smettem. It would appear he would rather the theatre were elsewhere and those spaces unoccupied.

Equally, local planning restrictions precluded all but a tiny and minimal fascia board on the street outside to attract the theatre going public. Also the Libraries Committee was playing the Arts Council at its own game and voting money provided its sums were matched by the Council, and the company was only able to reclaim losses months after they had been incurred.

Working conditions for Stephen's staff were poor to say the least. After nine years the Libraries Committee agreed to a water heater being fitted over the sink for the actors to wash off their make-up. After ten years P.B. was still having to pack up cups and saucers and take them back to the house to be cleaned. The working conditions for lighting and sound control were primitive. The stage management couldn't see the stage, and the control was up a ladder and over the actors' communal toilet. Stephen now insisted that unless there was a committment by the Library to provide more backup, 1965 would be his last season there.

He had applied to the Arts Council the year before for a grant to tour from Scarborough in the North of England, and Jo was initially sympathetic. That was until the possibility was put to him that Manchester University Theatre might be one of the touring 'dates.' By the middle of August Stephen heard from the Chairman of the Libraries Committee that they would take no action on his request to improve facilities at The Library. He had once again been a pawn in a game, so he announced that after the best attended season ever, his company would not be returning to the Library in 1966.

The management of the New Theatre Cardiff got in touch with him and were keen for him to take his company there as a permanent base. He appears to have seriously considered it as an option; but the New was a touring date with an annual pantomime and therefore a strictly proscenium theatre.

It was not only the Scarborough operation which was in trouble. The Victoria in Stoke opened on a financial time bomb. The Pilgrim Trust were not prepared to help further and business was so poor that an adviser was called in to give *An Assessment of Theatre Publicity* with recommendations for future development. Its author John Bennett met Peter Cheeseman, members of his company, the Editor and two reporters from the *Staffordshire Sentinel*, and questioned approximately 70 residents.

His first observation was that the Theatre frontage was dismal. When he first went there he passed the theatre without noticing it. The newspaper editor thought the theatre would have a hard battle to win an audience in the Potteries. "Several of the plays were for Hampstead but not for Hanley," he wrote. He only saw one of the 75 poster sights in his travels. He went from door to door, talked to all types, but found only one person who liked theatre "up to a point." Typical comments were, "I don't like this long haired stuff," and, "I never go to the pictures." There was no antagonism, only supreme indifference.

He gathered in conversation that Mr Cheeseman did not get on well with Mr Joseph who, he thinks, talks down to him! He made several recommendations, amongst which were the sale of confectionery in the foyer and a theatre Club.

He also noted that the company had a factory liaison scheme for inviting groups of factory workers to see the productions. "The importance of personal attention ... makes them feel warm ... and welcome," he noted.[9]

It was only eleven months before that Stephen had written to Jo that he was lucky to have someone of Cheeseman's enthusiasm to overcome difficulties. Something serious had happened in the interval. In the first place the Arts Council were only prepared to give the theatre £7,000 of the £17,000 it had asked for, less than half the sum it needed to continue. Stephen had agreed, in consultation with Jo, not to approach Stoke or Newcastle authorities until the company had been in operation for a year, and it was only six months down the line. He admitted privately that the Arts Council had not given him the support he had expected.[10]

Ayckbourn wrote the first Christmas show, which played to under 20% capacity, and another play that year did only 13% business. Drastic cuts had to be effected and Cheeseman asked his company to take a wage cut in order to keep going. They didn't heat the theatre either and the actors often had to stand in groups hugging each other to keep warm while awaiting their entrances during the show.[11] By April 1963 Stephen's directors had carefully considered the options and gone along with retrenchment plans. Jo wrote wondering whether he should have a word with Cheeseman.

The company had always been underfunded by the ACGB. In their first operating year their grant was £4,500 - about a third as large as those received by Birmingham or Coventry. Three years later it had risen to £6,400, still no more than a third by comparison, and pitiful when one considers the size and ambition of the company. Then in 1965/66 the ACGB increased their grant to approx. £15,000, but still the company overspent £3,000.

Stephen considered that Cheeseman was driving his company perilously close to bankruptcy, the retrenchment plans of '63/4 only began to be implemented six months later and only affected the actors. Single acting members were working for £9 per week; married actors were supporting their families on £12 per week. Stephen was now wondering whether he had to replace Peter Cheeseman, and asked Ayckbourn to meet him in Scarborough. There he asked him to take over the direction of the company, but Ayckbourn refused. Sensing the atmosphere Cheeseman was keenly interested to know why Ayckbourn had been sent for.[12]

Around this time also Jo sent for Cheeseman to discuss the situation and later wrote that he was taking on far too much work himself in order to save money,[13] but Stephen was not so sure. He pointed out "He has an assistant Manager, two box office people, a secretary and an accountant... I am highly suspicious of this overstaffing . . . Note he also has three producers on the spot."[14]

All the local authorities, trades and business associations were canvassed for support and, typically, it was Newcastle who came up with an offer of £1,000. The Arts Council offered an extra £1,000 also, if, Stoke Council stumped up £2,500. One wonders who was manipulating whom and why, and Cheeseman was complaining to Jo that that year's Arts Council report failed to mention the opening of the theatre or the fact that this was the only provincial company in Britain offering repertoire the whole year round with three weeks rehearsal. He wrote, "There is no question that we will not succeed here eventually, so there is no question in my own mind of giving up."[15] There can no doubt that Cheeseman kept the company going through this period by his own undaunted determination.

Still some of Stephen's friends were worried. Joan Macalpine wrote from Leatherhead:

> "Peter Cheeseman has asked me to go up to Stoke . . . I'm a bit worried lest he take over and you get squeezed out, but I expect I shall be able to sense the current political situation when I'm there. If I can I'll drop the idea that it might be a stroke of genius to persuade you to produce the epic . . ."[16]

Stephen was not invited and it rankled and P.B. fuelled his dissatisfaction by always speaking of Cheeseman 'as that little toad'. He found himself cast in the role of the interfering parent, and unwittingly he played that role.

On visits to the theatre, he was apparently never complimentary about a production, but grumbled of bulbs needing to be replaced, or of dirty cups. After one production he complained that the lighting was too dim, much to Cheeseman's annoyance who had meant it to be. The Lad had taken over the family firm and disliked Dad's criticisms, but Dad was still responsible at the bank! Dad too, was being highly critical of the Lad's achievement.

If Stephen was treating Cheeseman as Michael had treated him, it was because Cheeseman was behaving like a rebel without a cause. Letter after letter reflect Stephen's anxiety that the actors could be paid more if less money was devoted to administration and production. Because Stephen had no family of his own, perhaps he was using Cheeseman as a surrogate son. He wrote to Jo :

> It will be very difficult to turn the Victoria . . . into an entirely conventional theatre . . . but the details are becoming commonplace and a certain devastating excitement has gone.[17]

Alan Ayckbourn - *Victoria Regina*

Johnson Ward Ltd.

Chapter Twenty Eight

The Last War

Perhaps some of the excitement had gone out of Stephen's life also. After ten years slog, of hand to mouth existence he was leading an extremely fulfilled life at the University. He was called in as consultant on both the Leeds Grammar School Theatre and the new Theatre Laboratory at Lancaster University. In 1965 he was engaged by the University of Minnesota to conduct a survey of acting education in the UK, with particular attention to schools outside London, at a fee of $2,375.

His public talks were more than ever immensely stimulating, but, as ever:

> I am sorry you had so flabbergasted the conference that they couldn't even make a stab at shooting down some of the kites, the wit and zest with which you flew them . . . (they) treated you and what you had said so pompously and shabbily. . .[1]

As much as ever he was addressing his letters to Jo almost as to a father confessor :

> Senates of Universities are frightened of including acting as a university discipline. But it is the essence of drama . . . to study acting is not necessarily to train actors . . . God knows the theatre could do with some skilled and knowledgeable actors . . . Last time I went to Stoke I saw some good acting which is more than I had been able to find in half a dozen other theatres . . . the Phoenix at Leicester had a pretty mean lot of conventional pierrots parading as actors - alas the Living Theatre . . . But goody-goody, this is what fills the house! Let's have more awful mediocrity![2]

In the autumn of 1965 he was feeling tired. Early in 1966 he applied to the University to have a year's leave of absence. He wanted to complete work which had been rumbling on for almost ten years towards the Ph.D denied him in Iowa. In March he received £250 from the Arts Council in their scheme honouring

Awards to Living Artists Directors and Others Working in the Theatre.

There had been many times in his life when his digestion was not good. While teaching at the Hall he would often ask the secretary for Milk of Magnesia. A few years later Faynia Jeffery remembers feeding him indigestion tablets all the time and nursing him through an illness in Ashburnham Mansions when P.B. had not been there. She received a 'thank-you' scarf from Hermione. Alan Ayckbourn rounded a corner on his way to the Library one day and came across Stephen doubled up in excruciating agony, and still he ate digestion tablets like sweets.

Jo Hodgkinson's godson, as a guest in the house, would be woken in the night to accompany him on walks along the beach, and one of his undergraduates Sue Meredith walked him up and down the road, holding on to his hand. He squeezed it unbearably hard in an attempt to obviate the pain, and apologised to her, saying, "I don't know about the pain but it's done a lot of good for my street cred walking up and down with you."

On the 2nd of January, 1966 he went into hospital in Manchester. In a letter to Gwynneth he wrote, "the diagnosis cannot be delayed more than another week or so."[3]

Surgeons discovered a malignant tumour on the liver. He kept the information from all but a very few people, but of course Hugh Hunt had to be informed, and it must be assumed that through him to the Arts Council Peter Cheeseman became aware of the illness.

Also alarmed at the prospect of the theatre in The Library closing, Ken Boden contacted Rodney Wood and asked him to run the season in 1966, but when Stephen was asked for his opinion he was discouraging. Therefore Ken mounted a series of amateur productions to keep the theatre open. Wood directed the season, professionally, the following year, but by the end of the summer Stephen was confined to his bed. Hermione arrived at the end of October, ostensibly en route to do a few days filming in Ireland.

She had been no stranger in Stephen's adult life. When he bought his house in Scarborough she sent him £500 towards restoration (she sent the same amount to Leslie). In 1961 Stephen had flown for the day to California where she was to be the subject of *This is Your Life* on television and Stephen thoroughly enjoyed the prospect of a two way crossing within four days, packing nothing but a change of shirt in his briefcase. When he and Leslie appeared she said "You can't be my sons, you're both far too old;" and to an old lover she snapped, "Not a word!"

Mike Stott met her in Manchester when she was touring Britain in *O Dad Poor Dad Momma's Locked you in the Closet and I'm Feeling So Sad* by Arthur Kopit. Stephen was quite scared of her and of Stott, who had seen the show and had not liked it. Stephen advised him to say he hadn't seen it yet, because anything less than lavish praise would be lost on her. Over dinner one evening she launched into deep regrets about the small number of modern plays she'd done . . . most of all she regretted turning down a part in the World premiere of *Waiting for Godot* . . . Stephen, bemused, asked "Which part - *Godot*?" She stared at him and announced, "But of course, my darling! The only part worth having."[4]

At one point in the technical rehearsal the stage management had trouble with some equipment which wasn't working and Hermione said, "Wait till my son comes, he's a genius," and when Stephen arrived they waited to test his brilliance. With considerable embarrassment Stephen went to the plug, checked it, discovered a dead fuse, and was exonerated.[5]

For the performance of *O Dad,* Stephen climbed into a grey striped suit, with a white shirt and tie, and looked very uncomfortable. He had bought half a dozen tickets, Campton and P.B. went, and he invited Peter Thomson and his wife Rita. He was only on a lecturer's salary, but this was his Mum, so they sat in the gallery - front row of course. After the show Hermione insisted on Stephen being photographed with her for the *Daily Express*. "Stephen you must come with me," she cried, and from the dressing room Thomson heard her say "Mother and Child both doing well!"[6]

In Scarborough she was more trouble to P.B. than bedridden Stephen was. He had had his bed moved into the large old rectory drawing room with picture windows across the South Bay. "From my bed I can see the sea and the sunset over Scarborough town. It is a luxury way of being in bed," he wrote to Mrs Aubrey Collin. Hermione had to sleep upstairs and P.B. called on the assistance of several student friends to keep her occupied. Hermione kept having to call the local GP because she was unwell, and then collapsed in the upstairs toilet. She had to be more ill than Stephen. Some thought she could not allow herself to be upstaged, even by her dying son.

Campton escorted her round Rowntrees department store one day while she filled a trolley full of luxuries, but when she got to the check-out to pay, said, "I can get all these things on my account in Harrods," and left the assistants to replace their stock. Sitting over lunch with Chris and Sue Meredith, who had just got married, she bought them 1902 vintage champagne, and one day she inquired, "P.B. dear, this soup, does it come out of a can?" Of course P.B. had done her usual catering with the works, including fresh cream. "Oh really?

Well it tastes good enough to come out of a can," she added.

She was on the telephone often to her doctor in America, and before she left P.B. to finish ministering in peace, she had the latest thinking on cancer prescribed to Stephen in the form of injections of Vitamin B12, and they helped improve his quality of life. But something else gave Stephen the will to live. Public perception. What the Italians call 'bella figura.' One's own good image.

> In spite of the present boom in provincial theatre building indigenous regional drama is still a rarity in Britain, and it is hard to overestimate the importance of those few companies that do manage to reflect the life of the immediate community. One much publicized example is the Edinburgh Traverse, another, which so far has not had the attention it deserves, is the Victoria Theatre...[7]

The 'Vic' was about to receive attention.

Aware that Stephen's situation was pathological, Peter Cheeseman appears to have been concerned to reinforce his own position as the director in Stoke, and of the company Stephen controlled. It was a case of two men with paranoid tendencies mistrusting the motives of the other.

It appears likely that in his manoeuvres Cheeseman had the backing of one or two significant members of Stephen's Board of Management. Gwynneth Thurburn was no timorous lady. She ran Central School for 50 years. She reported that at a Directors' meeting in August 1966, while Stephen was undergoing surgery, Cheeseman threatened to resign if the directors did not give him a place on their board.[8] At the same time two 'local' men were elected to the committee, Roy Shaw of Keele University and Kenneth Cooper, a local businessman. One of the two men even wrote a letter to Hugh Hunt seeking his advice on how to run the Studio Theatre company. Hunt asked Stephen what was going on.

As it happened the election of Shaw and Cooper was illegal within the terms of the company constitution. Neither man owned a share in the company, and anyway their appointment had to be ratified by the Annual General Meeting called for November 1966. Stephen was lying inert one day, having given up the will to fight, when Campton mused, "Of course there is the Proxy Vote."

Stephen showed interest here and David Campton amplified. As a young man he had done a course in company law, so was au-fait with the legal complexities. Cheeseman attended board meetings ex-officio, but the only people allowed to be elected to the Board and to vote were those who owned an 'A' Share in the company. Stephen had been indoctrinated by his father, and in his Articles of Association no one was allowed to hold more than one 'A' share. If he obtained the Proxy votes of his friends, Stephen could outmanoeuvre his other directors and what he perceived as Cheeseman's attempt to gain control of the company.

From that day on he came back to life, and for the next nine months he fired off letters, telephoned, planned and fought with all the vigour he was capable of. In the first place he had the AGM annulled, because not only did he never receive notice of it, when he did his name had been left off the list of Directors. By the time three weeks notice had been given, he'd had time to get his proxies and Campton went to the AGM armed with them.

Two days before the AGM d'Arcy Orders and Stephen Garrett had a meeting with Jo Hodgkinson for an informal discussion. The printed resume of that meeting can be summarised. The Arts Council was satisfied with the work of the company in Stoke, and its grant was in no way dependant on the contribution of either Stephen Joseph or Peter Cheeseman. The Arts Council was opposed to the idea of Cheeseman being on the Board, feeling that a Board should be free to direct the artistic and business management without their decisions being hampered by those officers.

When told bluntly that the AGM would have to decide whether to vote for Joseph or Cheeseman, Jo Hodgkinson said he would wish the AGM to vote for Joseph. Jo went on to say it was a good thing for the Artistic Director to change every few years, adding that "Cheeseman has probably been at Stoke long enough." When asked if it would be easy to find a replacement for Cheeseman, Jo said, "Yes."[9] These were not the answers d'Arcy and Garrett were expecting and in the event Jo's actions belied those answers.

When they realised they had been defeated by Stephen's proxy votes the entire committee resigned. In the words of one of them, Neville Hunnings, "it was as if the whole thing had been orchestrated, the way they all resigned." Hunnings stayed on, and a new Board reassembled. Apart from Hunnings, Jack Clark later agreed to remain. He was chairman of an advertising company in London. The Hon. Anthony Lyttelton also agreed in solidarity to remain for a while, although he was far from well. The other new Directors were Owen Hale, who had been secretary when the company started at the Mahatma Gandhi Hall, Gwynneth Thurburn and David Campton.

In the interval Stephen went over alternatives. He had asked Ayckbourn a year or two before to take control in Stoke, he now asked a contemporary, Teresa Collard, but she wasn't in the business of rocking boats, either. "It would take me nine months to set the company on an even keel," she said to Stephen, and he replied, "Nine months is exactly what a woman needs." She also sought Jo's opinion, and he advised against packing her bags and whizzing up north. He'd monitored the situation, knew that Cheeseman had a great following at the Victoria, and would make a comeback within weeks.[10]

Whilst her story makes good 'copy,' Campton is quite emphatic. Stephen did write to her at Worcester, but his letter was returned unopened, as she had 'gone away.' She never received his offer! What is more Jo's remark that Cheeseman would make a comeback within weeks implies the situation as at February '67 not November '66.

So Stephen approached Oscar Quitak who was married to actress Andre Melley and lived near Primrose Hill. Quitak went to Stoke on Trent but the theatre was dark when he got there. The low red-brick, dank houses all around and the general air of seediness, in addition to the publicity material for a Potteries documentary outside, left him feeling hollow and uninspired.

When a Christmas card from Terry Lane landed on Stephen's bed, he lifted the telephone immediately.

> "I'm getting rid of Peter Cheeseman, and I want you to take over at Stoke."
> "Cheeseman won't go."
> "He'll have to go if I say so. It's my company."

That company had gone through many crises during the four years it had been in existence, and it must be said that its continuation had been achieved against incredible odds by Peter Cheeseman. The Arts Council were happy to have a change, greater fiscal rectitude was looked for, and Stephen wanted his theatre secured. As it was reported to Campton, Jo had told Stephen that Cheeseman ought to go.

If his replies to Orders and Garrett underline that message, the Arts Council archive merely hints at the assertion. There is nothing written, but, as with so much diplomatic activity, what is important is never written down. Terry Lane did not feel any of Ayckbourn's sense of conscience, so far as he was concerned it was Stephen's company, and the job was being offered him.

When he arrived in Stoke one of the first things Lane received was a phone call from Jo. "This is a pathological situation," he said, but to Lane there was a principal involved and pathology had nothing to do with propriety.

News of the dismissal was made public in the papers on the 9th of January, 1967 with Jo Hodgkinson asking everyone to play it cool. But it was front page news in the *Evening Sentinel* that day and the following. Indeed there were few days when the theatre was not leading the news. This scandal of local power politics was bled for all it was worth by the news-hungry local papers. Stephen was reported as saying:

> Cheeseman told me to my face there was not room for him and me in the organisation . . . When I fell ill, Cheeseman told the other directors he would resign instantly unless he was elected to the Board . . . He wanted to take charge, not only of the theatre, but of the Board as well . . .

When in 1966 the Board decided to increase the number of executives along with Arts Council grants, Stephen wanted Cheeseman to continue as Director but to hand administrative (financial) responsibility to a manager. Cheeseman refused to accept that situation and those were the grounds for giving him three months notice of the termination of his contract.

The Arts Council could be decidedly judgemental also and Jo was never sympathetic to what Stephen was trying to achieve with his company, as Ian Curteis has already been quoted as saying. Stephen's preoccupation was financial, and notes in his hand reflect his concern. In the first year average attendance had been only 28% and when Stephen asked Jo for an advance from the following years grant, Jo's answer was an emphatic NO.

The second years estimates show calculations for an estimated 30% audience - only a 2% increase. Over the five years of operations, the company had accumulated losses of £5,000 according to figures drawn up in January 1967, of which £3,250 was lost in 1966 alone. Stephen claimed, and declared himself prepared to prove it in a court of law, that Cheeseman was trying to bankrupt the company. To put it out of existence so he could assume total control of the theatre. Stephen said:

> The revenue account for last year, demonstrates in my opinion nothing less than the embezzlement of public funds . . . throughout the year Cheeseman continually kept accounts and returns from me and deliberately deceived me into supposing (the account) was balancing.[11]

It was to stem the losses that the Board and the Arts Council wanted tighter fiscal control in the theatre. In his public reply on the 16th of January, Cheeseman was quoted as saying :

> I believe that ultimate control by one man at theatre executive level is the only sensible way to run a theatre... And when Mr Joseph proposed that I should be 'Artistic Director' and one of a three man executive, he was not trying to lighten the burden of my work, but only severely limit my authority.

In complaining that Stephen Joseph was a one man director running the theatre at his whim, Cheeseman was overlooking his own statement above, that a theatre should be in the control of one man. In fact both men wanted a board of governors they could control as necessary. By failing to clarify why the two local men could not be on the board, Stephen lost the significant ground of public opinion.

Stephen played every card he was capable of. He circulated the correspondence to every member of parliament, and through his stepmother lobbied Lord Goodman, then Chairman of the ACGB. Cheeseman countered by circulating his version to local politicians and members of the Council of Repertory Theatres. Those members, running their own companies, were only too glad it was not happening to them, and were unlikely to rock any boats. The start of this chapter demonstrates how self interested and self satisfied they were when Stephen addressed them, and how pompously and shabbily they treated him then.

A reporter from *The Guardian* rang in search of copy, and in the middle of a very brief interview, Stephen put down the phone in a state of shock. Commenting on the struggle with Cheeseman the reporter had asked, "What's the point of causing all this trouble when you're dying?"

In all of this public and private parrying of words work had to go on. Lane had inherited a company which was totally hostile to him. In their manner and mockery they behaved no better than children in a playground. Any attempt at reconciliation or understanding was seen as weakness and a weapon, and Cheeseman had to be banned entrance to the theatre, as no doubt he knew he would be. Of course, that was further publicity.

The secretary spent her day typing Cheeseman's letters and the manager his, reporting every move and action. There were demonstrations outside the theatre with placards, and all the time Cheeseman continued to rehearse in the pub and operate from his council house.

A public relations sherry party by the Board of Directors turned into a public demonstration with more placards outside, and a patron, Mrs Katrina Hill, rounded on the directors saying that the storm over the handling of the theatre was a spontaneous reaction by local people who felt something precious was in danger. Some of those present thought the spontaneity rather whipped up. Placards cannot appear spontaneously!

By the 20th of January *The Sentinel* was trying to analyse the situation, having been secretly primed by Campton into the background of the affair. Lane had already announced that he would not alter any of Cheeseman's announced programme. *The Sentinel* reported:

> Mr Lane, virtually outside the crisis, despite being in the middle of it, remains as yet the enigmatic card in the pack.

There were seven weeks to go of repeated repertoire before *Julius Caesar* was scheduled to go on, and *The Sentinel* gave the new man plenty of warning when it reported that the company might refuse to work with him. So, acting upon the suggestion of his wife Ros, he played a trump card, and made contact with someone he had met whilst running the Traverse Theatre.

Iain Cuthbertson agreed to do the production. Not only was 'Big' Iain a tough man, he commanded a great deal of respect theatrically, having directed and acted at the Glasgow Citizens Theatre and the Royal Court Theatre in London. None of Cheeseman's actors were going to pass up the chance of having 'Big' Iain direct them.

A month after the 'sacking,' the Stoke on Trent City Council began considering plans to form a new local charitable trust to negotiate the take-over of the theatre's assets and liabilities. Lane's only companion was a young man who had recently graduated from Manchester, Chris Meredith. He had been one of the students who had corralled Scarborough folk into the Library the previous summer season, and was publicity assistant in charge of public relations. All Lane's telephone conversations were listened into by the secretary; the photo copying machine was used to copy all Cheeseman's press handouts and mailouts. Cheeseman's ex-staff were spending all their spare time working for him, so the business manager and play reader, who happened to be Mrs Cheeseman, were also paid off. More headlines.

Amid the over-current of hysteria, speculation, and fabrication every observation was broadcast and any attempt at discussion useless. On a visit to Scarborough, Lane let Stephen know that, in his opinion, Cheeseman was dug-in for the duration and would never go away, and that in that case he would be happier running the company elsewhere. Whilst disappointed with that analysis, Stephen and Lane began considering other options in the North of England, and planning a new form of theatre – Promenade - which Stephen had experimented with in Manchester.

With the departure of the business manager, Ian Watson, a Diploma student from Manchester joined the payroll to take over that job. Without a clear or firm direction from Jo Hodgkinson it was time to force the hand of the Arts Council. Their commitment after all was to the Studio Theatre company in Stoke on Trent, not to an individual. The the new team announced a three month programme to follow *Julius Caesar*.

Lane discovered that the Edwardian Music Hall star Gertie Gitana had been born in Stoke on Trent. Her lasting fame was as the singer of *Nelly Dean*. In the days before Karaoke everyone in the country knew the words by heart of this, one of the most popular songs ever. Not to be outdone in this theatre of dramatised documentary, he announced a *Victoria Palace of Varieties* in part to celebrate Gertie Gitana and in part to be the theatre's contribution to the Arnold Bennet centenary celebrations. Henry Livings' *Big Soft Nelly* was to open the season followed by a Feydeau farce, *The Birdwatcher*. The last play in the programme was Ibsen's poetic drama, *Brand*. The International Ballet Caravan were booked to play a week.

During a conversation with Gwynneth Thurburn, she said to Lane, "There is a young actor who has just left the school, he might be difficult to cast, but he has a quality . . ." So Tony Robinson joined for the production of *Caesar* and stayed on. Elizabeth Waghorn had been taken on to design and make costumes before anyone bothered to tell the artistic director that Catriona Trevelyan had already been engaged to do so. The two ladies worked well together, in fact they made over fifty costumes for the production in three weeks. Even with some voluntary assistance, that would have been impossible for only one designer.

With the guest director, and the salaries of Lane, Meredith and the extra designer, Caesar finished within budget. When it was announced Cheeseman was reported to have stopped the theatre's book-keeper in the street and asked,"How has he done it?"

> (Iain Cuthbertson) has insisted on retention of the poetry, perhaps unfashionably, at the Vic. The result is a beautifully spoken play, expressive and rhythmic, but not so verse ridden that poetry overlays drama . . . *Julius Caesar* arrives at (the Vic) as a triumph over the circumstances.

It can't have pleased those actors that their tantrums and lobbying had robbed them of half of their usual first night audience. An angry shopkeeper opposite the theatre, said "These actors claiming to represent the Potteries and going around dirty and grubbily dressed! What kind of reflection is that of the society they claim to represent?"

The man who signed himself 'an ordinary theatre-goer' cannot have been a lone voice. He wrote to Stephen asking him to make sure that the "Vic" did not come under the sole control of the Stoke Corporation and Peter Cheeseman. "Your point of view is appreciated by many who are not demonstrative," he said. He was unsurprised that his letter to the paper expressing this view had not been published.

For the first night of the new company, its presentation of *Big Soft Nelly* had a record number of paying customers. As they say in the 'business,' all publicity is good publicity. Writing to Jo, Campton was sure that the average theatre-goer hoped the theatre would not stay dark for long - no matter who was to be the director. The *Sentinel* reviewer was generous:

> Henry Livings invades private areas of personality in *Big Soft Nelly* and any self respecting bum who has been called by that name will watch this loaded farce nervously . . . This odd playwright has been dangerously used to introduce the new company . . . and the newcomers make an immediate good impression. . . . Sometimes the laughs beat the finish of a line, a tribute usually reserved for high speed comedians.

The company had arrived successfully, with a technically difficult play to do in the round, and back at the Vic after a week in Dartington the company opened *The Birdwatcher*. *The Sentinel* described the production as one which bounced on bedsprings and *The Stage*, in commenting that the company had already specialised as high grade farceurs, observed that 'the new company are certainly not losing any friends for this controversial little theatre.'

In between all the vicissitudes, Lane had been reading up about music hall with some trepidation. Cheeseman claimed to Jo that his documentary style had taken four years to develop and here was a new company whipping one up like a souffle. The old company had a high profile in the field of dramatised documentary, but Lane had never seen one. He hadn't either seen *O What a Lovely War* which popularised the whole genre. But he had Gertie Gitana as a lynch pin.

Using reminiscences of old Stoke, bits of music hall history and suitable songs, the company created their own personal documentary, incorporating magic, a vanishing act, drag and ventriloquism. One of the reviewers observed that : 'Someone in the new company has a quirky and inventive sense of fun.' It was a production designed to bring in the audience and it succeeded.

> Old-time music hall was welcomed back to the Potteries last night with numerous pleas for encores and the loudest applause ever heard at the Victoria Theatre . . . this hardly detracts from the merit of the nine brilliantly versatile performers, none of whom could have been born before music hall finished. The material is handled lovingly, like a family heirloom and tributes to great troupers . . . are made with total sincerity . . . there is no mistaking Gertie Gitana for whom we have to wait until nearly the end. Miss Craig, with the most difficult moment of all to bring off successfully, Nellie Dean . . . but the honours really go to Tony Healey for his chatty resume from a seat in the audience . . . last night's audience were not only captivated but sometimes helped the reminiscences along themselves.
>
> Only the beer is missing from Palace of Varieties but there are cockles and mussels on sale at the interval. This is a cheeky, noisy, audacious and entirely genuine homage to the Music Hall... (the) new team at the Vic have definitely arrived.

The company received a lot of fan mail, one regular theatre going lady said it was the best thing she had seen at the Vic.

While rehearsals for *Brand* went ahead, and needing to add to this a sense of consolidation, the company announced its programme for a further three months. Arnold Bennett's *Love Match* would be followed by a Victorian melodrama, *Black Ey'd Susan*, a world premiere from Scotland of Tom Wright's *Pygmies in the Colosseum*, and another documentary on the life of *Philip Astley*, founder of the European circus tradition, who had been born in Hanley, next door.

Successful though the company was, or perhaps because it was, Jo Hodgkinson pulled the plug.

He had only backed the three month programme on the strictest injunction that if it went over budget, there would be NO grant at all. Faced with a successful enterprise he panicked. There was to be no more money for further productions by Stephen Joseph's Studio Theatre Company. He wanted a local authority Trust to take over the running of a 'dark' theatre. An active theatre would have left Studio Theatre in business. A moribund theatre meant a lifeless company. In this he was partisan. Even in March, when the company were rehearsing *Caesar*, Jo contacted Dartington Hall and advised them to cancel the visit of the company that year. Richard Gill was teaching there. He had been in Stephen's *Hamlet* and a member of Lane's company at the Traverse, so the tour went ahead.

The company was actively discussing taking the Studio Theatre on to a theatreless town. Preston, Blackburn and Lancaster were surveyed, but Burnley seemed the most promising. However, Jo wanted the company to die with its founder. Jo admired Stephen personally, but not his theatre. Whilst the opening of Stoke was being discussed Jo snapped, "We've got one Theatre in the Round, we don't want more." During a later, heated mid crisis telephone call, Stephen said to him on the telephone. "Jo you're a bloody liar," and then turned to Campton and said in all innocence, "He's hung up! I didn't say anything to offend him, did I?"

Jo Hodgkinson was the supreme diplomat. All through the affair he tacked into the wind. Whatever the message he gave to Orders and Garrett, his every action suggested he was firmly behind Cheeseman and against Joseph. Stephen hated duplicity, and not for the first time in his life he saw it writ large, and he was dying.

Death concentrates the mind, and reports from his Directors and from Jo made him realise that even now he was abandoned. His two oldest friends from Cambridge had sold him short and were in support of Cheeseman. Jo, whatever his pronouncements, was a politician and supported the status quo. As with Goneril and Regan they were carving up his Kingdom before the funeral meats were prepared. As early as October 1966 the Stoke Directors of Studio Theatre, with Arts Council advice, had decided to change the company's Auditors, without reference to Stephen. So Stephen did what any self respecting man would do, he fought for his dignity and for his principle. He said:

> I do not see the sense in letting the Victoria Theatre go dark at the end of the present series of plays. It will do nobody any good whatever (except possibly Peter Cheeseman who is longing to see the Studio Theatre Company quit). I have some experience of take overs, including my Father's own firm, in which I am a Shareholder.[12]

It was not only Stephen who thought the Arts Council were behaving badly. The *Evening Sentinel* wrote

> "(The Arts Council), I fear, have not really distinguished themselves in their handling of this dispute. From the beginning they have failed to give good direction when so badly needed by both sides. Assurances, too, have not been fulfilled to satisfaction... *Why are they in such a*

hurry to see the theatre change hands?[13]

The Arts Council made sure that the Studio Theatre was penniless when the lease was handed over to the new local Trust. 'Good-will,' as Jo pointed out to Stephen, was not an item on the agenda.

Many people, sometimes the participants themselves, behaved shabbily in this affair. Equally, it is clear that the Arts Council were far from happy with the direction the theatre was taking, and the company might well have done no more than soldier on but for Stephen's intervention.

"What should Stephen have done?" The question was put to the author while he was researching details for this book. Ayckbourn was in no doubt he should have been more precise about his intentions at the start of the venture. Ayckbourn perceived Cheeseman to be thinking that assassins were lurking to get rid of him.[14] But Stephen was quite clear, as his letter of engagement to Cheeseman shows. To those who ask what he should have done, this author says, "What he did." If Cheeseman had been prepared to sit it out he'd have got rid of Stephen and controlled the board as he wished. He was the right person to assume Stephen's mantle in Stoke, but not in the way in which he went about it.

He has done exemplary work in Stoke on Trent and been a powerhouse of activity there. Actors who didn't like him agreed that he got things out of them which they did not consider themselves capable of. One cannot but admire his achievement and ability to inspire loyalty among his company and his having masterminded the building of a handsome new custom-built theatre. Even the way he missed a first night in order to make sure the builders did not take down trees on the site which were making construction difficult, gains respect.

To one observer, watching him in conference several years later : "Peter Cheeseman sat there talking like Stephen, sounding like Stephen . . . laughing like Stephen . . . preaching Stephen's gospel . . ." [15]

It was a transformation which had taken its toll. There were some who considered him not a little paranoid, talking of Alan Ayckbourn and Stanley Page as Joseph men, and there were times when he would be sitting in the theatre working alone at night, and would 'feel' Stephen's presence in the room with him. At which point, he had to pack up and go home!

Chapter Twenty Nine

Happily Ever After

Stephen's action forced the several local authorities to reassess their commitment to the Vic and significantly increase the funding to the new North Staffordshire Trust Company. The Arts Council also increased its funding level, so the Director started the new company with a substantially more comfortable seat, and with a theoretically reduced workload, because there was to be an Administrator appointed to look after the business of running the theatre - what Stephen wanted all along.

Not that Peter Cheeseman did not do his own thing. One Trust director complained,"We can't tell Peter anything... he says 'You're only here officially because you've got to be... I'm the person running this company.'"[1]

In negotiations with the Arts Council and the North Staffordshire Theatre Trust Stephen and Jo agreed a figure of £5,000 to include £4,000 in respect of assets and valuation fees, whilst the Arts Council accepted responsibility for the accumulated deficit, estimated at slightly under £5,000. By a sleight of hand the Arts Council reduced the accumulated deficit to only £679, saved themselves £4,300 and left the Studio Theatre Ltd. almost penniless.

Stephen died on the 12th September 1967, two months after his Company in Stoke on Trent was put out of business. The fact that he was dying does not detract from the obscene haste with which some attempted to disengage him from his achievement during his lifetime. He was not a perfect man. Alfred Bradley summed him up on one return from Scarborough - "I don't think we pick friends because of their qualities. I think we pick friends because of their faults. They're usually more interesting".[2]

Phyllis Leggett, secretary and treasurer of the Council of Repertory Theatres felt she had lost a good friend and a wise counsellor... "This is a very tragic loss to the theatre."[3] In Llandaff that year, Mary James (nee David) had lost the three most important men in her life as her poem shows:

> RIP Jo 1967
> Prude pride,
> Disapprover,
> Stopped me inviting
> Sympathy from Jo
> In my widowed sighing.
> O loved youth,
> Scorned lover —
> Forgive my not writing:
> I didn't know
> That you were dying.
>
> MJ

During Stephen's final illness Ayckbourn used to take a portable record player and records to play to him Tchaikovsky and sentimental classics, and Stephen would say, "Dear God I'm still alive," while they cut up bits of card without talking and constructed model theatres. While they built these cardboard dreams, between wheezes and grunts with Tchaikovsky churning over in the background, it would be, "Give me the thingummy," "Hand me the whadercallit," "Where's the Whatsit," and Stephen would smile and say, "By Jove Akers, it's a good job we speak the same language!"

Not that Ayckbourn was not scared stiff. Stephen had become a wizened, frail man with a kitten gifted to keep him company, and with the lights on Ayckbourn would say "Maybe next year we could..." and Stephen said "I'm dying, don't you believe what they tell you about it, once you accept your death everything becomes reasonable."[4]

Stephen told Stott that he had made a deal with the doctor to be given enough pills to end it, but the doctor chickened out and left his locum without instruction. Stott remembers: "After a long, drowsy ramble about how the Chinese could organise birth control, he looked around, and asked if there was any chance I could find a sledgehammer and hit him hard on the head?" Stott chickened out too, and Stephen said "Oh well, it won't take long now, anyway. 'Tis disgusting though, Love. Silly too, of course." And he winked, and slid back onto his pillow, and slept.

At a Directors meeting in his bedroom sat Owen Hale and David Campton. The discussion had barely got going when Stephen began to issue bizarre instructions. They were to get hold of the window dresser from Rowntrees and have everything re-arranged starting with the toys. After a while he seemed to doze while the two men sat in dazed silence, then he opened his eyes and said, "I've been talking complete drivel, haven't I?"

It was typical of Stephen that he was forthright with those who, whether they knew it or not, were able to bear reality. To Ken Boden and P.B. and even Campton he maintained perfect innocence and kept them going in the sublime belief that he did not know he was dying. To them he would talk of what he would do when he got better.

There were sixteen applicants for the new post of Artistic Director and it is unclear by what criteria the committee chose to interview those they did. In the event they short-listed four, two of whom appear to have been chosen at random. The young Bill Bryden had been one of the applicants.

Peter Cheeseman and Terry Lane were both short listed, but the latter was convinced that the whole procedure was a formality to re-appoint Peter Cheeseman, and he did not want to be a participant in what he perceived to be a 'show' selection. He took advantage of an alternative interview in Newcastle on Tyne the same day. Campton, as a Trust member, did not bother to make the journey from Leicester for a decision that had, he felt, to all intents and purposes already been taken.

Similarly there were nine applicants for the position of Manager/Administrator. After reading the Curricula Vitae it is difficult to assess how the three interviewed for the job were chosen, certainly not by merit. Two of them were ex managers, one Cheeseman's, one Joseph's.

Stephen bequeathed the monies remaining from William Elmhirst's personal covenant to the Victoria but the Directors of Studio Theatre were unhappy with the bequest. The Deed of Covenant was intended to be used on behalf of the theatre but entirely at the discretion of Stephen Joseph. Foreseeing the possibility of problems, Elmhirst would not make the donation to the Victoria Theatre. The point of the gift was that it should not be accounted for in the Company's records. The directors of Studio Theatre wanted to refuse the bequest, but the consent of the Charity Commissioners had to be obtained.

Donations from Margaret Rawlings and Gwynneth Thurburn had to be dealt with, and both ladies wanted their money to be used to swell the funds for the Memorial theatre Ken Boden was organising in Scarborough.

One of the last actions Stephen took was to return to his uncle the £200 he had lent him to help get the theatre off the ground. He left his valuable collection of theatre books to the Central School, hoping to establish a separate reference section in the school's library. There had been times in his life when he was known to spend a month's salary on a precious theatre book. In drawing up his will, Stephen had tried to leave his house to P.B., which after her death, would revert to Shirley. His lawyers advised that reversion was not possible, so he allowed the house and his money to be left to P.B., which in turn devolved to her children. She was always incapable of coping with finance. During his last illness she had run up a personal bill in Rowntrees for £400, and when he got to hear about it Stephen bailed her out.

Shortly before he left the University he took out an insurance on his life for £6,000, and it and most of the royalties from his books went to her also. One of the first things she did was buy a new tea service, and give a large donation to the Stephen Joseph Theatre Fund. So of course she ran out of money and had to sell the house. Ayckbourn bought the old vicarage from P.B. and maintained her in it till she died.

By 1974 the committee of the company had been meeting annually to discuss what to do with the £1,600 at its disposal. Several options were mooted, and eventually it was suggested they pay £1,000 to P.B. to produce a biography of Stephen. The contract was drawn up, but she hesitated in signing it, and had a stroke before she could. She died that year.

Eventually the Company were struck off the register for non function, and the directors once again had to consider how to dispose of £1,600. Neville Hunnings was still a board member, and by then also on the board of the Society for Theatre Research. It was agreed to donate the funds from one charity to the other of which Stephen had been a member, and so the money formed the basis of the Society's Research grants. Very shortly thereafter another society member, Anthony Downing, died and left them a very considerable sum, so that now the Society for Theatre Research uses the Stephen Joseph grant to make an annual award to a suitable research project.

As Secretary of the Scarborough Theatre Trust and later Theatre Manager (which occasioned the retirement in disgust of Alfred Bradley who wanted to ditch Ken and find a 'professional'), Ken Boden kept the whole dream alive. He wrote, cajoled, reasoned, liaised, sold dreams in the shape of bricks, canvassed members of the theatrical profession, architects, professors, peers and ladies. Within three years he had raised £20,000, but the ability to collect enough to buy whichever building they considered next continued to elude him.

Plans to convert premises moved from old churches, Claremont and St. Paul's, to a revived scheme to build a community centre in Crescent Gardens. Architects drew up plans to build a new theatre between Esplanade Road and Avenue Victoria. For each new scheme, each new appeal, Ken fought. He struggled on for the next eleven years with the trust running the seasons in The Library. The Librarian continued to hamstring them by placing difficulties in their way. In 1969 for instance Ayckbourn wanted to run morning matinees specially for children but Mr Edwards winkled out a 1933 Act which precluded the Library Theatre from catering solely for child audiences.

Alan Ayckbourn was Director of Productions in 1967, 1969 and 1970 with Alfred Bradley or Rodney Wood joining him, or producing in between. Then in 1972 he left his job as a BBC radio director in Leeds to work full time running the Scarborough company. With his commitment the seasons became extended until the company kept going all year. In 1976 the North Yorkshire County Council offered them a lease on the ground floor of the former Boy's Grammar High School at Westwood. The move was swift and dramatic. From the time the builders moved in to the first night, the total conversion took just over 60 days.

The last performance in The Library was with *Just Between Ourselves* on the 11th of September, 1976 and they opened at Westwood with *Mr Whatnot* on the 26th of October that year. They remained there for almost twenty years until the Scarborough Council made available the former Odeon Cinema in the centre of the town opposite the railway station. In the interval Scarborough had lost four cinemas, two theatres, the Open Air Theatre had fallen into ruins and the Opera House, originally built as a circus venue and which still had elephant walks to the stage, had been burned out.

Dona Martyn - *Martine*

Chapter Thirty

The Full Round

Stephen Joseph had been the first person in Britain to conceive a Stage Management course in a drama school, the first to recommend Speech Therapy as a University subject and the first to recommend that an acting course should concentrate the production of a play in a three week period rather than an entire term.

He was the first person in Britain to hold playwriting courses, and one of the first to advocate Local Radio (1946). His was the first full time Theatre in the Round company in Britain and the first company to champion new as opposed to West End writing.

He was certainly the first person to startle his listeners by advocating a Fish & Chip Theatre - years before Pub performances gained ground, and his Promenade Performances in Manchester rank as the first of their kind in Britain.

His was the first company of his generation to encourage in-house writers/ dramaturgs, and was also one of the first to advocate all day uses for theatres, to encourage those huge buildings not to be idle for twenty two hours of the day.

Although he did not start the First Degree course solely in Drama at Manchester University, he did give the department its reputation which attracted young students like Antony Sher and Roland Joffe and produced technical designers like Geoff Joyce who designed the New Victoria Theatre in Stoke on Trent.

Stephen was unconventional, eccentric and revolutionary and he was aware that society is afraid of anarchy. Its leaders, rulers, those in positions of authority, attain those positions because of the powers inherent in them, and he was opposed to power. If he was not, himself, a 'good' director, it was because he was opposed to the power it implied.

> He was an extremist for the round, but then . . . he was an extremist about everything . . . being a pioneer makes you extreme: you have to

take an extreme point of view to get your point across . . . he didn't like . . . the compromises that came up - (for example) thrust stages. He believed that you should go the full Round or not at all.[1]

Therefore the essential difference in character between the Victoria Theatre in Stoke and the Library in Scarborough was not one of policy but of leadership. Between the interpretive and the creative artist.

In Stoke on Trent Peter Cheeseman encouraged interpretation. Actors queued up to work for him. His was the scholarly, intellectual, academic approach to studying a play - the Stanislavskian method of directing. If you were playing a nuclear scientist you have to become a physicist and to have read all the books on the subject.[2]

It was a method popular with many actors, as his stable of fine and accomplished performers testifies. Ken Campbell and Bernard Hill and Robert Powell were in the company together with RSC director Ron Daniels. Heather Bell and Heather Stoney (the present Lady Ayckbourn) spent several years in Stoke, and Bob Hoskins and Ben Kingsley are two other notable actors whose careers were in a sense launched by Cheeseman, who also developed the dramatised documentary which further characterised the work of the Vic.

In Scarborough Stephen was the catalyst for the creative artist, and many mostly playwriting-careers benefitted by his enthusiasm and confidence.

He had been the first person to stage Robert Bolt and James Saunders, whose works had previously only been broadcast. He inspired others, like TV writers, Antony Marriot and Ian Curteis. If Colin Wilson had only one short play performed by the company, it was because playwriting was secondary to his other interests as a writer.

Joan Macalpine spent years working on the *Cornish Mysteries* never to see them performed, but the company did her adaptation of *David Copperfield* years before her *Tom Jones* was seen in the West End.

Richard Gill remembers his play *Station People* as a 'wretched piece, best forgotten,' but Stephen agreed to stage it. He would have preferred to do Gill's earlier play, *Travellers*, abortively premiered at the Lyric Hammersmith, but Cheeseman wanted the premier. Stephen accepted Stott's *Mata Hari* even though Stott admits he had done very little work on it and that it had structural weaknesses. It too launched him on a career as a writer and his later play, *Funny Peculiar*, enjoyed a lengthy West End run.

David Campton and Alan Ayckbourn are the two best-known writers who have enjoyed longest service and good conduct in writing, but only Ayckbourn earned the gong.

Campton had his *Soldier from the War Returning* performed at The Comedy Theatre in what John Russell Taylor describes as an ill-assorted triple bill of One Act plays with Saunders and Pinter.[3] Campton had already written for a radio series compered by Richard Murdoch and had revue sketches performed in *One Over the Eight* and *On the Brighter Side*.

Campton's style of writing had been well honed and generically linked with the school of writing which became known as *Comedy of Menace* and which preceded the works of Harold Pinter. His first full length play, *The Cactus Garden*, was performed by the Everyman Repertory Company in Reading the same year that Stephen used his *Dragons are Dangerous* to open the first Scarborough season.

It was Campton's shorter comedies of menace, influenced and often inspired by Stephen, which attracted the attention of the critics. The Menace school of writing was a post-script, or extension of the *Theatre of the Absurd* playwrites defined by Martin Esslin in his book of that name. The style was exemplified by writers such as Samuel Beckett and Eugene Ionesco.

Campton's plays were born out of his preoccupations of the day:

> To my mind the Theatre of the Absurd is a weapon against complacency (which spreads like a malignant fungus). The weapon of complacency is a pigeon-hole. Pigeon-hole an idea, and it becomes harmless. (We have a clean bomb). It is difficult to be complacent when the roots of one's existence are shaken, which is what the Absurd at its best does. [4]

In his long One Act play *Little Brother Little Sister* Campton not only displays his unease with contemporary society, but wears his social conscience unequivocally on his sleeve.

Many actors are critical of Stephen's production methods - Ayckbourn and Gill and Rosamund Dickson - thought him a lousy director, but it is difficult to reconcile this opinion with his pedigree. His productions in Budapest would not have been invited on to Warsaw had they been without merit, nor his Footlights successes been earned if talentless.

If he personally did not want to 'make the grade' as a notable director, we should remember that it was his productions of Ayckbourn and Campton which showed their plays off to their best advantage.

Stephen produced Campton's *Comeback* in the summer of 1963, when it was seen by Donald Albery, a London Manager, who bought an option for production in the West End. The fact that it died on its way to London may have had as much to do with director and cast as with the fact that it was retitled *Honey I'm Home*. Having bought the option Albery let it lapse. So the rights to present *Comeback* were then taken on by a director and presented for a pre-London tryout at Leatherhead under the H.M. Tennant management.

The play had an all star cast. Paul Rogers and Betty Marsden led the company, but it never went into town, because Paul Rogers mid rehearsal, was offered a part in a new Pinter production destined for the West End. The actor preferred to be seen in the West End in Pinter rather than Campton, so gave notice to quit. His decision left the company in an impossible situation. A leading actor cannot be replaced at such short notice by another 'star' so the production collapsed, therebye robbing both Stephen and Campton of the possible accolade of established success.

Alan Ayckbourn was more fortunate. He had grown up in a house where his mother wrote constantly, producing stories for magazines and books for children. His first plays he describes as Pirandello-ish. Stephen had read one or two, without comment. It was not until they were rehearsing for Campton's *Ring of Roses* in Newcastle under Lyme that Ayckbourn complained about the writing. Stephen smarted, and said, "If you can write a better play do so and I'll put it on. Write a good part for yourself. Make sure it is popular, because if it doesn't bring in an audience the company will 'fold.'"

Ayckbourn remembers the rehearsals as being for *Bell, Book and Candle* [5] but Campton is equally emphatic that they were for *Ring of Roses*.. The difference of recollection may have something to do with the natural competition between the two writers.

We have already seen the circumstances which led to Ayckbourn's first play being bought by a London management. *Standing Room Only* also died, under the weight of requested re-writes. However the manager, Peter Bridge, was loyal and an enthusiast, no doubt recognising the potential rather than the actual. The play was raw, and Ayckbourn has not let it be published, nor performed elsewhere.

With the opening of the Victoria in Stoke on Trent in 1962, Ayckbourn remained with the company there for eighteen months as an actor and a director. His *Christmas versus Mastermind* played to the worst business in the theatre's history, but undeterred, his next play *Mr Whatnot* opened a year later in November 1963.

It was an unusual and effective piece of daring theatrical experiment, inspired in part by the tradition of the silent screen greats such as Chaplin, Keaton and Tati. Some reviewers likened in to the films of Labiche. The central character in the play, a piano tuner, never speaks. It was a confection of mistaken identity, stereophonic sound effects, and mime. *The Guardian* reviewer thought the in the Round presentation vital for the form of experiment. Using actions rather than words, the play creates a kaleidoscope of car chase, garden fête, sleepless guests mistaking each other for ghosts and so on.

Mr Whatnot was also bought for the London stage by Peter Bridge and opened at the Arts Theatre, then managed by Michael Codron, nine months later. Only Peter King as Whatnot went from Stoke with the production, whose cast included Ronnie Barker and Marie Lohr.

Reviewers were unkind. Only two were complimentary, the *Birmingham Post* thinking that Ayckbourn was a hopeful saboteur at the heart of modern drama. *The Spectator* considered it a joy and a minor technical triumph, but others a circus trick or a nursery hallucination of Christopher Robin after a debauch of cream buns. The *Telegraph* described it as hanging on a gossamer thread, a desription echoed by reviewers of his next play.

Mr Whatnot never transferred into 'Town.' It failed, but it failed in a big way. Ayckbourn was noted.

It also marked his departure from Stoke on Trent. He had committed himself to Stephen's theatre, but Stephen was no longer running it, and as he says himself in *Conversations with Ayckbourn* he did not, then, see eye to eye with Peter Cheeseman who was at that time running the Vic. In 1964 he applied for a job being advertised, that of director with the BBC Radio Drama department in Leeds, under the leadership of Alfred Bradley, himself an innovatory radio director. Ayckbourn was given the job in Leeds and spent several years there.

In 1965 when Stephen was planning his last season in Scarborough under the direction of Campton, he asked Ayckbourn to write a play for the company of four actors. Ayckbourn agreed. When it didn't materialise, Stephen contacted him and asked what the play would be about so that he could prepare advance publicity. Ayckbourn didn't know, so Stephen said he would describe the play as one of mistaken identities.

Still no manuscript came from Leeds, so Stephen once again made contact with Ayckbourn and asked for the title. Still Ayckbourn was uncertain. Stephen said he would announce the play as *Meet My Father*.[6]

The programme was announced. Stephen had agreed to do a play he had not read, and which Ayckbourn had not yet written!

Stephen was unconventional.

His 1965 production of *Meet My Father* established Ayckbourn as a successful writer. It was Alan's eighth play to be staged by Stephen's company, and on its passage into the West End became retitled *Relatively Speaking*.

Meet My Father was welcomed in Scarborough as a feather-light farce, at times brilliant, with Ayckbourn's brittle wit shimmering through. Most of the laugh lines depending almost entirely upon timing. Scarborough's *Evening Sentinel* reviewer noted: It is a tribute to the entire cast and producer Stephen Joseph that (the play) came off without a hitch.[7]

In London *Relatively Speaking* had a superb cast led by Michael Horden and Celia Johnson with Richard Briers and Jennifer Hilary as the young lovers. It also had Nigel Patrick directing. He had been a debonair leading actor on stage and in films for almost 35 years before turning his hand to impeccable sophisticated productions.

The *Sunday Times* thought the London Stage had decidedly taken a turn for the better. "Nigel Patrick's direction was tirelessly inventive," crowed the *Guardian* and yet another observed a sly gloss which, without his hand, would have made the play more obvious. "Nigel Patrick drives the joke along superbly," said the *Evening News* whilst the *Financial Times* remarked that the performances coalesced under direction into hair-trigger teamwork of a rare kind.

In the *Telegraph* W.A. Darlington noted that the moment you begin to look into the plot it disintegrates into incredible nonsense, remarking that "The imagination quails before the picture of what it might have been like, clumsily staged . . . " "Light as a souffle," trilled *Punch*. Ayckbourn had arrived, with a play which his agent, Peggy Ramsay, said was a tiny play - a baby could hold it in the palm of its hand.[8] One critic likened it to a house of cards, always just escaping collapse.

The plot is as gossamer fine as that of *Top Hat*, the Astaire-Rogers film, in which characters avoid calling each other by their names and rarely finish any sentence that might reveal what is going on. It is the high-wire performer's trick of making his audience believe that at any moment he might fall.

If in part Ayckbourn owed his success to Nigel Patrick, one cannot help but notice that the quality of production in London had also been achieved at Stephen's hands in Scarborough. With light comedy and farce, he was at his most inventive.[9]

More than that, in his determination to project the talents of his star disciples, he was also more indulgent than his critics and the Arts Council of their right to fail. Only by giving his stable of writers a platform on which to fail could they succeed.

Within a year of the Vic and the Traverse being established, other new companies had opened. One in a warehouse in Brighton, the other in Chester, where the director was a man who had acted at the Traverse. Stephen's advice was sought constantly by the two young ladies running the theatre in Chester, and both had contacted Lane before setting up in business.

In 1966, the year Stephen left Manchester a lecturer from Loughborough finally persuaded the authorities in Bolton to build a fully adaptable theatre, capable of in the Round performances. He was Robin Pemberton Billing and the son of P.B. Two of the administrators of the company were ex-Stoke men and several of the cast had acted in Stoke and Scarborough.

Out of Manchester, Roland Joffe ran a season of plays in Promenade style with the Young Vic in London. Apart from *Timesneeze* he did both *Scapin* and *Waiting for Godot*. Sydney Bernstein never set up a drama school in Manchester but did fund the establishment of the Stables Theatre, which in turn became the Royal Exchange Theatre in the Round housed in what looks suspiciously like a geodesic dome. A group of directors who had formerly been scathing in their criticism of the medium directed in it.

Arnold Wesker directed the Centre 42 in Chalk Farm on similar lines. Faynia Jeffery, who painted Stephen's flat black, was the first director of Glasgow's Tron Theatre and Tony Robinson one the the first actors there. From Manchester Claire Venables went on to direct an alternative company, The Monstrous Regiment of Women.

In fact Fringe Theatre became an accepted part of the theatrical scene, many of them open plan, thrust stage or in the round. *Contacts* published annually by *The Spotlight* lists almost a hundred such in 1990.

Frank Dunlop's production of *Joseph and His Amazing Technicolour Dreamcoat* at the Edinburgh Festival was in the round and a company from Italy presented a promenade *Orlando Furioso* there. R.G. Gregory, who had his first play directed in Scarborough in 1962, set up Word and Action which performs exclusively in the round, touring 'instant' theatre to schools in Europe, and organises a Round Festival in Wimborne Minster every year. The unconventional has become accepted.

The Other Place in Stratford upon Avon, the New Swan, the open plan Barbican and National stages, quite apart from the New Globe Theatre, all testify to practitioner and audience delight in the new relationship between actor and audience. *Larkrise* was directed by Bill Bryden promenade at the National Theatre. The first of several promenade productions there, and in 1997 its Olivier Theatre was converted to a space for in the round performances both intimate and epic which several reviewers hoped would be used often.

Stephen's advice to his students had been that when a group of people are in one place, they should act as a group, creatively.[10] His dictum was that if drama happened in the street, a crowd would gather round to watch, just as in ancient times people gathered round to observe corn threshing, ritual, or dance. At boxing matches or football the spectators surround the spectacle, and in that way generate maximum excitement - the thrill of being present at the moment of creation, the sort of feeling one gets walking around Rodin's group sculpture, the *Burghers of Calais*.

What he was after was an actors' ensemble - there is no director - the production is the collective creation of actors, stage management, choreography, and music. Productions are developed through a process of improvisation and experiment within the group, one in which the production is not a finished entity until after the last performance. This is precisely the manifesto of the Footsbarn company, now resident in France. They came together as a group in 1971, just four years after Stephen's death. There was no direct link: the founders have never heard of Joseph. But fifteen years earlier Theatre in the Round would not have been an option for them.

Stephen spent the last ten years of his life fighting for his dream. He himself admitted that he wasn't always sure what shape it should take, or what style he wanted to develop, so his career had been an adventure, and one in which he carried other people along. He was in the front seat of an intellectual roller-coaster and those he carried with him were inspired by his example. He generated not only inspiration but enthusiasm and love. He was a catalyst, and not one it is always possible to give credit to.

Bernard Shaw once observed that the weakness of America was that it was lumbered with a fixed constitution. If Stephen never himself achieved directly what he wanted, it was because he wanted to leave his options open for further development. If he had ever crystallised a philosophy it would have fossilised.

A creed is a system of beliefs, whilst anarchy represents an absence or lack of government. As an anarchist Stephen recognised that to embrace a creed or a cause, was to become its slave. Freedom of action is lost, or proscribed by the need to advocate the ideal, be it Brechtianism, Stanislavskianism, Freudianism, Communism, or Theatre in the Roundism. Freedom was all. His mind was ever alert to fresh fields.

In his time he had been an artist, scene designer, scene painter, actor, director, writer and teacher. His stage lighting caught the attention of commentators from his student days on, yet he was always practical. "It doesn't matter how arty the lighting is if you can't see the actors," he would remark.

It was undoubtedly his enthusiasm and determination that carried the inception of the ABTT and his resolution to capitalise, at last, on his expertise which brought about the Society of Theatre Consultants. He was an apparently tireless champion whose followers were left to carry the day, which in part explains Peter Thomson's observation, that Stephen was greater than anything he achieved.

He championed Theatre in the Round to rediscover the role of theatre and break the barriers between actor and audience, to revitalise the relationship between the two. His example of what was possible on a small scale was of enormous influence

In 1990 Peter Brook was reported as saying:

> Today, it is universally recognised by all serious experimenters in theatre that, until we know what really is going to be the society and its needs in the 21st century, what one needs is a free space that can be used in many different ways and doesn't impose an 18th or 19th century concept.[11]

It was not a statement he would have made thirty years earlier.

It is indeed a funny old world. Stephen never lived to see how his inspiration influenced so much and so many other people. He was indeed greater than anything he achieved, and it was left to others to dilute his often outrageous ideas[12] into a more thoroughly acceptable form:

> If, when mankind finally disintegrates,
> whoever created him has been stimulated and amused,
> man-kind will have accomplished something great.[13]

Two years after his death Sir Bernard Miles of the Mermaid Theatre in London, supported by Laurence Olivier at the National and John Clements from Chichester, was making vitriolic attacks on the experimental shape of the new design for a Sheffield Theatre. In the pages of *Plays and Players*[14] it was writers Alan Plater, David Rudkin, David Campton, Alan Ayckbourn and director Peter Cheeseman who rode to the rescue and laid low the attack. The champion of new writing in the theatre had been defended by playwrights.

The cathartic element with which he toiled can only be judged subjectively in the present. Performances are meant to be of lasting value to their audience, not to history. There can be no great plays, only great performances, and perfomances vary from night to night, which is what makes theatre going so exciting. You never know what will happen and every performance is both different and subjective. In the view of this writer it is easier to give an acceptable mediocre performance of Beethoven or Mozart than Othello.

So the mystery and magic of being at a live theatre performance is to be alone with one's own imagination and to be sharing the experience with others. Stephen called for a re-examination of theatre and its place in society. The problem for the Theatre in the 1990s was one which existed mid fifties for other reasons. Then thinkers were hexed on the nuclear issue, now, it is the environmental one, and perhaps theatre has ceased to give people what O'Neill asked of it - a meaning in life. It has become like the church, its members mutually exclusive to non-celebrants, and if you are not a member you can't take the host.

Instead, like the modern church, theatre confronts people with their own day-to-day problems, just like Coronation Street or Eastenders. It spends too much time examining its own navel, and if it can't do better than that, no wonder it is in such a bad way. Where are Stephen's disciples now, and what should they do to revitalise Theatre?

Bring back Blood and Thunder. Bring back Spit and Sawdust. Bring back Fire and Brimstone. Bring back Hanging and Flogging if you like, but for pity's sake -

Bring back Catharsis!

Geoffrey Todd - *Big Soft Nelly*

THEATRE IN THE ROUND

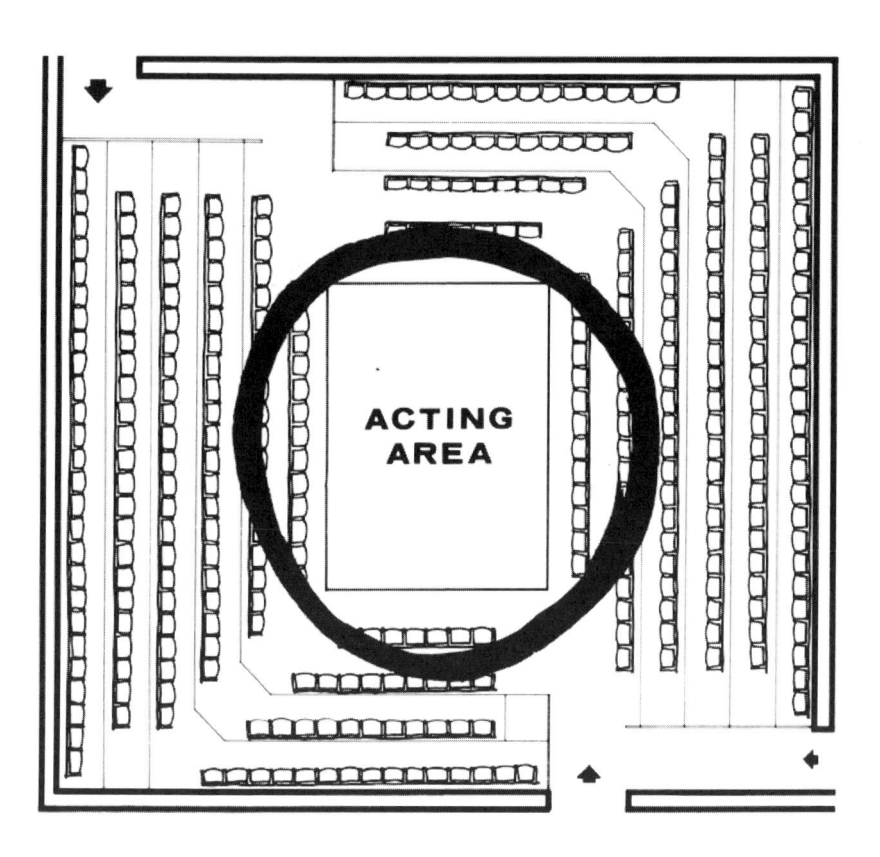

Charles Parker & Stephen Joseph

The Footlights Dramatic Club
(Founded 1883)

At the kind invitation of J. W. Pemberton

PRESENTS

1947
MAY WEEK REVUE

JUNE 15th
AMBASSADORS THEATRE
LONDON

LIBRARY THEATRE SCARBOROUGH

Licensee and Manager for Studio Theatre Limited : STEPHEN JOSEPH

VERNON ROAD

EVERY NIGHT (EXCEPT SUNDAYS) AT 8 p.m.
WEDNESDAY MATINEE AT 2.30 p.m.

THEATRE IN THE ROUND

Seats may be booked at W. Rowntree and Sons Ltd., Westborough, Scarborough Theatre Booking Office in York Place entrance

Price 5/-

CHANGE OF PROGRAMME EVERY THURSDAY

JULY 14 TO JULY 20	**CIRCLE OF LOVE**	A romantic tale by **ELEANOR D. GLAZER**
JULY 21 TO JULY 27	**'PRENTICE PILLAR**	A strange legend told by **RUTH DIXON**
JULY 28 TO AUG. 3	**DRAGONS ARE DANGEROUS**	A comedy by **DAVID CAMPTON**
AUG. 4 TO AUG. 10	**CIRCLE OF LOVE**	A romantic tale by **ELEANOR D. GLAZER**
AUG. 11 TO AUG. 17	**TURN RIGHT AT THE CROSSROADS**	An exciting adventure by **JURNEMAN WINCH**
AUG. 18 TO AUG. 24	**'PRENTICE PILLAR**	A strange legend told by **RUTH DIXON**
AUG. 25 TO AUG. 31	**DRAGONS ARE DANGEROUS**	A comedy by **DAVID CAMPTON**
SEPT. 1 TO SEPT. 9	**TURN RIGHT AT THE CROSSROADS**	An exciting adventure by **JURNEMAN WINCH**

An Exhibition of photographs and drawings showing theatre-in-the-round on the continent and in America will be open to the public daily from 10 a.m. to 6 p.m. except Wednesday when it will close at 1 p.m. Admisson free. This is in the exhibition room of the Public Library in Vernon Road.

Derrick Gilbert & Faynia Jeffery - *Soldier from the Wars Returning*

Alan Ayckbourn & Rosamund Dickson - *Five Finger Exercise*

Stanley Page, Alan Ayckbourn & Patricia England - *The Dolls House*

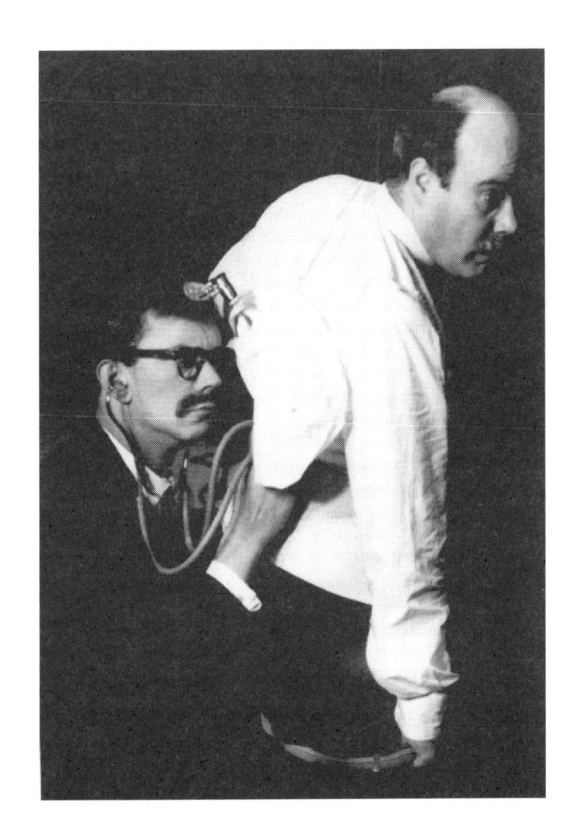

Alan Ayckbourn
& David Campton
- *Love After All*

Robert Fyfe - *Alas, Poor Fred*

Tony Healey - *Big Soft Nelly*

PROGRAMME
SUMMER 1964

Obituaries

STEPHEN JOSEPH

Shirley asked Hugh Hunt to deliver a funeral address:

This is not an occasion for sorrow, but rather one of joy. Joy that a man has passed through our midst, touching our lives at various points, leaving each one of us the richer for his passage.

Stephen has given us so much from the wealth that he discovered in life that there can be no-one who came into contact with him who did not receive some fresh revelation, some surprising insight, some flash of inspiration which will have thrown a new light on their problems, their work, their hobbies, or on the humblest of their daily tasks. I suppose that each one of us has tried to discover the particular secret that made Stephen so different from the majority of the men we meet. What was the key to his unbounded enthusiasm?

What made us so anxious to share his company, and to share his views even when we disagreed with him? I believe that it was a very simple secret - it was his ability to look on the world and all that happens in it as something that is happening for the first time, as a discovery that must be made by each one of us. as if it had never been seen or felt before, as a challenge which demands the full use of the faculties which God has given us. Not that he denied the wisdom and experience of others, but that he believed in man's right to question, to probe for the truth, to discover for himself.

Life was for Stephen an adventure, a challenge, a question and an endless wonder. He met it with the eyes of a child and the mind of a man. Eyes that saw everything as if for the first time, unblurred by the preconceptions of tradition and a mind that he had trained to distinguish between truth and falsehood, emotion and sentiment and, above all, between beauty and its many imitations.

For Stephen, beauty lay in the way a man works as well as in the completed work itself. He taught us to endow each work we undertake

- however humble - with the care and love of a craftsman. It is as a craftsman that many of us will remember him - as a man who worked with his hands as well as his head.

For him there was no such thing as a menial task - the skill of the stagehand was equal to the skill of the playwright. Workmanship was the basis of all art. If he was a perfectionist it was as a lover of a simple task well done, rather than an ambition to create a master piece or become a public figure. For Stephen beauty was to be found in all humble things - even more perhaps than in the complexities of creation. The beauty of a leaf, of a kitten at play, the beauty of carpentry, the beauty of an old-world melodrama or an early film. It was, I think, this love of simple craftsmanship that led him to champion the course that will ever be associated with his name – Theatre in the Round.

He was drawn to this form of theatre - not that he despised other more elaborate forms - for a variety of reasons. He saw it as a challenge to the outworn conventions of a theatre that was rapidly losing touch with humanity. He saw it as a stimulus to a new approach by actors and playwrights as an opportunity to create more vital relationships between actors and audience, but above all he saw in Theatre in the Round the simplest form of performance, springing from the earliest days of man's history when poet, actor, and artist were united as craftsmen.

This unity of man's God-given faculties - the unity of head, heart and hands - is the quality that Stephen championed. It is the challenge that he holds out to those of us who loved and admired him. This love of simple things, this pride in our work however humble, this perpetual discovery of life for ourselves, this neverending search for truth - these are the secrets Stephen discovered, the riches that he leaves behind. Stephen is not dead so long as we preserve these things. He lives on, in us and with us.

8 Oct 67

Hunt did not deliver the address well. Nor had he studied dramatic composition, for the fourth paragraph should have been the last one. As it was, the address was downbeat, and John Wood afterwards commented, "Stephen deserved a better boss."

KEN BODEN

Ken Boden

Scarborough Evening News - 5 June 1964

As a footnote to this epoch, it is fitting to record Alan Ayckbourn's address at the funeral of Ken Boden.

The very first season I ever came to Scarborough I came as Stage Manager of the Library Theatre.

I had never been to Scarborough before - I had no idea even where it was. Near Leeds said someone. But nicer. Indeed I was not to meet Stephen Joseph until I had been employed by him for six weeks.

How was an eighteen year old Stage Manager expected to cope? How, whilst rehearsing in London, was he to find props and furnishings for four different plays, due to open three hundred miles away in two weeks time?

In desperation I phoned my predecessor, the Stage Manager from the 1956 season.

"Scarborough," she said, "Oh, that's a doddle. A summer holiday. Listen. Write down all the props you need, right? Then write down all the furniture you need, right? Then write down anything else you need, right? Then put it in an envelope and post it to Ken Boden. B-O-D-E-N. Right? ... No, he's not. No, I don't know what he does, actually. Insurance or inland revenue. Something like that. But he's amazing at finding props and furniture."

I arrived in Scarborough to find the set and props for The Glass Menagerie and An Inspector Calls piled up in the middle of the Library Theatre dressing room floor. "There you are, lad," said a big, gruff, genial, every-Southerner's-idea-of-what-a-Yorkshireman-should-look-like Yorkshireman. "It's all there. If you want anything else give me a call. Boden's the name."

It was the start of a long professional relationship and friendship with Ken. Although twenty years my senior, the sheer energy and time he devoted to that tiny, virtually unknown theatre was remarkable. In fact it is, of course, a matter of record that without Ken, there would probably be no full time professional theatre in Scarborough today.

For almost fifteen years we worked side by side, administrator and artistic director. Ken's support was invaluable. His ability in times of economic crisis to conjure up extra money from nowhere - a secret fund we came to refer to as Ken's Left Sock - his care never to interfere with the artistic decisions but nonetheless unfailingly to support them - for these things and more, I shall remember him with gratitude.

As a footnote, it's perhaps a little known theatrical fact that Ken once appeared as an actor in a world premiere of one of my lesser known one act plays. Less known still is the fact that I appeared in it with him. To the maxim, never act with animals and children, I quietly added the words 'or with Ken Boden.'

I saw him last a few weeks ago at the theatre. "How's it going, lad?" he asked. "Fair enough, Ken," I said. "Good. I'm glad lad," he said. That's another thing I'll miss him for. He's probably the last man who will ever call me 'lad' again.

HERMIONE

Hermione outlived both of her sons, and both of her husbands, dying in May 1987. She was almost ninety years old. She was occasionally visited by one or another grandchild, who would be astonished when an African man opened the door. Each time they visited, it would be a different face. She had taken a leaf from Waugh's writing and become a Mrs Beste-Chetwynde.

She lived in an apartment in New York, and had to call the police on several occasions to report robbery. Her jewellery or whatever, was never recovered, and indeed the New York City police were quite convinced that her robberies were inside jobs.

She had been entertaining the world for the best part of seventy five years, and went on doing so when, the year after her death, her surrogate daughter became her executor and had the autobiography *How to Grow Old Disgracefully* published. It was an instant best seller.

Hermione Gingold

Acknowledgements

Michael Joseph's advice to writers was to start a story as if you have just entered a room and said "I've just heard the most remarkable thing." In writing the biography of his son I thought it very good advice. In this book I am telling a story; it happens to be a true one, and although I appear as one of the characters there were so many unexpected facts which came to light while I was researching the book, that I felt I was telling the story for the first time.

I only express one opinion in this account in response to the question put to me on page 212. All statements are taken from contemporary documents, letters, books and newspapers available to any researcher. Stephen Joseph was the most charismatic and inspirational person and my intention in writing the book was to put his role as catalyst for experimental theatre into perspective.

I also wanted to explore the way in which upbringing impinges upon the development of individuals. In this respect Dr Alice Miller's *For Your Own Good* was my springboard to understanding Stephen's parents.

I am especially grateful to Walter and Freda Martyn, to Jan MacDonald of Glasgow University and to Simon Trussler. I must thank Alan Ayckbourn, David Campton, Paddy Greene, Charles Lewsen, Peter Thomson for their generously given time; also Janet Kinrade Dethick, Richard Kent and John Sawyer. To Mary David I was indebted for most of the information concerning Stephen's student life at The Hall, in Llandaff and at sea – without her archive of photographs, programmes, letters and the early manuscripts, Stephen's formative years would have been much more obscure.

My thanks to the staff at the John Rylands Library in Manchester and to those in the Arts Council of Great Britain. I am deeply indebted to Richard Joseph for rescuing me from computer mishaps, his sister Shirley, and to everyone who wrote, telephoned or otherwise gave me their time, duly acknowledged in the proper place.

The author wishes to acknowledge his indebtedness to the Society for Theatre Research, whose scholarship award assisted in making possible the researches necessary to the completion of this work.

Whilst every effort has been made to contact copyright holders, it has not always been possible to discover with whom copyright lies.

Castiglione del Lago

Bibliography

Brook, Peter, *The Empty Space*. Penguin Books, 1968
Callow, Simon, *Orson Welles*. Jonathan Cape, 1995
Chambers, Colin, *Peggy*. Methuen 1998
Cole, Marion, *Fogie*. Peter Davies, 1967
Gingold, Hermione, *How To Grow Old Disgracefully*. Gollancz, 1988
Gascoigne, Bamber, *World Theatre*. Ebury Press, 1968
Hewison, Robert, *Footlights*. Methuen, 1983
Jones, Margo, *Theatre in the Round*. McGraw Hill, 1951
Joseph, Richard, *Michael Joseph Master of Words*. Ashford Press, 1986
Kendall, Henry, *I Remember Romano's*. Macdonald & Co, 1960
Kettle, Michael, *Salome's Last Veil*. Hart Davis McGibbon, Granada Publishing 1977
Leacroft, Richard & Helen, *Theatre & Playhouse*. Methuen, 1985
Lusty, Robert, *Bound to be Read*. Jonathan Cape, 1975
McColl, Ewan, *Journeyman*. Sidgwick & Jackson, 1990
Maschwitz, Eric, *A Taste of Honey*. Constable, 1924
Maschwitz, Eric, *No Chip on my Shoulder*. Herbert Jenkins, 1957
Miller, Dr. Alice, *For Your Own Good*. Virago Books, 1987
Nichols, Peter, *Feeling Your're Behind*. Weidenfeld & Nicholson, 1984
Osborne, John, *A Better Class of Person*. Faber, 1981
Poggi, Jack, *Theatre in America 1870-1967*. Cornell Univ. Press, 1968
Priestley, J.B., *Art of the Dramatist*. Heinemann
Racine, Jean, *Phedre*, transl. Margaret Rawlings. Faber 1956
Rowell, George, *Robert Atkins*. Society for Theatre Research, 1994
Shaw, Bernard, Preface *Back to Methuselah*. Penguin 1954
Bernard Shaw, Preface *Man and Superman*, Penguin 1962
Taylor, John Russell, *Anger and After*. Penguin Books, 1963
Trewin, J.C., *John Neville*. Barrie & Rockliff, 1961
Tynan, Kenneth, *He That Plays the King*. Longman, Green & co., 1950
Watson, Ian, *Conversations with Ayckbourn*. Faber, 1988
Wood, Rodney, *Stephen Joseph*. Unpublished thesis.

Stephen Joseph's bibliography of written material.

– these are the published works I have been able to identify. The unpublished works are either in the John Rylands Library, or where indicated, in the possession of the author.

PUBLISHED

1948	Project for a Cambridge University Radio Station
1948	*Outlook for Décor,* Cambridge Writing, editor, Young Writers Group
1948	*Cambridge Verse One,* editor Young Writers Group
1948	*Cambridge Verse Two,* editor Young Writers Group
	In Histrionic Circles, Joseph & David Eady (?)
1948	*La Vie Cambridgienne* Sketches & Musical items for Footlights revue, some bought by Samuel French Ltd - including
	How To Make a Cup of Tea Joseph
	Carnival SJ, Peter Tranchell & Ted Cranshaw
	Dancing Through Joseph
	Cymbolic Joseph
	Potted Carmen
1954/5	Beginners, Please! *Encore,* the voice of vital theatre
1955	Theatre in the Round, *Plays and Players,* August
1957	No New Playwrites, *Encore* Vol 3 No 5
1957	Theatre in the Round, *Drama,* winter - open correspondence between Ivor Brown & Joseph
1957	No New Playwrights? *Encore,* No 2
1957	Theatre in the Round, *Tabs,* Sep
1958	To the Barricades! *Encore,* Vol 4 No 3
1958	Letter to *Encore,* Vol 5 No 2
1958	Review, *Medieval Theatre in the Round, Encore* Vol 4 No 4
1958	Review, *Medieval Theatre in the Round,* Tabs Apr
1959	The Unique Theatre, *Encore* No 4
1959	The Celebration of Miraculous Man, *Umbrella,* summer. see also spring no.
1959	Theatre Go Round, *Theatre World,* Mar
1960	Review, Shakespeare's Wooden O, *Encore* No 1
	New Patterns in America, *Encore,* no. 1
1960	Letter to Encore, *Encore,* Vol 7 No 2
1960	Three Hundred Years After, *Encore,* Vol 7 No 5
1962	Review, Seven Ages of Theatre, *Tabs,* Apr
1962	*Adaptable Theatres,* editor, ABTT
1962	*Planning for New Forms of Theatre,* Strand Electric & Engineering Co. Ltd.
1962	Newcastle under Lyme Civic Project, *Adaptable Theatres,* ABTT
1962	Proscenium Madness, *New Theatre Magazine,* Jul/Sep
1963	Theatre in the Round in the Potteries, *Prompt,* No. 3
1963	*The Story of The Playhouse in England,* Barrie and Rockcliff

1964	Stephen Joseph writes from Manchester, *New Theatre Magazine* IV.4
1964	Stage Lighting for Theatre in the Round, *Architects Journal* (Aug)
1964	Stage Lighting for Theatre in the Round, *Tabs*, Sep
1964	Notes on School Theatres, *Tabs*, Vol 22 No 4
1964	*Actor and Architect*, editor, Manchester University Press
1964	Letter to a Ratepayer, *New Theatre Magazine* V.4 written under a pseudonym
1964	*Scene Painting and Design*, Sir Isaac Pitman & Sons Ltd
1965	Leeds Grammar School, *Tabs*, Vol 23 No 3
1965	*Civic Theatres* - Report of a Conference & 'Brains Trust'
1966	*Tabs* Vol 24 No 2
1966	Towards Tomorrow's Theatre, Perspective, J*ournal of the York & East Yorkshire Architectural Society* 8.66
1967	*Theatre in the Round*, Barrie and Rockcliff
1968	*New Theatre Forms*, Sir Isaac Pitman & Sons Ltd

UNPUBLISHED

1938	*Beauty and the Beast* (Author)
1938	*Haman* (Author)
1939	*Wild Sonata* (Author)
1939	*The Time Has Come* (Author)
1940	*Cinderella* no trace of MSS
1941	*Gold and Scarlet* (Author)
1948	*What Happened in the Bedroom* Manchester papers/Author
1948	*Come to Codwyn Bay*, music Peter Tranchell Mr. papers
1952	*What Would Mildred Have Said* Iowa Thesis, (Author)
1952	*Murder My Legacy* (Author)
195 ?	*The Key* no trace of MSS performed in Budapest & Prague
1958	*The Law of the Drama* Ferdinand Brunetière. Translator

The Private Secretary filmscript synopsis adapted from The *Justified Sinner.* Manchester papers

Henry Esmond synopsis and episode Manchester papers

Abracadabra, Mel Dinelli & Stephen Joseph (Author)

196? *The Ring at Eastborough* unfinished mss. Manchester papers

References

Stephen's Father

1. Charles Pick, in conversation with author 1990
2. Lusty, *Bound to be Read.*
3. ibid
4. ibid
5. Joseph, *Michael Joseph Man of Words*

Stephen's Mother

1. Stephen Sondheim, interviewd by Michael Ratcliffe – programme note – *A Little Night Music,* Royal National Theatre, 1996
2. Tynan, *He That Plays the King*
3. ibid
4. Kendall, *I Remember Romano's*
5. Reuth Ambre in conversation with author
6. Gretchen Franklin, letter to author
7. Gingold, *How To Grow Old Disgracefully*
8. ibid
9. ibid
10. *I Remember Romano's*
11. Margaret Keays in conversation with author
12. *I RememberRomano's*
13. *How to Grow Old Disgracefully*
14. ibid

Bringing Up Baby

All references are taken from *How to Grow Old Disgracefully*

The Co-Respondent

1. Lt. Ames, letter to author
2. Maschwitz, *A Taste of Honey*
3. Maschwitz, *No Chip on my Shoulder*
4. ibid
5. ibid
6. *How to Grow Old Disgracefully*

The Wicked Stepmother

1 David Campton, in conversation with the author
2 Shirley, Mrs Diana Simmonds, in conversation with the author
3 Michael Savage, letter to the author
4 Joseph, *Michael Joseph*
5 Shirley
6 Margaret Joseph, in conversation with the author
7 Reuth Ambre (Bernstein) in conversation with the author

Clayesmore

1 School brochure
2 Michael Balfour, in conversation with author
3 Carl Verrinder, in conversation with author
4 Clayesmore School Records
5 Reuth Ambre
6 *How to Grow Old Disgracefully*
7 Robert Lusty in conversation with the author
8 Shirley
9 Reuth Ambre
10 Margaret Joseph in conversation with the author

The Hall

1 Cole, *Fogie*
2 ibid
3 ibid
4 Gwynneth Thurburn in conversation with author, 1992. She could not clearly recall his terms of entry but thought it was a scholarship. An examination of the programmes does not suggest a shortage of male students
5 Victor Lucas, letter to the author
6 Mary David, letters and conversations with the author
7 Victor Lucas
8 Mary David
9 *Haman,* Stephen Lane (Joseph), unpublished mss. It is interesting to note that both Haman and Hitler had Jewish blood and were denying their origins in order to curry favour with the masses and fuel anti-semitism.
10 Reuth Ambre
11 Victor Lucas
12 *The Times*, 28 Dec 38

13 *Viva Voce*, No. 27, Dec 39
14 ibid
15 Victor Lucas
16 ibid
17 *Viva Voce*, No. 27, Dec 39

Playwright as Biographer

1 Reuth Ambre

The House of David

1   Victor Lucas
2   David Campton
3   Stephen's own undated letter from early 1944 from Royal Naval Hospital Bristol talks of his going to revisit Braidlea School.
4   David Campton
5   Lisbeth David. Anne's portrait in oils from 1939 now hangs in the Board Room of the Stephen Joseph Theatre in Scarborough.
6   Mary David
7   Mary David
8   Beryl Dunn, letter to Mary
9   Mary David
10 ibid
11 Catherine Lambert, letter to the author
12 ibid
13 *Llandaff Society Occasional Paper 6*
14 ibid
15 Catherine Lambert

The Cruel Sea

Details of Stephen's war records are as supplied by the Ministry of Defence. The official dates do not on all occasions match the addresses on letters written by him at the time. What is more he frequently left letters undated, in which case the addresses or indistinct postmarks have been used to fit them within context

1   David Campton
2   Stephen to Shirley 30 Apr 42
3   Lt. Ames, letter and conversation with the author
4   A.C. Myers, letter to the author
5   *Newbury Weekly News*, 10 Feb 94 in its Fifty Years Ago column

6 Shirley
7 Stephen to Shirley, undated
8 Shirley
9 Ministry of Defence letter 29 Jul 91
10 Stephen to Mary David 26 Mar 45
11 ditto – Apr 45
12 ditto – May 45

Salad Days

1 David Campton
2 Wood, *Stephen Joseph.*
3 David Campton
4 Shirley
5 Stephen to Shirley, letter
6 Stephen in conversation with the author 1962
7 Shirley
8 Rodney Wood
9 *Cambridge Writing*
10 ibid
11 Two slim volumes *Cambridge Writing* included in the Manchester papers. One priced at 6d and the other at 2s.6d.
12 Richard Baker, letter to author 17 Jun 91
13 Peter Tranchell, letter to author
14 *Project for a Cambridge University Radio Station.* Manchester papers
15 Richard Baker, letter to the author
16 Rodney Wood
17 Martin Wigglesworth in conversation with the author
18 Joseph, *What Happened in the Bedroom*
19 Hewison, *Footlights*
20 Peter Tranchell
21 Stephen Joseph, Manchester papers
22 Richard Bebb, letter to the author
23 d'Arcy Orders
24 Hewison, *Footlights*
25 d'Arcy Orders
26 Martin Wigglesworth
27 *Daily Telegraph,* Quoted by Rodney Wood
28 d'Arcy Orders
29 Michael Savage
30 ibid
31 Martin Wigglesworth

32 Robert Lusty
33 Michael Savage
34 Martin Wigglesworth

Hard Times

1 Harold Clurman, director of the first production as quoted in the Lowestoft programme
2 Brochure – Under Thirties Theatre Group 1948 – Manchester papers
3 d'Arcy Orders
4 ibid
5 Joseph & Tranchell *Come to Codwyn Bay*
6 Vivienne Wood, letter to the author
7 Trewin, *John Neville*
8 Joseph, *Ring at Eastbourne* unpublished mss.
9 Trewin, *John Neville*
10 Jack Mitchley in conversaton with author
11 *Lowestoft Journal* 24 Dec 48
12 Stephen Joseph, draft Manchester papers
13 Stephen Joseph to J.C. Trewin, 13 Jul 61
14 Vivienne Wood
15 *Lowestoft Journal*
16 Trewin, *John Neville*
17 Vivienne Wood
18 Shirley
19 Richard Joseph
20 Mary James (Lolly), mother of Alan Ayckbourn
21 Ronnie Scott Dodd in conversation with the author
22 Joseph, *Scene Painting and Design*
23 John Osborne, letter to the author
24 Anthony Knowles, in conversation with the author
25 Osborne, *A Better Class of Person*
26 Nichols, *Feeling You're Behind*
27 Anthony Knowles
28 John Osbourne, letter to the author
29 d'Arcy Orders says Knowles & Gradwell were
30 Rodney Wood, quoting Oscar Quitak
31 Oscar Quitak in conversation with the author
32 Joseph, *Scene Painting and Design*
33 Oscar Quitak
34 David Campton
35 Gwynneth Thurburn, *The Times* obituary, 26 Mar 93

36   Margaret 'Shosh' Tabor, afterwards Mrs Peter Copley
37   *The Independent* obituary, 26 Mar 93
38   Gwynneth Thurburn in conversation with the author, 13 Apr 91
39   Ralph Nossek, in conversation with the author
40   Gwynneth Thurburn
41   Vera Sargeant, in conversation with the author 13 Apr 91
42   Pamela Hamilton, letter to the author
43   Marie Sutherland, letter to the author
44   RodneyWood
45   Heather Black in conversation with the author
46   Alison Edmonds, letter to the author
47   Diana Bateman, Mrs Ken Willis, letter and conversation to the author
48   Marie Sutherland
49   Joseph, *Scene Painting and Design*

The New World

Unless otherwise stated all information in this section is taken from a *Confidential Report on a Years Visit to the U.S.A.* submitted to I.T.I. by Stephen Joseph, Nov 1952 – and from Iowa brochure and programme – Manchester papers

One Great Vision

1   Shirley Jacobs
2   Heather Black
3   Patricia (Paddy) Greene
4   Bryan Kendall
5   Ibid
6   Stephen Joseph to Gwynneth Thurburn, 3 Oct 53
7   Bryan Kendall
8   Paddy Greene
9   Bryan Kendall
10 Paddy Greene
11 Bill Lawford
12 *Manchester Guardian*
13 David Campton
14 Rodney Wood
15 Paddy Greene
16 David Campton

256

17 Rodney Wood
18 Bill Lawford
19 Ronnie Scott Dodd
20 Rodney Wood
21 Heather Black
22 Gwynneth Thurburn
23 Vera Sargeant
24 Gwynneth Thurburn
25 *The Times* Ian Brunskill
26 Ronnie Scott Dodd
27 Patricia Greene
28 Shirley Jacobs
29 Shosh Tabor
30 Shirley Jacobs & Manchester papers
31 Patricia Greene
32 Shirley Jacobs
33 Shirley Jacobs
34 Patricia Greene
35 Shirley Jacobs
36 Patricia Greene
37 Shirley Jacobs
38 Patricia Greene
39 Shirley Jacobs

Worlds End

1 Heather Black
2 d'Arcy Orders
3 Stephen Joseph Manchester papers
4 James Bree, company member
5 David Campton
6 ibid

To The Barricades

1 Jones, *Theatre in the Round.*
2 ibid
3 Gascoigne, *World Theatre*
4 Rowell, *Robert Atkins*
5 Callow, *Orson Welles*
6 Leacroft, *Theatre and Playhouse*
7 Callow, *Orson Welles*, *New York Post*

8 *The Stage*, 20 Jan 1955
9 Joseph, *Scene Painting and Design*
10 Jones, *Theatre in the Round*
11 Poggi, *Theatre in America*

Thrift

1 Jeremy Kemp in conversation with the author
2 Margaret Boden in conversation with the author
3 Joseph, Theatre in the Round.
4 Ibid
5 Letter in Manchester papers – Warren and Browne were Hermione's Agents
6 Priestley, *Art of the Dramatist* (Reprinted by permission of the Peters Fraser & Dunlop Group Ltd.)
7 Clifford Williams in conversation with the author

P.B.

1 For information about P.B. I am indebted to Barbara Stoney for letting me see parts of her unpublished biography of Noel Pemberton Billing
2 Kettle, *Salome's Last Veil*
3 Barbara Stoney also Robin Pemberton Billing in conversation
4 Mike Stott also author, (though Barbara Stoney is dubious of the information)

Beside the Seaside

1 John Sherlock
2 *Yorkshire Evening News* 15 Jun 55
3 *Manchester Guardian* 15 Jul 55
4 Tyrone Guthrie, letter to Stephen 30 Nov 54
5 *Daily Express*, 21 Jul 55
6 *The Stage* 28 Juil 55
7 John Sherlock
8 Hermione Gingold letter to SJ 28 Jul 55
9 Ibid, signed "your sorrowing, grey, blond haired Mum."
10 David Campton
11 *The Times* 27 Jul 55
12 Shosh Tabor
13 David Campton
14 John Sherlock

15 *The Stage* 23 Jun 55
16 *Scarborough Evening News* Aug
17 *Scarborough Evening News* 29 Jul 55
18 *Manchester Guardian* 2 Sep 55
19 Joseph, *Theatre in the Round*
20 *Journeyman*

Postscript: "He left me £20,000. He left me the farm. That was what it was worth at the time. It was bought in his name. Actually there were mistakes over the will . . . he had always said the farm would be mine. Anthea went berserk. He hadn't left her any money – ony a Top Hat insurance (I don't know what it was worth. I imagine it was quite a large amount). She was hysterical . . . two small children . . . this friend of hers came to see me and said he'd intended to make another will – well he was always terribly up to date with wills and I absolutely believe he would not have made a mistake and left me £20,000 and this place unless he'd meant to. Anyway this man came and made me feel absolutely awful, as if Anthea was going to be penniless and here were we were . . . He thought we should give up this (the farm). My husband, who was a very rational person said, "Which do you value more, the £20,000 or Anthea?," and I decided I valued her friendship more . . . and then she became madly wealthy because immediately her aunt died and then her mother left her a fortune, and then she went to work for Michael Joseph and worked her way up and built up the company . . . I always admired Stephen for that – he never showed he cared." Shirley in conversation.

In his Manchester papers there is a letter from Anthea in which she says to Stephen, "Richard seems to be going to come out of this richer than any of us."

Mahatma Ghandi

1   Michael Westmore in conversation
2   For a fuller account see *Contemporary Dramatists*
3   David Campton
4   John Sherlock
5   Faynia Jeffery
6   David Campton
7   Bunny Wedder, Manchester papers
8   Jean Bullwinkle in conversation with the author
9   Allan Prior
10 Harold Hobson to SJ, 17 Oct 57
11 Harold Hobson to SJ, 24 Oct 57
12 Keith Baxter, letter
13 Margaret Rawlings in conversation with the author

14 Joseph, *Theatre in the Round*
15 *The Times,* 11 Nov 57
16 *News Chronicle,* 18 Feb 58
17 Keith Baxter
18 Stephen letter to Margaret Rawlings 19 Feb 58
19 David Campton
20 Shirley
21 Letter to Stephen from Ernest Borneman, *Granada TV Network*
22 Stephen to T.C. Worsley 17 Dec 57

Scarborough

1 Chris Meredith
2 Ian Curteis, letter to the author 8 Jan 93.
3 ibid
4 Alan Ayckbourn to Stephen 15 Nov 58
5 Ian Curteis letter 14 Oct 92
6 ibid
7 The Lord Chamberlain, 21 Jan 59
8 Arts Council Memo, Richard Linklater to Jo Hodgkinson
9 Ian Curteis letter 14 Oct 92
10 ibid
11 Watson, *Conversations with Ayckbourn*
12 ibid
13 *Manchester Guardian,* 6 Aug 60
14 Stephen to Jo Hodgkinson 9 Jul 60
15 Ian Curteis
16 *Yorkshire Post* 10 Jun 61
17 ibid
18 Watson, *Conversations with Ayckbourn*
19 Stephen to Hermione 19 Aug 61
20 Stephen to Mary David 6 Jul 62

Makeshift

1 Secretary General ACGB to the Pilgrim Trust
2 Pilgrim Trust to ACGB 1 Jan 58
3 *Manchester Guardian,* 26 Jun 57
4 Stephen to Jo Hodgkinson 25 Sep 59
5 Stephen Joseph Progress Report to Mr Field ACGB Oct 58
6 Richard Linklater to Jo Hodgkinson ACGB Memo
7 *Leicester Mercury,* 10 Mar 58

8 *Birmingham Post,* 10 Jan 59
9 Harold Pinter letter to Stephen 2 Oct 58
10 Draft for Press Release, Joan Macalpine, Dec59

A Long Long Trail

1 Stephen to Jo Hodgkinson 4 May 58
2 Stephen to Jo Hodgkinson 24 Dec 58
3 Stephen to Jo Hodgkinson 4 Mar 59
4 Jo Hodgkinson to Charles Lister 27 Feb 59
5 *New Concept for a Playhouse* – press release for Theatre Conference Aug 59
6 Jo Hodgkinson to Secy. General ACGB memo 13 Jan 61
7 Kilmaine to Williams 16 Jan 61
8 Kilmaine to Stephen, 6 Feb 61
9 Williams to Kilmaine, 7 Feb 61
10 Margaret Rawlings to Stephen 18 Dec 61
11 *The Times* 6 Feb 61
12 Stephen article in Manchester papers
13 Stephen to Roy Shaw 15 Sep 61
14 Ibid
15 Stephen to Peter Cheeseman, undated

The Potteries

1 Stephen to Jo Hodgkinson 3 Feb 62
2 Kilmaine to Williams 19 Feb 62
3 Linklater to Secy. General ACGB 22 Feb 62
4 Kilmaine to Linklater 5 Mar 62
5 Stephen to Jo Hodgkinson 20 Jun 62
6 Jo Hodgkinson to Stephen 4 Jul 62
7 Stephen to Jo Hodgkinson 17 Jul 62
8 *Manchester Guardian* 22 Aug 62
9 Ibid , 9 Nov 62
10 Linklater to Jo Hodgkinson, memo 9 Nov 62
11 ibid

Catching On

1 Jo Hodgkinson to Stephen 1 May 63
2 Jo Hodgkinson to David Campton 10 May 63
3 David Campton to Jo Hodgkinson 11 May 63
4 Linklater to Stephen 1 Nov 63

5 *Scarborough Evening News* 5 Jan 64
6 Ibid 18 Aug 64
7 Ibid 27 Aug 64
8 Ibid
9 Ibid
10 Stephen to David Campton 21 Oct 64

The Fellow

1 Joseph, Notes Towards a University Drama Department, undated, addressed Ashburnham Mansions.
2 David Campton
3 *The Independent,* Allan Davies 1 May 93
4 *The Observer,* John Heilpern
5 Wood, *Stephen Joseph.*
6 *The Independent,* Chris Baugh, 1 May 93
7 Peter Thomson - unless otherwise stated the descriptions of activity in Manchester are based on conversations with Professor Peter Thomson
8 David Campton
9 *The Observer,* John Heilpern
10 Peter Thomson
11 Mike Stott
12 ibid
13 Mike Stott
14 Stephen Joseph Manchester papers
15 ibid
16 Shaw *Back to Methusela*
17 Chris Baugh
18 Mike Stott
19 David Campton
20 Chris Meredith
21 Stephen Joseph, Manchester papers, 23 Nov 65
22 Hugh Hunt, letter to author 16 Feb 93
23 Stephen Joseph *Report on Theatre*
24 Stephen, Manchester papers
25 Notes on Practical Work, Stephen Joseph, Apr 66
26 Bruntière, *The Law of the Drama*
27 *Sylvester H'an Drhagon,* programme note
28 Roland Joffe letter to Stephen 7 Jan 65, Manchester papers

Trouble Brewing

1. Joseph *Adaptable Theatres*
2. Stephen to Ian Albery 10 Apr 64
3. *Toronto Telegraph* 1 May 65
4. *Manchester Guardian,* John O'Callaghan 6 Dec 63
5. Stephen to Leslie Fairweather, *Architect's Journal,* 20 Jun 64
6. Henry Livings letter to the author 19 Apr 93
7. Stephen Croft memo to Jo Hodgkinson
8. Jo Hodgkinson to Stephen 6 Jul 65
9. *Assessment of Theatrical Publicity* – John Bennett, Mr. Papers
10. Stephen to d'Arcy, 23 Mar 63
11. Alan Ayckbourn in conversation with the author
12. Ibid
13. Jo Hodgkinson to Stephen 9 Aug 63
14. Stephen to Jo Johdgkinson 10 Aug 63
15. Peter Cheeseman to Jo Hodgkinson 15 Oct 63
16. Joan Macalpine to Stephen, '65 referring to her *Cornish Mystery Cycle*
17. Stephen to Jo Hodgkinson 27 Dec 63

The Last War

1. Linklater to Stephen, 19 Feb 65 Address to Council of Repertory Theatres
2. Stephen to Jo Hodgkinson 27 Dec 63
3. Stephen to Gwynneth Thurburn 1 Jan 66
4. Mike Stott in conversation with the author 14 Aug 91
5. Chris Meredith in conversation with the author
6. Peter Thomson
7. *The Times* 18 Jul 66
8. David Campton letter to John Abberley
9. Studio Theatre Ltd., Notes of a meting held at the Arts Council on 5 Dec 66, between Jo Hodgkinson, Stephen Garrett and d'Arcy Orders
10. Teresa Collard letter to author 3 Aug 91
11. Stephen to Jo Hodgkinson 23 Jul 66
12. Stephen to Jo Hodgkinson 7 Apr 67
13. *Evening Sentinel* 14 Apr 67
14. Alan Ayckbourn in conversation with the author
15. Teresa Collard letter to the author 3 Aug 91

Happily Ever After

1. Stanley Page in conversation with the author

2 Mike Stott 14 Aug 91
3 Phyllis Leggatt to Hermione 6 Oct 67
4 Alan Ayckbourn in conversation

The Full Round

1 Watson, *Conversations with Ayckbourn*
2 ibid
3 Taylor, *Anger and After.*
4 Ibid
5 *Conversations with Ayckbourn*
6 Alan Ayckbourn in conversation with the author
7 *Evening Sentinel* 9 Jul 65
8 Chambers, *Peggy*
9 David Campton
10 Chris Baugh
11 *The Guardian* 31 Oct 90
12 Peter Thomson
13 Stephen Joseph, *Sylvester H'an Drhagon*
14 *Plays and Players* Dec 69

Index

Several people in this narrative are listed under their proper names but referred to familiarly. Thus Gingold becomes Hermione and the Joseph family are indicated by their given names, although Diana I call Shirley, because that is how Stephen always referred to her. Orders is most often referred to as d'Arcy and Hodgkinson as Jo. Stephen retains his name throughout, although many people referred to him as Jo.

Adamov, Arthur, 133
Adler, Alfred, 35
Adrian, Max, 38
Albery, Bronson, 117
Albery, Donald, 176, 222
Aldridge, Kara, 126
Aldridge, Michael, 136
Alison, Dorothy, 124
Allen, Campbell, 133
Allen, Maud, 116
Andreyev, 81
Arlott, John, 50
Arnason, Benedikt, 94
Appia, Adolphe, 105-106
Apps, Edward, 102
Ashcroft, Peggy, 35
Aston, Richard, 64
Atkins, Robert, 40, 106
Attenborough, Richard, 131
Austen, Jane, 8
Ayckbourn, Alan, 8-9, 112, 121, 144-148, 149, 151, 163, 189, 194, 196, 200, 203-204, 212, 214-217, 221-225, 228, 233, 243

Baker, George Pierce, 102
Baker, Richard, 63-64, 67-68
Balfour, Michael, 32, 133
Barker, Ronnie, 223
Barry, Michael, 135
Bateman (Willis), Diana, 67, 82
Bateman, H.E. 67
Bates, H.E., 5
Baxter, Keith, 9-10, 136-137
Bayliss, Lilian, 18
Beckett, Samuel, 221
Bell, Heather, 220
Bennett, Arnold, 161, 208, 210
Bennett, John, 195
Benson, Sir Frank, 35

Bentham, Fred, 191
Bergman, Ingmar, 15
Bernard, Jean Jacques, 162
Bernstein, Ruth, (later Reuth), 36-38
Bernstein, Sydney, 180, 182, 225
Binns, Pamela, 104
Black, Heather, 44, 81, 92, 101
Blanchflower, Danny, 131
Boden, Ken, 112, 167, 176, 200, 215-217 233
Boden, Margaret, 111
Bolt, Robert, 220
Boucicault, Dion, 186
Boys, Barry, 163-164,
Bradley, Alfred, 112, 177, 193, 213, 216-217, 223
Brambell, Wilfred, 133
Brecht, Bertolt, 44, 108
Bridge, Peter, 152, 222-223,
Bridges, Robert, 67
Briers, Richard, 224
Broadhurst, Alan, 37-40, 71-76
Bronte, Anne, 122
Brook, Clive, 123
Brook, Peter, 72, 181, 227
Brown, Ivor, 106
Browne, E. Mrtin, 37
Browne, Lord & Lady Ulick, 112
Bruntière, Ferdinand, 188
Bryden, Bill, 151, 215, 226
Bryson, Bill, 84
Buchanan, Jack, 23
Burke, Alfie, 133
Byng, Douglas, 24

Campbell, Ken, 220
Campton, David, 49, 102, 112, 118-127, 131-132, 139-140, 149-150, 156, 158, 162, 164, 175-178, 189, 192-194, 201-211, 214, 221-223, 228

Carter, Patrick, 95
Casals, Pablo, 36
Casey, Harry, 111
Cecil, Lord David, 116
Chekov, Anton, 133
Cheeseman, Peter, 168-171, 195-197, 200, 202-206, 208-213, 215, 220, 228, 243
Churchill, Winston, 116
Clark, Jack, 203
Clements, Ian, 68
Clements, John, 228
Codron, Michael, 223
Cody, Buffalo Bill, 84
Collard, Teresa, 204
Collin, Aubrey, 200
Collin, Philip, 157-158,
Cooklin, Shirley, 81
Cooper, Kenneth, 202
Copley, Peter, 80, 95
Coward, Noel, 11, 23,140
Craig, Edward Gordon, 106
Craig, Pam, 193, 210
Craig, Wendy, 94, 102
Cromwell, Oliver, 121
Curteis, Ian, 8, 146, 148-149, 205, 220
Cuthbertson, Iain, 207-208
Curtis Browne, 28, 31

Daniels, Ron, 220
d'Arcy, 64-67, 72, 78, 113, 135, 150, 176, 203-204, 211,
Darling, Lord Chief Justice, 116
Darlington, W.A., 68, 224
David, Mary, 36-40, 44, 49-52, 54, 57, 152-153, 213
David, Prince of Wales, 27, 117
David sisters, Anne & Lisbeth, 44, 49-52
de Keyser, David, 133
Davies, Robertson, 102
de Leon, Jack, 123
Delius, Frederick, 121
Dent, Alan, 134, 138
Derbyshire, Eileen, 194
Devine, Alexander, 31
Devine, George, 122, 157
Dexter, John, 89
Dickens, Monica, 11
Dickson, Rosamund, 173, 207, 221
Dinelli, Mel, 103
Dixon, Ruth, 123
Dodd, Ronnie Scott, 93-94
Dostoevski, Fyodor, 133

Downing, Anthony, 216
Dryden, John, 93
Du Maurier, Daphne, 11
Duncan. Ronald, 76
Dunlop, Frank, 226
Dunn, Beryl, 37, 50

Eady, David, 75, 68, 113
Eccleshare, Colin, 75
Edinborough, Arnold, 64
Edwards, Hilton, 106
Edwards, Jimmy, 68
Edwards, Mervyn, 150, 152, 178, 194, 217
Eliot, T.S., 35, 37, 84
Elizabeth, Queen Mother, 112
Elliot, Michael, 182
Elmhirst, William, 148, 163, 171, 192, 215
Empson, Professor, 168
Esslin, Martin, 221
Ewstrell, Tony, 16
Evans, Edith, 35

Fagan, Gemma, 84, 112
Fairbanks, Douglas, 131
Farmer, Elsie Veronica (see P.B.)
Fenby, Eric, 121
Feuillère, Edwige, 138
Fields, Gracie, 71
Fogerty, Elsie, 35-40, 44, 79-80
Fonteyn, Margot, 50
Foster, Barry, 133
Francis, Barbara, 89
Franklin, Gretchen, 101, 129
Freeman, Les, 9
Frost, Edna, 27-28, 33-34, 77, 125
Fry, Christopher, 32
Fuller, Buckminster, 159
Fyfe, Robert, 176

Gabb, W.H., 50
Garrett, Stephen, 62-63, 113, 164-165, 203, 204, 211
Gartside, Mrs, 166
Geddes, Norman bel, 106
Gertler, Mark, 49
Gielgud, John, 35
Gielgud, Val, 23
Gilbert, W.S., 102
Gill, Richard, 211, 220, 221
Gingold, Hermione, 13, 15-19, 21-22, 24, 28, 31, 33, 35-36, 49, 54, 67, 69, 72, 79, 82-83, 90, 94, 101, 113, 122-125, 135, 144, 148,150, 200-201

266

Gingold, James, 17
Gingold, Margaret, 17
Ginner, Ruby, 37
Giradoux, Jean, 133
Gitana, Gertie, 208-210
Glaister, Gerard, 133
Glaser, Eleanor, 122
Glock, Clement, 112
Goethe, Johann W. von, 105
Goff, Lewin, 86, 176
Gollancz, Victor, 11, 24
Goodman, Lord, 206
Goodwin, Clive, 95-96, 145
Gordon, John, 122
Gordon, Richard, 11
Gorky, Maxim, 106
Gradwell, Ben, 68, 72, 75, 78
Grahame, Kenneth, 46, 116
Gregory, R.G., 226
Greene, Patricia (Paddy), 94, 96-98, 102, 133, 193
Grenfell, Joyce, 44
Guiness, Alec, 71
Guthrie, Tyrone, 108, 123, 151, 181

Hale, Owen, 133, 203, 214
Hall, Peter, 191
Hardwick, Cedrick, 88
Harper, Gerald, 136
Harris, Robert, 38
Hartnell, Norman, 68
Hauser, Frank, 144
Hayes, Lawrence, 80
Healey, Tony, 210
Heilpern, John, 180
Helpman, Robert, 71
Henty, George, 67
Higgins, Norman, 68
Hilary, Jennifer, 224
Hill, Bernard, 220
Hill, Katrina, 207
Hird, Thora, 122
Hitler, Adolf, 37
Hobson, Harold, 111, 135, 138
Hodgkinson, Jo, 134, 135, 145, 149, 150, 152, 156-158, 163, 169, 176, 194,196, 200, 203-205, 208-211, 213
Hodson, Anthea, 77, 125, 192
Hoffnung, Gerard, 155
Hogg, James, 102
Holm, Ian, 133
Horden, Michael, 224
Horsfall, Bernard, 138

Hoskins, Bob, 220
Houseman, Laurence, 8
Hudd, Walter, 80, 91, 95
Hudson, Leslie, 21
Hunnings, Neville, 103, 112, 203, 216
Hunt, Hugh, 10, 159, 179-181, 184-188, 200-202, 241
Hunt, Caroline, 193
Hurst, Brian Desmond, 79
Hutch, (Leslie Hutchinson), 23
Hutchinson, Walter, 22
Hutton, Barbara, 62

Iliffe, Alan, 165-166, 170
Ionesco, Eugene, 221
Ireland, Kenneth, 174
Isherwood, Christopher, 24

Jacobs, Shirley, 90, 98, 118, 126
Jackson, Barry, 76, 158
Jaffa, Max, 122
James, Henry, 133
James, Mary (Lolly), 77, 121, 144, 148, 151, 153
Jarrett, David, 176, 193
Jeffery, Faynia, 132, 200, 225
Jenner, Caryl, 10
Joffe, Roland, 132, 189, 193, 219, 225
John, Sub. Lt. 54
Johnson, Celia, 224
Jones, Griffith, 38
Jones, Margot, 108-109
Jones, Owen, 117
Jonson, Ben, 105
Joseph, Leslie, 16, 21, 23, 28, 33-34, 44-47, 125, 150, 200
Joseph, Lionel, 12, 124-125, 138
Joseph, Michael, 11-13, 17-18, 21-22, 24, 27-28, 33-34, 45, 50, 56, 67, 76-77, 121, 124, 125, 135, 140, 144, 197
Joseph, Moss and Rebecca, 12, 19
Joseph, Richard, 77, 125
Joseph, Diana (Shirley) 28, 56, 61-62, 67, 77, 90, 125, 140, 150, 216, 242
Joyce, Geoff, 219

Kalkowska, Eleanor, 40
Kean, Charles, 105
Kemp, Jeremy, 92, 111
Kendall, Henry, 16-7
Kenny, Sean, 181, 191-192
Kerr, Walter, 83
Kettle, Michael, 115

Kilmaine, Lord, 156, 165, 169
King, Peter, 193, 233
King, Sub. Lt., 54
Kingsley, Ben, 220
Kipling, Rudyard, 144
Komisarjevsky, Theodore, 106
Kopit, Arthur, 201
Knowles, Anthony, 103
Krishnamurti, 9, 183

Lacy, Catherine, 38
Lambert, J.W., 50-52
Landis, Harry, 90, 95, 101
Lane, Mrs., 38
Lane, Terry, 173-175. 177, 193, 204-209, 207, 215, 225
Lassaly, Walter, 95
Laughton, Charles, 88, 121
Laughton, Tom, 121-122, 126
Law, Bonar, 115
Leacroft, Richard, 157
Lean, David, 79
Leggett, Phyllis, 213
Leigh, Vivien, 107
Leonardo da Vinci, 113
Levy, Ben, 24, 112
Lewsen, Charles, 126
Lingwood, Tom, 71, 76
Linklater, Dick, 157, 169, 172, 177
Lister, Charles, 161-3, 170
Littlewood, Joan, 68, 108
Livings, Henry, 194, 208-209
Llewellyn, Richard, 11
Lloyd George, David, 116
Lohr, Marie, 223
Lorrimer, Enid, 136
Lorne, Constance, 137
Lord Chamberlain, 66, 147
Lucas, Victor, 36-40, 49
Lugne-Poe, 106
Lusty, Robert, 11
Lyttleton, Anthony, 112, 145, 203

Mabie, Edward C., 83-87
Macalpine, Joan, 151, 159, 167-8, 189, 197, 220
McCowan, Michael, 38
McKay, Fulton, 71
Macintosh, Kenneth, 32
McLean, Fitzroy, 57
Malcolm, John, 173-5
Marlow, Anthony, 129
Marlowe, Christopher, 185

Marriot, Antony, 220
Marsden, Betty, 222
Marshall, Norman 191
Martyn, Dona, 148, 157, 163, 193
Maschwitz, Eric, 23-24, 33-34, 54, 64, 69
Massie, Paul, 90
Masters, John, 11
Maughan, Somerset, 104
Mawer, Irene, 37
McCowan, Michael, 38
McKay, Fulton, 71
Medici, Giuliano & Lorenzo, 87
Meiningen, Duke of. 105
Melley, Andre, 204
Mercer, David, 194
Meredith, Chris, 200-201, 207-208
Miles, Bernard, 108, 157, 228
Miller, Alice, 46
Miller, Arthur, 83
Mills & Boon, 23
Miranda, Carmen, 51, 67
Mitchell, Tom, 173-174
Mitchley, Jack, 74-75
Mond, Karis, 71
Moorehead, Agnes, 88
Morley, John, 68
Moro, Peter, 191
Morrell, John, 144
Morris, William, 11
Morris, Wolfe, 133
Mosley, Oswald, 37
Muir & Norden, 68
Murdoch, Rupert, 221
Murray, Stephen, 38
Myers, A.C., 55

Neil, A.S., 182
Nelson, Gwen, 133
Neville, John, 71-76, 167
Norfolk, W.F., 171
Nossek, Ralph, 126, 133

O'Casey, Sean, 102
Odets, Clifford, 71, 83
O'Donnell, Michael, 62, 68
O'Farrell, Bernadette, 71
Okhlopkov, Nikolai, 106
Olivier, Laurence, 35, 61, 72, 228
O'Neill, Eugene, 38, 83, 102, 133, 228
Orders, see d'Arcy
Osborne, John, 78
Ost, Geoffrey, 168
Owen, Alun, 131

Page, Stanley, 171, 212
Parker, Charles, 68
Pasco, Richard, 133
Patrick, Nigel, 224-225
P.B., 104, 114-118, 126, 132, 144,148, 174, 195, 197, 200-202, 215-216, 225
Pemberton Billing, Noel, 46, 115-117
Pemberton Billing, Robin, 225
Pericles, 146
Perry, Morris, 126, 128-9, 133
Phipps, Simon, 68, 75
Pick, Charles, 11
Pickard, Helena, 136
Pilbrow, Richard, 133, 191
Pinter, Harold, 158-159, 221-2
Pirandello, Luigi, 133, 222
Plater, Alan, 194, 228
Plows, Maurice, 177
Poel, William, 18, 105
Poole, Kenneth, 68
Powell, Robert 220
Pratt, Desmond, 133, 151
Priestley, J.B., 38, 112, 140, 143, 168
Prior, Allan, 135, 139
Prudhoe, John, 183-5
Purcell, Henry, 8, 93

Quitak, Oscar, 71-73, 78, 103, 204

Racine, Jean Baptiste, 133, 139
Ramsey, Peggy, 224
Rattigan, Terence, 87
Rawlings, Margaret, 135-139, 166, 171, 215
Read, Catherine, 50-2
Reinhardt, Max, 105
Reynolds, Oliver, 89, 91-92
Richard III, 121
Richardson, Ralph, 61
Ripman, Walter, 37
Robinson, Tony, 208, 225
Rodney, Jack, 82
Rogers, Paul, 222
Rothrock, Richard, 7, 9, 186-187
Routh, Jonathan, 64
Rudkin, David, 228
Rylands, George, 64

Sackville West, Vita, 11
Sargent, Malcolm, 36
Sargeant, Vera (Sarge), 80. 92, 159
Saroyan, William, 133
Saunders, James, 220-221

Savage, Michael, 62-63, 67
Schiffler, Harold, 87
Schofield, Paul, 91
Sears, Ann, 136
Shaffer, Peter, 72
Shakespeare, William, 105, 108, 138, 185
Shaw, Bernard, 21, 32, 91, 162, 183, 189, 227
Shaw, Roy, 202
Sher, Antony, 219
Sherlock, John, 126-128, 131
Shiner, Ronald, 103
Silberman, Jerry, 87
Simmons, Monty & Anthony, 95
Sitwell family, 122
Smettem, W,H., 111, 125, 194
Southern, Richard, 181, 191
Spearman, Alec & Diane, 112
St Denis, Michel, 92
Steinbeck, John, 133
Stoney, Heather, 220
Stopes, Marie, 22
Stott, Mike, 8-9, 181, 183-4, 193-4, 201, 214, 216, 220
Strindberg, August, 113, 162, 176
Sweeting, E.L., 10
Swift, Jonathan, 67

Tardieu, Jean, 133
Tabor, 'Shosh' (Mrs Peter Copley), 118, 126
Taylor, Ann, 136-138
Taylor, Peter, 95
Taylor, John Russell, 221
Tennants, H.M., 103
Thompson, James, 104
Thomson, Peter, 8-9, 182, 184-187, 201-203, 227
Thorndike, Sybil, 72
Thurber, James, 15, 64
Thurburn, Gwynneth, 79, 80-1, 89-92, 95, 102, 112, 200, 202-203, 208, 215
Tieck, Ludwig, 106
Todd, Ann, 79
Tolstoy, Leo, 101
Tranchell, Peter, 63-68, 72-73
Tree, Sir Herbert Beerbohn, 18
Trevelyan, Catriona, 208
Tunnard, Viola, 40, 44
Thorndike, Sybil, 72
Turner, Clifford, 37
Tynan, Kenneth, 15, 123, 138
Ure, Mary, 91, 94

Ustinov, Peter, 103

Van Druten, John, 73
Van Gogh, Vincent, 101
Venables, Claire, 193, 225
Verrinder, Carl, 32
Volonakis, Minos, 112, 133, 144

Yeats, W.B., 40

Waghorn, Elizabeth, 208
Wadja, Andrei, 98
Wallach, Eli, 88
Wallace, Hazel Vincent, 71, 103, 144, 168
Wallis, Mr., 128
Walter, Kate, 17
Waterhouse, Alfred, 31
Watson, Ian, 208
Webber, C.E., 82
Weller, Mike, 181
Welles, Orson, 83, 106-108

Wesker, Arnold, 225
Westmore, Michael, 8, 68, 72, 131-2
Widdicombe, David, 63
Wilde, Oscar, 116
Wilder, Gene, 84, 87
Wilkinson, Arthur, 37-40, 49
Williams. Clifford, 113-114, 133, 149
Williams, Tenessee, 83, 108
Williams, William Emrys, 156, 158
Willis, Ken, 67
Wilson, Colin, 220
Winch, Joan (Jurneman), 128
Wilton, Terence, 193
Wolfit, Donald, 144
Wood, John, 111, 232
Wood, Rodney, 144, 200, 217
Wood, Viviene, 71
Worsley, T.C., 140
Worthington, Arthur, 186
Wright, Tom, 210